WHITE-COLLAR
BLUES

WHITE-COLLAR BLUES

THE MAKING OF THE TRANSNATIONAL TURKISH MIDDLE CLASS

MUSTAFA YAVAŞ

Columbia University Press   *New York*

Columbia University Press
Publishers Since 1893
New York   Chichester, West Sussex
cup.columbia.edu

Library of Congress Cataloging-in-Publication Data
Names: Yavaş, Mustafa author
Title: White-collar blues : the making of the transnational
Turkish middle class / Mustafa Yavaş.
Description: New York : Columbia University Press, [2025] |
Includes bibliographical references and index.
Identifiers: LCCN 2024054908 | ISBN 9780231213608 hardback |
ISBN 9780231213615 trade paperback | ISBN 9780231559935 ebook
Subjects: LCSH: Quality of work life—Turkey | Work-life balance—
Turkey | Middle class—Turkey | American Dream
Classification: LCC HD6957.T87 Y38 2025 |
DDC 305.5/509561—dc23/eng/20250331
LC record available at https://lccn.loc.gov/2024054908

Cover design: Milenda Nan Ok Lee
Cover photo: Laurence Berger/Shutterstock

GPSR Authorized Representative: Easy Access System Europe,
Mustamäe tee 50, 10621 Tallinn, Estonia, gpsr.requests@easproject.com

CONTENTS

ACKNOWLEDGMENTS

W riting these lines feels like writing a love letter to the village that helped me put everything between these two covers and allow it to see daylight. Expressing my gratitude to many people who animated *the labor process* behind this book is very meaningful for me.

I would like to start thanking my interviewees for their time, the increasingly elusive and precious element of our day. Time may be even more precious for business professionals behind corporate wheels who try to live as humanly as possible in ever-so-busy global cities. Over many lunches, coffees, and drinks, they opened their hearts to me, sharing their memories, experiences, hopes, and frustrations. From where they stand, most made it to the conceivable peak of the social pyramid (the steepness of which sits at the very center of many troubles), occupying high-pay, high-status occupations thanks to their educational credentials and hard work. As I learned and wished to share in this book, however, such achievement does not inoculate these elite workers against the ills of being embedded in an exploitative socioeconomic system running on inequalities. Like many working poor but unlike the wealthy who do not need to labor for a living, they too feel that they lack autonomy over their labor and, by extension, their lives. They too fall short, albeit in different ways than most workers, of flourishing and living a fulfilling life. I am thankful to my interviewees for their generosity and sincerity, which enabled me to tell this underappreciated story of meritocracy and capitalism. I hope I am doing justice their accounts. I also hope they realize they do have more power than they presume to push back against those ills.

In its infancy, this book was shepherded by great mentors at Yale University. My deepest gratitude goes to my brilliant adviser Julia Adams. I am tremendously lucky to be her student, and I wish I could articulate how indebted I feel for her mentorship. Julia has been my rock and a role model as an excellent sociologist, a multifaceted and dedicated academic, and a dear human being and friend. I am more than grateful for all her feedback, which always provided me with improvements in my writing, including this very manuscript. From the bottom of my heart, thank you, Julia!

Emily Erikson, Phil Gorski, and Amy Wrzesniewski also helped me very much with the early versions of this manuscript. Emily's comments were influential in shaping my argument, making it hold the book together. I thank Phil for encouraging me not to shy away from asking big questions. I have been privileged to tap Amy's expertise on work and getting her immensely productive feedback. Amy also kept refreshing my faith in the importance of this research, for which I am thankful.

At Yale University, I also had the privilege of getting help from Fred Wherry for the research design, Rene Almeling for my interview schedules, and Ron Eyerman for immersing myself in the Frankfurt School. The Comparative Research Workshop of the Sociology Department has been my intellectual home, and its participants were all helpful in crafting my argument in this book. The dear companionship of Till Hilmar, Dolunay Uğur, Dicky Yangzom, Dana Hayward, Gülay Türkmen-Dervişoğlu, Andy Cohen, and Shai Dromi during my PhD studies was also formative in the kind of sociologist I became and the kind of manuscript I produced. In this regard, I also want to acknowledge the precious support I received at my beloved alma mater, Boğaziçi University. Yaman Barlas and Gönenç Yücel taught me the art of modeling and systems thinking, which indelibly shaped my intellectual taste and vision. I couldn't be where I am without their mentorship. And thanks also to Filiz Garip for role modeling and helping me take a leap of faith and build an academic career in sociology upon my industrial engineering background.

Some parts of the manuscript benefited from several colleagues' close reading. Phi Hong Su, Zeynep Özgen, Evren Savcı, and Cihan Tuğal's critical feedback helped me with chapter 2 and, more broadly, with the historical aspects of my argument. Kinga Makovi, Blaine Robbins, and Malte Reichelt provided many useful comments for chapter 4, portions of which appear as an article published in 2024 in *American Sociological Review*. Elisabeth Anderson and John O'Brien were generous with their time to discuss at length both chapters and beyond. I am also grateful to Stephanie Mudge for her support and sharing useful feedback for the manuscript. The book also benefited from anonymous reviewers' generous and thoughtful comments.

I would like to thank Eric Schwartz for believing in this project and supporting me to write a book I want to read myself. I also thank Alyssa Napier for her help throughout the book's production. I am also grateful to Isabella Furth for her meticulous editorial help with the manuscript. Working with her was a joy, and she helped me produce a manuscript that reads much better. Attending Laura Portwood-Stacey's book proposal workshop was also useful in developing an x-ray of my manuscript and then its key argument.

I thankfully acknowledge the financial support I had from Yale's MacMillan Center, the MacMillan International Dissertation Research Fellowship, and the Çağatay Summer Travel

Fellowship, which made my fieldwork in Istanbul possible. My postdoctoral fellowship at New York University Abu Dhabi provided me with the financial resources and the respective peace and quiet to craft this book. I also want to thank İlayda Özdemir and Adi Baurzhanuly for their assistance with historical data collection, and Büşra Mahmutoğlu for her assistance with qualitative data analysis.

As the living, breathing author of these pages, I also want to share the indirect yet invaluable help that went into the making of this book. Yes, I am talking about the social support that help me keep it together and carry on. My *consiglieri* Melih Barsbey and Ekrem Başer blessed me with their unwavering support, lending their sharp intellects and gracious ears to me whenever I needed. Nazım Can Serbest, Suna Kafadar, Melis Gülboy Laebens, Ufuk Topkara, Sertaç Kaya Şen, Cihan Çelik, Can Görür, Mashuq Kurt, Çağlayan Başer, Korhan Koçak, Matteo Nori, Thomas Marlow, Anju Mary Paul, and Şafak Yücel all supported me with their friendship from near and far and in various ways that neither they nor I are probably even aware of.

I am also grateful to my dear parents Handan and Ömer and my sister Betül for the family they have fostered. Beyond tolerating my geographical distance and supporting me with their warmth and love, it was also always helpful to chat about Turkish history with my parents to put things in the historical context from the ground up. My dear white-collar sister Betül also helped me find some interlocutors for my research. I also thank the Stokes family, who have blessed me with joy, love, and support in a way and in an amount more than I can say. And special thanks to Uncle Chris for introducing John Hartford, whose beautiful song "In Tall Buildings" serves as epigraphs for the introduction and conclusion in this book.

Last but not the least of my thanks goes to my dear wife Corinne. Your cheerfulness, charm, calm, and even chaos have become the light of my life. I am impressed by and trying to learn from your determined positivity. Thank you for bearing with me, weathering my gloomy, seeing-the-glass-half-empty days and letting the sunlight come in nevertheless.

COPYRIGHT ACKNOWLEDGMENTS

WHITE-COLLAR
BLUES

INTRODUCTION

White-Collar *Blues*?

Someday, my baby, when I am a man,
And others have taught me the best that they can,
They'll sell me a suit, they'll cut off my hair,
And send me to work in tall buildings.

—JOHN HARTFORD, "IN TALL BUILDINGS"

On a lovely Sunday afternoon in early May, I was waiting for Ozan, my interviewee, an investment banker, at a coffee shop somewhere around Wall Street. Although Manhattan skyscrapers framed my view of the blue sky, I decided to wait outside to enjoy the beautiful spring weather. Late to our appointment, he texted me, telling me that his manager would not let him leave. I replied that it was all right. I had time. When he finally arrived an hour later, he first asked me the Wi-Fi password of the café while he rushed to set up his laptop:

OZAN: I should be seen online on the company's communication
    channel. The folks are working, and they can see who is online
    and who is not. Disgusting, it's disgusting. These are all going
    to pop up in our conversation, you know.
MUSTAFA (THE AUTHOR): What was the deal with your manager?

OZAN: Just kept asking "Shall we add this, too? Should we reconsider this part?" [Eating a piece of pie while talking] I mean . . . in the US . . . the corporate culture . . . maybe not the whole US, but particularly for the companies in New York, and particularly consulting, finance, and in fact many other corporations . . . the workweek is seven days, six to seven days. You can't leave work at 5 P.M. on Friday to come back at 9 A.M. on Monday. With these [smart]phones, everybody has to be online all the time. Emails are always pouring in and you are expected to reply immediately. It is really not acceptable in the US anymore to reply to an email after an hour. Because you always have your phone with you, you should reply even if you are not working. So . . . Monday was good actually because I worked until 9 P.M.

MUSTAFA: Wait, it was good?

OZAN: Yeah, because I worked until 5:30 A.M. on Tuesday, that is, until Wednesday morning. Then I slept three hours and I worked until 1:30 A.M. on Wednesday. Thursday, again until 1:30 A.M. On Friday, I came to work around 9:30, and then I worked until 7 to 7:30 [P.M.]. I went out for a drink or two on Friday night. The emails started pouring in again on Saturday [morning], you know, "Let's finish this part first. You fix this and that." I left [work] around 2 P.M. for a friend's birthday, [but] I requested my two analysts [his subordinates] to cover for me. One of them told me that they were coming back from a brunch and could continue working from home. The other said they were already leaving for home. Then, the two swapped by 8 P.M. . . . When the director [his own manager] pushes for something over the weekend, you try to cover each other, you know, one of you goes for a brunch for two hours and comes back. . . . I mean, the system of the city is actually appropriate for this, everywhere is just a short distance away.

Many corporate people's [business professionals'] lives in New York . . . working from 9 A.M. to 8 P.M., coming back home for dinner and keep working by replying to emails until 11 P.M., and then sleeping at midnight. . . . That's how you spend your weekdays. And when it's the weekend, as a New York classic, you go to a brunch and a bar . . . but you always *sprinkle* these on your working hours. You are primarily working. And then you go for a brunch for two hours but you think, "While I eat, my analysts would finish this part, and then I would be home by then and I finish that part." . . . In this corporate life in New York, and I guess in the US overall, you sprinkle. Your hobbies, you try to squeeze in . . . I mean, for example, this is actually my coffee break. . . . And I am available if there is an urgent question. I am online, and they can reach me via this in-office communicator. You can see who's working, who's not, who's online or offline, who has not touched their computer for ten minutes. And folks check it out and poke you. "Why have you been away for two hours?" . . . I went to this music festival last year for three days, and it is a festival, right? But I was work-ing during the days, at least three straight hours. . . . We were at a friend's house with a pool and everything, you know, to chill out for the weekend. But I get an email every hour, I leave the pool, go upstairs, and find a room and work. Then, I finish it and come down again, just about to take a sip from my cock-tail, [and there's] another email with requests. You just *cannot free up* your mind from work!

Born and raised in Turkey, Ozan was in his thirties at the time of our interview and working at a prestigious transnational cor-poration as an investment banker. He was a success story of the transnational Turkish middle class. He was always at the top of his academic class, and his high school and university alma maters were among the best in Turkey. As we continued talking about his corporate career, he told me that he would actually have loved to be an academic and that he tutored math and science during college. His eyes brightened while he shared how much fulfillment he got from teaching, such as witnessing "the progress of a student," and feeling that "my labor was appreciated." However, he also reasoned:

I am not sure, why it was [that fulfilling], whether because it was also my *own* business or because I liked what I was doing? . . . I was working for myself, and I was not reporting to anyone. You know, in corporate life, it frequently happens that . . . you get confused about for whom you are working. For your company? Or for your immediate manager? Or the owner of the company? . . . Particularly at the large American corporate firms, you get confused. Who is the owner of this business? Where is this money going? What am I doing? I have my salary every month, okay. [But] that feeling of ownership, it is really difficult to develop it.

He also remembered his semester abroad in college during which he worked at a research lab, designing improvements for a product to be used in multiple industries. He compared this with his current job:

[At the lab] you are producing something at the end of the day, and you think "How can I make this better?" Using your intellect and selling your own product to a customer is a unique satisfaction. Corporate life is very different; it is a different setup because you are not really creating a product. Because someone tells you what to do every five to six hours or three hours, and you do it on paper [as opposed to something tangible] with three to four hours of deadlines. This corporate [life] lacks satisfaction so much. Really.

In his senior year in college, Ozan had considered pursuing a PhD in engineering in the United States but could not get into the programs that he aspired to. Although he got other offers, they were not good enough for him; they were not among the "top" programs. Instead, he began to work at a prestigious transnational corporation in Istanbul. After some years of work experience in finance, he pursued an MBA degree at one of the most well-known business schools of the world, and later he found himself at a Wall Street firm. He reflected, "Once you're inside the corporate world, they shape you in a such way that . . . you [should] get an MBA, you [should] go more corporate." He felt trapped, that he was on a one-way street, and although it pointed socially upward and toward the type of better life that many people aspire to, he did not seem contented with taking this path.

While Ozan's story highlights some extremes of the corporate work culture of Wall Street, he also quite accurately pointed out that this was not restricted to Wall Street, New York, or the United States. Thanks to transnational corporations (TNCs), a sizable number of which hail from the United States, and their increasing overseas operations in the past decades, this all-consuming work culture is a global phenomenon.[1] Indeed, Ozan was not an exception in having such a surprisingly low quality of working life; his experience of feeling detached from his labor was representative of many Turkish business professionals who comprise the transnational Turkish middle class.[2]

Best and brightest of their cohorts, these individuals have been successful throughout their lives. They have attended the best high schools and universities in Turkey and beyond; some have attended Ivy League colleges in the United States. In addition to their grit and hard work—or, as some might put it, their compliance for delayed gratification—they are often the products of "concerted cultivation" of their middle- or upper-middle-class families.[3] They typically major in engineering, management, and economics, majors that are sought after in the elite labor market of prestigious TNCs such as the companies in the *Fortune* magazine's Global 500 list. They have a global orientation to their lives and careers, and often pursue exchange semesters and summer internships abroad even before they kick off their transnational careers. Passing through selective recruitment processes and navigating the labor market successfully in their senior year of college, they immediately find employment at prestigious TNCs, mostly in Istanbul though sometimes in other global cities such as New York and London. Looking at their parents, many of whom were state employees or civil servants (the main modes of employment that brought about a relatively secure middle-class life before Turkey's neoliberalization), they consider themselves upwardly mobile, both in terms of income and consumption, but not wealthy.[4] They are ambitious with respect to their careers; they seek promotions within their companies, always keeping an eye on the market for a better position at another company or in another country. Many pursue MBA degrees from the most acclaimed business schools in the United States and Europe to secure or boost such upward mobility. Some of them are future CEOs, and most will make it to higher levels of management at top-notch companies.

Despite the backdrop of such prestigious participation in the global elite labor force and having enviable levels of income and consumption practices, many members of the transnational Turkish middle class do not feel contented. As Ozan's story demonstrates, they feel disappointed, exhausted, and trapped, and they have the nagging sense that the high income and prestige they have worked so hard to attain are in fact impoverishing their lives—in a word, they suffer from what I call the white-collar blues.

These white-collar blues represent more than a few malcontents. The theme resonates across an emerging genre of literature, including novels, satires, and stand-up shows written and produced by white-collar workers. These works tell the stories

FIGURE 0.1 The covers of popular books written by and for Turkish white-collar workers

of Turkish business professionals and managers, often via sarcasm and a stereotype of *beyaz yakalı* (white-collar worker). Figure 0.1, for example, shows the covers of five popular Turkish books exploring themes of white-collar discontent. The first, *Tebrikler Kovuldunuz!* (Congratulations! You're Fired!) was written by a former banker, now one of the most famous stand-up comedians in Turkey, who frequently draws from his white-collar work experience.[5] The second book is *The Profesyonel*, and its subtitle reads, "Put your business card down slowly and start turning the pages . . ."[6] The middle one, *Mezeleri Güzel: Bir Beyaz Yakalının İtirafları* (Appetizers are Tasty: The Confessions of a White-Collar Worker), displays a constricting necktie covered with a red-stained white napkin.[7] The cover of the next book, *Fabrika Ayarlarına Dön* (Reset to Factory Settings), shows a white-collar worker against a verdant natural background; his eyes, though, have been transformed into bolts, which are being tightened by a wrench.[8] The title of the last book, *Beyaz Ya-la-ka: Kariyer İçin Hayat Feda Etme Sanatı* (The White Collar/Bootlicker: The Art of Sacrificing Your Life for Your Career), contains a play on words that transforms the word *yaka* (collar) to *yalaka* (bootlicker).[9] The cover displays a man in a suit with his head on fire.

These books are full of self-reflective insights about white-collar employees' lives and working conditions. They describe various experiences and stories of alienation while satirizing having bourgeois dreams and the realities of middle-class life, including distinction seeking, aspirational consumption and the accompanying credit card debt; status anxiety, lost self-respect, and lack of sincere social ties; and the discontents of working life in corporate workplaces, such as meaninglessness, boredom, burnout, and stress. The back jackets of these books often include a promise that the book will speak to the reader, an echo of the Latin phrase famously used by Karl Marx in the preface of the first volume of *Das Kapital*: "De te fabula narratur! [It is of you that the story is told!]."[10] This kind of white-collar literature—which has emerged organically and not from ideologues or vanguardist intellectuals—could be interpreted as a sign of the formation and maturation of a new middle-class identity. We can even talk about the emergence of a class consciousness—if not an outright oppositional consciousness to culminate in "a class for itself"—in the sense of an awareness of a shared life experience. The strong participation of well-to-do Turkish white-collar professionals and managers in the Gezi Park Resistance—a nationwide uprising that shook Turkey in 2013—suggests this consciousness entails a pervasive dissatisfaction with "quality of life": a set of grievances that can be traced back to neoliberalism and aggressive commodification that have provided even middle classes with a tasteless life.[11]

And yet this pervasive dissatisfaction is puzzling: scholarship on "new middle classes" in general and the transnational Turkish middle class in particular highlights these highly educated, transnational business professionals as the winners of neoliberal globalization.[12] That this class is discontented is also surprising from fundamental class perspectives: it is surprising from a production-centered Marxian class perspective because these professionals surely are not in the same or remotely similar conditions as those of the proletariat. It is surprising from a market-centered Weberian class perspective as well because these workers are at the top of the Turkish labor market and can enjoy global mobility. It is also unexpected from a consumption-centered Bourdieusian class perspective because their consumption practices are aspired to and emulated; they are the trendsetters. So, how do we make sense of white-collar blues?

WHAT'S WRONG WITH "GOOD JOBS"?

Most resource-centered studies of inequality assume that high income levels and occupational prestige equal the good life.[13] Focusing on the discontents of business professionals through the lenses of worker consent and alienation, however, exposes the inherent limits of such an approach. I argue that the relative scarcity of in-depth empirical research on professional-managerial employees or "elite workers,"[14] in particular their quality of working life, chiefly stems from taking the job quality of such highly educated and well-employed white-collar workers for granted as opposed to the often undesirable job quality of blue-collar and precarious service-sector workers. This book problematizes the enviable jobs and lifestyles of business professionals and seeks to understand white-collar blues both by situating these blues in the intertwined processes of globalization and middle-class formation and by attending to these workers' lived experience of quality of working life via in-depth interviews.[15]

Through official documents and historical sources on foreign investment and employment in Turkey and the secondary literature on the Turkish middle classes, I show how the definition of "good jobs" that bring about a solid middle-class life has changed over the last fifty years. During Turkey's developmentalist era of the 1960s and 1970s, the main role models for "making it" were state-employed doctors, lawyers, and engineers. However, the post-1980s neoliberal era, marked by increasing foreign direct investment and Turkey's tighter integration into the global economy, witnessed the emergence of new hegemonic archetypes of success: professional-managerial employees of TNCs. As capital became increasingly mobile and transnational under the aegis of neoliberalism, world-renowned companies such as McKinsey, Deloitte, Microsoft, and Procter & Gamble opened offices in Istanbul, making it an emerging global city with "tall buildings" while also engendering new trajectories for upward mobility. As TNCs, with their higher salaries and prestige, outshone the Turkish state and companies in attracting highly educated professionals, the *best* jobs in the Turkish labor market have increasingly concentrated at TNCs. Turkish *yuppies* have sought employment at these brand-name firms, whose ample salaries enable them to consume more and better. These companies also hold out the promise of a *global* upward mobility by easing immigration to the Global North;[16] that these workers' credentials have the seal of approval of Fortune 500 companies legitimizes their membership in the global elite labor market. This equation of the good life with white-collar jobs at TNCs emerged in the context of a neoliberal welfare retrenchment that undermined public employment and made educational attainment more costly and competitive.

This book examines an underappreciated flip side of this equation: the way that fast-track careers at TNCs, despite providing higher incomes than most Turkish companies and state jobs, in fact have impoverished the quality of working life for many of the best and brightest of Turkish millennials. Drawing from more than one hundred in-depth interviews in Istanbul as well as New

York, I follow these Turkish members of the global elite workforce through selection into, surviving within, and (for some) opting out of sought-after jobs at TNCs. Being good sons and daughters and honoring their families' sacrifices by studying hard and acing one high-stakes test after another in an increasingly competitive Turkish education system, they have learned foreign languages, survived demanding extracurricular activities, and graduated from top colleges—and now, as masters of delayed gratification, these elite workers have developed high expectations for their careers. Such chronic overachievement makes them susceptible to experiencing relative deprivation, particularly in the form of underemployment qua overqualification (partly structured by the scarcity of high-skill jobs in the Turkish labor market). These elite workers also tend to suffer from burnout because of the increasingly demanding corporate work culture spearheaded by TNCs since the late twentieth century. However, high income levels and upscale consumption patterns, mortgage and credit card debt, and a pernicious status anxiety tend to tether these workers to their jobs, despite the discouraging quality of their working life. Still, some professionals do break free and abandon their corporate careers. Those who do report that they typically work fewer hours, are more fulfilled by their noncorporate jobs, and become more contented with their lives despite earning less.

This book offers a window into the processes that govern the middle-class boundaries and the nature of middle-class-ness itself. In my exploration, I raise three interrelated questions: Who can (and can't) get high-prestige, high-salary white-collar jobs at TNCs? Once they have landed these jobs, how do Turkish elite business professionals think about the quality of their working lives? And why and how do some of them end up opting out of these supposedly enviable corporate careers?

STUDYING WHITE-COLLAR BLUES

To answer these questions, I marshaled empirical materials from two waves of fieldwork in Istanbul and New York City in 2017 and 2018 comprising over one hundred interviews with various constituencies of the transnational Turkish middle class in both cities. The interviews revolved around my subjects' educational backgrounds; career trajectories; recruitment experiences; and reflections on their jobs, careers, and lives. My questions were mostly open-ended, aiming to capitalize on how my respondents interpreted and found (or failed to find) meaning in their own experiences. To account for respondents' varied backgrounds and experiences, I used semistructured interview schedules and improvised whenever it appeared fruitful to do so. I also employed a vignette instrument (see the appendix) to elicit respondents' work orientations, ideal work narratives, and how these compared with their actual experiences.

Throughout my data collection and analysis, I followed abductive reasoning, which actively seeks surprising empirical phenomena (i.e., results unexplained by existing theories) and synthesizes deduction and induction with an iterative approach, "a recursive process of double-fitting data and theories."[17] Doing my fieldwork in two waves with a spatial and temporal break in between facilitated an iterative approach that abductive analysis favors. For example, in my first round of interviews with business professionals (seventeen in New York and seventeen in Istanbul), I learned that part of my respondents' disappointment stemmed from their high expectations for corporate careers. This finding shaped my second round of fieldwork in Istanbul in 2018, leading me to interview fifteen graduating university seniors who were about to join the elite workforce, in addition to fourteen more business professionals. After my first round of interviews, I also wanted to explore what comes after disappointing and exhausting work experience, which led me to interview seventeen people who had opted out of their corporate careers. When I learned that some business professionals see therapists to cope with their problems, I added interviews with five psychotherapists, in which I asked about the complaints their white-collar patients usually bring into therapy and how these patients make sense of their work-related problems.[18]

My research purposefully focused on the generations born in the 1980s and after. These people were raised in a neoliberalizing Turkey. Hence, my sample of elite workers, which I describe in more detail in chapter 3 and the appendix, consisted mostly of young adult business professionals and midlevel managers, ranging in age from twenty-five to forty-four years (31.4 is the average). Gender distribution was even, and almost one-fifth of my subjects were married. Another sampling decision I made was to focus solely on subjects who were born and raised in Turkey at least until college to make sure that my interviewees had experienced the social trans-formations of Turkey's neoliberalization in their formative years. Based on my survey of their self-perceived class locations with respect to their consumption or purchasing power and income lev-els as well as self-declared salaries, respondents spanned the range from middle to upper class, coalescing around upper middle class. Most experienced some level of upward mobility compared to their families' class background, most commonly from middle to upper middle class. The term "yuppies" (young urban/upwardly mobile professionals), which became popular in the 1980s in the United States and then circulated globally, squarely fits them. Note that they were not executive-level managers (with a single exception) and did not yet occupy the commanding heights of the corpora-tions they work for. Hence, they are most aptly defined as "elite workers"; not *the elites* who own or rule, but the elite *of workers* who occupy the high echelons of labor markets thanks to their presti-gious educational credentials and skill sets.[19] Of course, as they age and keep climbing the career ladder, some of them might become executives of TNCs or large Turkish companies and join the ranks of *the elites* or even *the global elite*. The majority, however, will continue being part of the transnational middle class because of the pyramidal shape of corporate organizations; after all, there can be only so many CEOs, as one of my respondents pointed out.

I relied on referrals for initial access following the advice on eliciting qualitative data from elite professionals.[20] I used LinkedIn's premium accounts for scouting purposes and leveraging my network. Being an alumnus of Boğaziçi University and having worked briefly for Procter & Gamble as a business professional granted me an insider status, helping me with recruitment as well as building rapport with my subjects, many of whom considered me socially and culturally close to them. One sign of the fruitfulness of these attempts is the frequent overflow of my interviews beyond their prearranged duration: it was common for me to schedule a forty-five-minute slot, typically during lunch, to accommodate my respondents' busy schedules, but then end up extending interviews much longer in response to their desire to continue our conversation. My interviews with business professionals and managers averaged around ninety minutes.

I also made ethnographic observations during my fieldwork in Istanbul, chiefly to better understand the population I studied by increasing my "exposure."[21] In this respect, I mobilized my white-collar past; I reached out to former colleagues as well as classmates pursuing fast-track careers, spent time with my white-collar friends, visited them in their offices, and took every chance to join their social gatherings while actively listening to them. I occasionally joined them in their morning commutes and observed subway stations during rush hour. I spent time in the Levent district of Istanbul, where most TNCs have their offices; I frequented the coffee shops and restaurants there, particularly during lunch time because it is almost a sacred ritual for business professionals in Istanbul (unlike New York City) to go out for lunch. In all these excursions, I actively observed and listened to business professionals and took field notes on my phone when appropriate. These efforts improved the quality of my interviews because I learned my respondents' vernacular and cultural scripts in their everyday lives and beyond.

TRANSNATIONAL CORPORATIONS AND MIDDLE-CLASS ALIENATION

This book develops a theory of middle-class alienation rooted in the way that middle-class investments in education and high hopes for corporate careers clash with the reality of poor work-life balance, low intrinsic satisfaction, and lack of meaning in labor. The fact that these "good jobs" can fail their occupants at work—just like "bad jobs"—while also colonizing most of their waking hours justifies extending alienation theory beyond blue-collar labor and precarious service-sector work. I recast alienation as a condition independent of skill and salary—a malady that can be found even in high-echelon labor markets when work is characterized by exhaustion and unfulfillment. Against the backdrop of high expectations and the major investment in cultural capital required to land these "good jobs," my historically grounded empirical analysis of Turkish elite workers shows how professional-managerial employment at TNCs can structure a discouraging quality of (working) life by failing to provide elite workers with intrinsic satisfaction and meaning from work while suffocating their non-work-life spheres. They know that they have to keep selling their intellectual labor in corporate workplaces (which are almost always located in expensive global cities) to earn the upper-middle-class living they have aspired to, so they feel constricted, powerless, and dominated by the human capital that they built themselves with their hard work and success. If playing by the rules and doing everything right, that is, if winning all the contests of school and work cannot yield a fulfilling and happy life, what can?

I also argue that TNCs have been responsible for cultivating such alienating work conditions. Running on high-performance work systems that rose with post-Fordism in the Global North, TNCs helped spread the corporate culture of greedy work—demanding an undivided commitment to work over everything else in life—around the world. Moreover, many TNCs have exacerbated skill mismatch, especially overqualification, in the high-skill Turkish labor market by replicating the Taylorist design/execution binary along the hierarchy of headquarters versus branch offices. Put simply, the headquarters of TNCs in the North *design* and their branches in the South *execute* following that design, which reproduces the uneven global division of labor.

This book examines how burnout and disappointment, enabled by a lack of worker control over labor, taint the transnational Turkish middle-class identity; it also looks beyond the socioeconomic rewards of such jobs and demonstrates how a life lived well requires autonomy and the ability to derive intrinsic satisfaction and find meaning in work. I hope this exploration, by revealing the hidden costs of sacrificing these essentials for higher pay and status, and how trading freedom for financial security spoils business professionals' lives, will encourage us to revisit our relationships with work, the activity that occupies most of our waking hours.

This book advances scholarship on globalization and inequality. Theorizing " 'middling' forms of transnationalism,"[22] it expands the literature's dominant binary foci of the global ruling elites and the immigrant poor.[23] It also restructures the consumption-centered middle-class analyses that dominate the scholarship on

professional-managerial employees in the Global South by propos-
ing an employment-centered theorization of transnational middle
classes through an organizational approach to inequality.[24] Much
like comparing workplaces of professional-managerial employees
reveals earnings and occupational prestige differentials, examining corporate recruitment practices reveals who can or cannot join
the ranks of transnational middle classes. Focusing on brand-name
firms also sharpens our inquiry; unlike exclusive consumption
practices—the majority of which could be achieved on credit—the
prestige of working for a world-renowned TNC cannot be imitated
and affords greater distinction in "the classification struggle."[25] In
other words, "bringing employers back in" and at the center helps
us parsimoniously capture socioeconomic and cultural aspects of
middle-class formation, elucidating the dynamics of economic and
cultural capital accumulation as well as social and symbolic boundary making during the neoliberal transformation of many Global
South countries.

This analysis also contributes to the empirical study of the
Global South's emerging middle classes by focusing on Turkey,
an underappreciated case that reveals TNCs as influential agents
of middle-class formation and social change. It shows how the
advent of TNCs in economies where protectionism once prevailed
transforms domestic labor markets, alters earnings distributions
and status hierarchies, engenders new social mobility pathways,
and reworks the cultural makeup of the middle classes. The fact
that Turkey witnessed these changes despite consistently attracting rates of foreign direct investment that were lower than those
in many middle-income countries allows us to offer an a fortiori
argument that TNCs have been crucial mechanisms of middle-class
transformation across the Global South, as can be seen in countries
such as Mexico, Poland, and others that attracted higher rates of
foreign direct investment.[26]

This book contributes to the burgeoning literature on elite labor.[27] In the vein of a "critical economic sociology of labor,"[28] it enriches our understanding of how assessing merit in the elite labor market dominated by TNCs is often entangled with the reproduction of inequality. The book also develops a novel critique of global capitalism by detailing how even the most privileged workers have failed to lead fulfilling lives because of alienation from their labor. Focusing on the winners of neoliberal globalization in the Global South—the business professionals employed at TNCs—and highlighting the consequential importance of work's nonfinancial aspects, my book complicates the "good jobs, bad jobs" discourse, which relies primarily on the conventional divide of *collar color*.[29] Moving this debate forward with empirical analysis, I revisit the perennial sociological question of how the division of labor we inhabit affects our well-being, and especially how it contributes to our *ill-being*; along the way I extend the alienation theory from manual labor to knowledge work to better account for a broader chunk of postindustrial and globalized working conditions. While alienation theory has recently made a comeback in contemporary sociological scholarship,[30] its labor-related aspects have remained underappreciated.[31]

This book challenges the widespread assumption that high-salary corporate jobs make people happy and content. There is a human cost to overwork and unfulfilling labor—even when the work is secure and pays well. By examining the harms of getting caught up in the rat race and showing how inequality hurts even the upwardly mobile, the book emphasizes that stronger social security measures, revalorization of public-sector jobs, a universal reduction in the workweek, and a stronger emphasis on liberal arts in higher education represent crucial contributions to our individual and collective well-being.

OUTLINE OF THE BOOK

To make sense of how the holders of so-called good jobs could experience white-collar blues, I peel back the layers of middle-class formation, shifting my level of inquiry progressively from macro to micro. The book continues with a historical examination of the rise of a transnational middle class in Turkey, followed by three empirical inquiries into *becoming* a member of the transnational Turkish middle class, *enduring* as such, and (in some cases, at least) *opting out.*

Chapter 1 contextualizes my inquiry theoretically and historically. I begin by situating the problem of white-collar blues within the middle class in general and within the transnational aspects of new middle-class formation in particular. I argue that the Turkish economy's global integration and increasing embrace of neoliberalism since the 1980s constitute the key macrolevel processes undergirding transnational middle-class formation in Turkey. Starting with how most countries in the Global South increasingly left protectionist economic models and subscribed to the Washington Consensus, I later center on TNCs as consequential agents of neoliberal globalization. Marshaling empirical evidence from official documents and historical sources on foreign direct investment and employment in Turkey and the secondary literature on Turkish middle classes, I reveal how TNCs transformed the Turkish high-skill labor market by connecting it to the global one, offering above-market rates of pay, and providing higher occupational prestige. The increasing prevalence of TNCs in Turkey and their emergence as the primary employer of its most educated labor force marked the rise of a Turkish "yuppiedom" vis-à-vis its old middle class, whose primary employer was the Turkish state. In contrast to the developmentalist era of the mid-twentieth century, during which public-sector doctors, lawyers, and engineers were popular role models, the business professionals of famous TNCs became the new forebears of modernity, champions of meritocracy, and hegemonic symbols of success, thus redefining the "good life" for the masses. This contrast also reveals that this ascendant new middle-class culture is centered around a competitive individualism that manifests itself in career aspirations of global mobility and transcending Turkey, in addition to the oft-mentioned consumerism. This chapter lays out the political-economic processes and accompanying cultural changes that my respondents were born into, helping us to grasp how their aspirations and expectations have been shaped.

I turn to meso-level, organizational processes in chapter 2. Conceptualizing recruitment as a critical moment of gatekeeping and social closure, I ask, Who can land the prestigious entry-level professional jobs at prestigious TNCs, who cannot, and why? I answer this question by thoroughly covering both the supply and demand side of the Turkish elite labor market through my interviews with senior undergraduates from an elite public university who were in the labor market during my interviews; with human resource professionals who engage in their recruitment; and with business professionals and managers who have been on both sides of hiring.

These interviews reveal that the hiring processes at these companies begin by targeting students from a select group of universities—a practice that, given the increasing privatization of education in Turkey since the 1980s, privileges wealthier families. Even though university admissions in Turkey might seem to be meritocratic, governed as they are by nationwide centralized exam scores, acing these tests requires dedicated preparation and support from private tutors and cram schools, which has raised the costs of middle-class reproduction. Furthermore, my examination of the subsequent stages in the hiring process highlights the importance of transnational forms of cultural capital—English-language skills, quality of international experience, and a cosmopolitan outlook and taste—which in turn depend heavily on class background. While the increasingly global nature of labor process at TNCs could justify such a predilection, the job interviews at these firms—particularly the final rounds conducted by revenue-generating managers instead of human resources professionals—also tend to suffer from class homophily, that candidates from affluent backgrounds are often subtly yet systematically preferred. I explain such biased assessments with the rise and prevalence of high-performance work systems at TNCs that have championed teamwork since the 1980s. I find such bias often takes place while assessing "the fit," that is, whether a candidate fits well with the team. For instance, having similar high-end hobbies, elite high school backgrounds, and international travel experience can help create an emotional resonance between job candidates and the managers who would be their immediate supervisors. Such biased assessments happen more frequently at elite professional service firms because they often lack human resources divisions or rely on their revenue-generating managers for assessing talent and "fit."

These findings emphasize that, in addition to economically undergirding the transnational Turkish middle class, TNCs help with its cultural formation as well, demarcating these workers as a relatively exclusive group with a homogeneous class culture. Such exclusivity, combined with the job candidates' history of hard work and overachievement, raises their expectations of corporate careers and their future lives and structures their future experiences of relative deprivation and alienation.

Chapter 3 turns to a micro-level analysis of class formation and takes a deep dive into the lived experience of workers suffering from white-collar blues by analyzing the quality of the working-life narratives of the transnational Turkish middle class. Drawing mainly from my interviews with business professionals and managers, I develop a fourfold typology of overall experience of quality of work life by identifying two significant dimensions of satisfaction and discontent: experiencing work as fulfilling versus lacking intrinsic satisfaction and meaning from work, and having a good work-life balance versus being overworked. Analyzing the narratives of my respondents based on these dimensions, I find that while a small portion of white-collar workers feels contented with their jobs, most feel disappointed, exhausted, or both. Despite having the best corporate jobs in the labor market and high hopes for their careers, disappointment and exhaustion loom large in the lived experiences of Turkey's transnational middle class. Throughout the chapter, I discuss how such job quality became more prevalent in the context of post-Fordism and high-performance work systems of the corporate workplaces in the Global North. This historical perspective helps us to conceptualize TNCs, most of which hail from the United States, as the global carriers of "greedy work" culture and to understand better the work-related aspects of how global capitalism is manifest in the Global South, including Turkey. Such a discouraging quality of working-life experience, while grounding my extension of alienation theory toward elite labor, also raises the question, Why do Turkish business professionals continue to put up with alienation?

Chapter 4 examines how middle-class discontent spurs some Turkish business professionals to forego their hard-earned corporate careers. Drawing comparatively from interviews with business professionals who were actively working and those who had resigned, I consider these resignations as the withdrawal of worker consent. I find that while desiring freedom from alienating labor is a primary motive for quitting, the decision to opt out is contingent on how much the push factors of the workplace resonate with the pull factors of nonwork spheres of life. Moreover, a strong fear of falling, heightened by the lack of safety nets in an era of privatized risk, discourages many from taking the leap, while debt-dependent lifestyles keep their consent fresh.

Competition has been the name of the game under the aegis of neoliberalism; gone are the days of the lifelong employment model, and social security institutions are gradually eroded because of austerity measures in the Turkish economy's "structural adjustment." In the absence of social safety nets such as the efficacious unemployment benefits that their northern European peers rely on, Turkish business professionals' desire to resign can be actualized to the extent they can mobilize personal safety nets. Personal savings and/or financial help from family and friends are of critical importance, as is ongoing social support. Note that despite these workers' high incomes, the increasingly exorbitant costs of living in Istanbul—typical of emergent global cities—prevents many business professionals from feeling financially secure and fully exercising their freedom when they are faced with important life decisions. Mortgages and credit card debt accrued in the name of aspirational consumption—the signature feature of the yuppie lifestyle that arose with the introduction of expensive Western imports and consumer credit since the 1980s—serve as golden handcuffs, constraining workers' ability to quit their unfulfilling and draining careers. Such constraints are stricter for parents, who also deal with the increasing cost of private education, which has become critical for ensuring their offspring's upward mobility. Even when there is solid financial security, a social insecurity in the form of status anxiety can inhibit many from quitting corporate positions that grant status. In Marxist parlance, while "[t]he proletarians have nothing to lose but their chains,"[32] the white-collar salariat indeed feels like they have a lot more to lose than their (golden) chains.

If and when they can break free from such overdetermined consent, those who opt out typically work fewer hours in their new noncorporate jobs, get more fulfillment from their labor, and become more contented with their lives despite earning less. Upon resignation, their immediate postcorporate trajectories consist of four possible paths "back" to a more balanced life: (1) back to one's self by taking time off and soul searching, especially in the context of extensive travel; (2) back to family by becoming more involved with childcare and other family responsibilities; (3) back to a simpler life via what I call urban flight; and (4) back to labor that flourishes via occupational change, which often involves cultivation of new skill sets and credentials. Providing an important benchmark and empowering narrative for elite workers, these opt-out narratives also inform the immanent critique of global capitalism that I lay out in the conclusion.

The conclusion expands my analysis of the making of the transnational Turkish middle class by locating it in the broader context of Turkey's middle classes and of transnational middle classes in the Global South and North. This broader context sets the stage for an immanent critique of global capitalism and an extension of the alienation theory to include elite labor. In this model, alienation can be generalized as the experience of feeling disconnected from labor—be it manual, emotional, aesthetic, or intellectual labor—and an accompanying impoverished life experience marked by self-domination, relative deprivation, underemployment, and overwork. I conclude by discussing the book's broader policy, mobilization, and future research implications for quality of (working) life, higher education, and the middle classes and middle-class-ness.

In the subsequent chapters, we will try to understand how Ozan and some of his peers ended up with white-collar blues.

1

TRANSNATIONAL CORPORATIONS
AND REMAKING THE TURKISH
MIDDLE CLASS

For the vast majority of my respondents who were about to enter the workforce, the only acceptable option for an employer was a prestigious transnational corporation. Several of them spoke of their reluctance to work for a "no name company." The international prestige and fame of a company, while correlated with important factors of quality of working life such as salaries and workplace culture, was also important in and of itself in my respondents' career choices because they too wanted to be known and valued. When I probed Ezgi, a graduating economics senior who was going to work at a startup, about what she felt was most important in looking for a job, she put the "brand" of her workplace at the top of her list:

MUSTAFA (THE AUTHOR): If you were to look for a job now, which one would you say you would prioritize? Is it the industry? The company? Or the department, and by department, I mean what you do at work every day.

EZGI: I understood your question. Yes, all of them are relevant differently. I mean, the thing is, what sticks to you is the company [label]. Industry is also something I'd care a bit about but, yes, I think after my internship, I understood that the department is the most important thing, that is, what you spend time on from nine in the morning to five in the evening, but on the other hand . . . the thing is . . . it is also important how I answer the question, "Where do you work?" For example, a friend of mine is doing an internship at Uludağ [a Turkish soft drink producer], and marketing is what he actually does, but . . . I wouldn't want to work at Uludağ. It's because, you know, it is Uludağ. . . . It does not sound like you are doing much work [there]. . . . But Red Bull, for example . . . I think what it [company name] evokes is very relevant.

MUSTAFA: Then, can we say it is the brand of your workplace?

EZGI: Yeah, its brand, its image . . .

MUSTAFA: How about, say, Coca-Cola? Would you say "yes" to working there?

EZGI: Yeah, yeah, I mean, if I were searching for a job, I would be fine with it. . . . It matters how it seems on your CV. One says Uludağ, the other Coca-Cola.

Many respondents made these local versus global comparisons for their prospective employers—so much so that almost none of them even mentioned Turkish corporations as potential workplaces. Bülent, a graduating engineering senior who was about to start work at a Big Three firm,[1] stated:

The name [of the Big Three firm] is important and great because I do not have to explain [about my work]. I mean, it is like the key of a BMW car, a label of myself, and I like this. For example, last week, I made a surprise visit to Paris to see my girlfriend for her birthday. Among thirteen French people, I was the only Turkish person, and they liked me and when I said I will start working for [the Big Three firm], they immediately recognized it, and this is nice.

As Bülent's quote illustrates, one of the key expectations of this stratum of young people is that they envision their lives on a global scale, beyond the confines of Turkey. Hence, transnational corporations (TNCs), with their global networks and their world-scale operations, become an important vehicle for entering into a new identity that *transcends* Turkey.

The global expansion of foreign direct investment (FDI) and commodity chains has been a boon for TNCs, most of which hail from the Global North.[2] Apple Inc., for example, designs its products in Silicon Valley, California, but manufactures them in the Global South, where manual labor is considerably cheaper. Such practices raise significant labor, human rights, and climate change concerns.[3] Nonetheless, TNCs have become such a fixture of the global economy that headquarter–foreign affiliate relations can inductively map global urban hierarchies.[4]

Such interpenetration of national economies has also complicated the periphery-semiperiphery difference in the world system,[5] increasing working populations' incomes in the Global South and expanding the "global middle class."[6] Scholarly discussion of this middle class focuses mostly on the working classes of India and China, but the term also includes business professionals from the Global South. This population, also labeled the "global middle classes,"[7] has been noted for their aspirational consumption and Western lifestyle.[8] Unlike their counterparts in the Global North, the Southern middle classes display a distinctively *trans*national orientation to their lives and careers, often deploying cultural capital (e.g., prestigious educational credentials, fluency in English, international experience, and cosmopolitan tastes) to *transcend* their nation of origin and distinguish themselves from their own compatriots.[9] For example, Diane Davis noted that Bangalore's engineers bear more resemblance to middle-class American and European counterparts "than to their brethren in the rest of the state of Karnataka" and observed that the preferences of China's "investment-savvy, car-owning, urban-based professionals" distinguish them "from both their own pasts as well as many of their countrymen."[10]

How can we explain the emergence of a distinct category of professional-managerial employees across the diverse economies of the Global South? These individuals are now broadly considered role models of upward mobility and the good life. Although what caught the most attention is their convergent consumption patterns and lifestyles, it is striking that their workplaces are in fact identical. What unites most of them in the first place is their employers, mostly TNCs such as the Fortune Global 500 firms. References to TNCs and yuppies seem to go hand in hand across the Global South, including in Mexico,[11] postsocialist countries such as Hungary and Poland,[12] and Turkey.[13] Even so, scholarship on the middle class in the developing world has focused mostly on this population's consumption patterns,[14] leaving their employment in the background or taking it for granted.

But I would argue that employment is in fact at the heart of transnational middle-class formation. The circulation of capital in the form of TNCs has shaped contemporary middle classes across the Global South, insofar as TNCs compete with domestic employers and dominate local high-skill labor markets by connecting them to global counterparts. Emerging as the most desired employers in the Southern labor markets, TNCs have altered local hierarchies of income and status, made middle-class reproduction more competitive, and acted as gatekeepers of middle classes via selective hiring. Against the backdrop of neoliberalization and the erosion of the state-sponsored fractions of middle classes through curtailed public employment and welfare practices, TNCs have engendered new upper middle class fractions that I refer to as *transnational middle classes*.[15] During the developmentalist era of the 1960s and 1970s, state-employed doctors, lawyers, and engineers were the role models of "making it," but during the neoliberal era of the 1980s and 1990s, professional-managerial employees of world-renowned TNCs assumed that status, becoming hegemonic symbols of success, ideal citizens, and new forebearers of modernity in the Global South.

This chapter traces the emergence of this TNC hegemony through the history of FDI and employment in Turkey where protectionism once prevailed. TNCs have transformed domestic labor markets, altered earnings distributions and status hierarchies, and engendered new pathways for social mobility—and along the way they have dramatically reworked the cultural makeup of Turkey's middle class. As we saw from the respondents quoted at the beginning of the chapter, Turkey's new transnational middle class embraces a particular identity: success-driven, cosmopolitan, and globally mobile.

THEORIZING MIDDLE CLASSES

But what is middle class to begin with? This deceptively simple question has kept sociologists busy since the dawn of the discipline of sociology. There is still no consensus on how to draw the boundaries of the middle class or how to define what remains inside, although one of the earliest definitions goes all the way back to Aristotle. The plural term "middle classes" is often used to account for this ambiguity. One basic reason for why "middle class" is so hard to pin down is that the political stakes are high when it comes to the boundaries of the middle class; it has come to be viewed as something good per se: the larger it is, the better off a society is. It signifies not only higher life standards but also democracy.[16] As a desirable (and possible) end in itself (e.g., the American dream of upward social mobility), a middle class also ameliorates the conflict in a society polarized between capitalist and working classes or, more popularly put, between the haves and have-nots; creates consent for capitalism; and fosters its hegemony.[17] Much like sociologist Georg Simmel's contention that triadic relations can offer more stability in social settings than dyads, the concept of the middle class often appears to work as a deus ex machina of societal stability, resolving the conflict between the haves and have-nots.[18] The most intuitive and popular way to think about the middle class is to define it through what it is not, as a residual category: it is neither working nor capitalist class, and its members are neither poor nor rich. Contrary to Karl Marx and Friedrich Engels's famous punch line about the proletariat in *The Communist Manifesto*, middle classes, especially the upper middle classes, have more to lose than their chains; however, they feel they still have to work and sell their labor, albeit in a white-collar way, to keep earning a middle-class living.[19]

Amid the broad category of the middle classes, white-collar workers, particularly those with professional and managerial jobs who enjoy high salaries and status, have long posed a conceptual problem—what Erik Olin Wright memorably termed an "embarrassment" for students of class analysis,[20] especially of Marxist persuasion. As the category evolved in the latter part of the twentieth century, theorists examined the transformation of the "old" middle classes in the core economies, mostly small entrepreneurs, into "new" middle classes,[21] mostly white-collar workers—ranging from clerks to managers, from receptionists to professionals.[22] Three fundamental approaches within new middle-class theories are also vital in understanding middle-class formation in the Global South: the production-centered (Marxist), labor market–centered (Weberian), and consumption-centered (Bourdieusian) lenses.[23]

Marxist approaches to middle-class analyses center around labor conditions and their political aspects.[24] The most prominent approach in this vein was advanced by Erik Olin Wright, who argued that exploitation rather than authority relations in society or technical division of labor should be the basis of neo-Marxist class analysis.[25] Embracing the presence and complexity of the middle classes, Wright's theory of "contradictory class locations" provides us with a richer class map than the tripartite one with proletariat, bourgeoisie, and petty bourgeoise (i.e., self-employed) because exploitation occurs not only along the axis of economic ownership but also through control over the physical means of production and control over other people's labor power. The additional dimensions of skills and authority in the workplace grant a privileged location to elite workers compared to nonskilled workers. Many white-collar workers, according to this map, populate the in-between, contradictory class locations: between proletariat and bourgeoisie there are managers—including top- and midlevel managers as well as low-level supervisors such as forepersons—and between proletariat and petty bourgeoisie there are semiautonomous employees with relative control over labor processes—including professionals and experts such as engineers or accountants.

John Ehrenreich and Barbara Ehrenreich conceptualized Wright's managers and semiautonomous employees as a distinct class, the "professional-managerial class."[26] Inspired by the significant involvement of college-educated white-collar workers in the social movements of the 1960s and 1970s and the U.S. New Left, the Ehrenreichs maintained, that in addition to the common denominator of being salaried mental workers, the members of this grouping make a coherent and mature class because they coalesce around a common culture, lifestyle, and consciousness as well as common interests. Loïc Wacquant summarized this point as follows: "the PMC [professional-managerial class] has evolved its own organizations (professional associations), its own ideology (technocratic liberalism), and its own centers of recruitment and indoctrination (elite universities)."[27]

Weberian approaches, on the other hand, center around the notion of "life chances," or, more accurately, how well individuals fare in the market. Labor relations constitute a significant part of this picture, and expertise and managerial control—elements also introduced by Wright—are important factors in determining market outcomes and social mobility.[28] The most prominent Weberian class analysis was advanced by John Goldthorpe, who synthesized these insights into yet another concrete class schema, arguing that what matters most in distinguishing one class from another among employees is whether they enter a "service relationship" or a labor contract with their employers.[29] The former is characterized by a salary, a career ladder with progressive incomes, and varying levels of autonomy in the workplace, whereas the latter is characterized by wages, stationary career trajectories, and little to no autonomy in the workplace. Goldthorpe's class schema thus highlights managers and professionals as a "service class" while distinguishing them from white-collar workers who engage with routine work, such as clerks. Further differentiated within itself into an upper and lower service class, owners of large enterprises (i.e., bourgeoisie) are interestingly considered part of the upper service class, while small employers are not part of the service class; they are noted as petty bourgeoisie.

These Marxist and Weberian approaches, or " 'production-centered' and 'market-centered' " streams of middle-class research, show significant convergence[30] because of their shared structuralist understanding of class centered around labor. While they provide us with a valuable analytical lens and enable international comparative class analysis, these schools of thought have been criticized for being "static and ahistorical"—too concerned with structures and typologies at the expense of accounting for the dynamics of class relations and the boundaries of middle classes.[31] Just as

E. P. Thompson famously emphasized agency and lived experience of class against Althusserian structuralism,[32] this critique favors a Bourdieusian class analysis that emphasizes studying the struggle between social groups and their "strategies of distinction, reproduction, and subversion."[33]

The work of Pierre Bourdieu provides us with (among other useful concepts) the conceptual machinery of *capital*, most notably "cultural capital."[34] Shifting the conceptual emphasis from a static class structure to a more dynamic social space, Bourdieu argued that the distribution of class fractions in a social space is a matter of both the volume of economic and cultural capital a class fraction commands as well as their ratio of economic to cultural capital.[35] Through an inductive class analysis of France in the 1970s, Bourdieu curiously located professionals, engineers, and senior executives in the dominant class because of their high volume of both economic and cultural capital; office workers and junior executives, however, were placed in the middle class.[36]

While Bourdieusian class analysis could be seen as the ultimate synthesis of Weberian and Marxian approaches (as well as those of Louis Althusser and E. P. Thompson), it is used most fruitfully to make the case for a *consumption-centered* approach to middle classes. Bourdieu's illustration of how taste is weaponized in "classification struggles" pioneered a rich stream of middle-class research on how consumption patterns as well as lifestyles of social groups can have *classifying* effects.[37] What people buy and consume, and the accompanying lifestyles, allow them to draw, highlight, solidify, or negotiate social and symbolic boundaries,[38] to engage with social closure and police those boundaries,[39] and to reproduce class inequality writ large.[40] As I will demonstrate below, however, Bourdieusian insights can be applied to labor market and work situation as well, and doing so can provide us with a clearer understanding of middle-class formation.

TRANSNATIONAL ASPECTS OF MIDDLE-CLASS FORMATION IN THE GLOBAL SOUTH

The theories of the middle class outlined above, although they give us a relational understanding of middle classes in workplaces, labor markets, and the world of consumption, all lack a transnational dimension.[41] Their methodological nationalism can take us only so far today, and it is difficult to disregard the transnational aspects of class formation from the late twentieth century onward, particularly for middle classes in semiperiphery countries. However, critical globalization studies and the burgeoning empirical research on the emerging middle classes of various countries in the Global South have applied a transnational lens to class analysis in general and to middle-class formation in particular—one that takes cross-border flows of capital, labor and people, goods and commodities, and cultural scripts seriously.

This macro view has highlighted a significant shift during the late twentieth century "from a world economy to a global economy"—in other words, from an economy dominated by national accumulation processes and the international trade of finished goods to the transnational accumulation of capital and a globally integrated production system animated by value chains.[42] Such interpenetration of national economies has been driven mainly by liberalized capital circulation across national borders, principally as FDI.[43] The global expansion of capital flows from core economies and the organization of those flows into TNCs have led some scholars to posit the rise of a "transnational capitalist class,"[44] and even a "transnational state."[45]

The expanding and deepening interconnections between national economies has also been enabled by fundamental transformations in the Southern economies. Throughout the twentieth century, many so-called third world countries, such as Iran[46] and

Mexico,[47] sought to "catch up with development," often through state-led modernization projects and protectionist economic policies like import substitution industrialization (ISI).[48] State-led industrialization with a nationalist ethos provided citizens with white-collar employment, accessible public education and health care,[49] and meaningful unity with the nation,[50] all of which served to reproduce and extend national middle classes in the Global South.[51]

With the shift to a global economy, however, a new set of factors came into play.[52] The specific transitions varied, but countries looking to integrate into the emerging global economy often adopted market-oriented principles (later designated the Washington Consensus) such as removing restrictions on international trade and FDI, forgoing fixed currency regimes, avoiding budget deficits, reducing public spending, and privatizing state-owned firms.[53] These and other policies were often prescribed by the International Monetary Fund (IMF) and World Bank as *loan conditions*,[54] and they were meant to address matters like the Latin American debt crisis of the 1970s, the Asian crises of the late 1990s, and the Turkish crises of the late 1970s and early 2000s. These structural adjustments pushed many Southern states to renounce their role as middle-class benefactors; austerity policies necessitated cutting welfare spending, while privatization shifted middle-class jobs to the private sector, often causing existing middle classes composed of state employees to shrink and stagnate.

The transition from ISI to export-led growth models and integration into global markets writ large led to significant fragmentation in these nations' middle classes and the emergence of new middle-class fractions.[55] Such bifurcations propagated mostly along a rift between domestically and internationally embedded sources of employment. For example, as Saskia Sassen observed, "emergent global classes," including a "transnational professional class," developed in the wake of the globalization of production and the

constant expansion of financial markets.[56] The offshore operations of many TNCs increasingly spanned the world via the global
expansion of FDI.[57] Their foreign affiliates or branches—mostly run
by the local managers and professionals who constituted this new
class—began to populate not only the global cities of the North[58]
but also the major cities in the South—transforming many of the
latter, including Istanbul, into emerging global cities.[59] Located
"[b]elow the global elites," these "high-income professionals and
technicians" have occupied structurally equivalent positions in the
national and global stratification schemes and have "share[d] more
culturally with their counterparts in different countries than with
their fellow nationals of the lower classes."[60]

Another burgeoning literature focused on empirical case studies of the Global South from Latin America to East Asia, examining
the emergence and convergence of these classes. In contrast to the
emphasis of critical globalization studies on political-economic processes, this literature scrutinizes globalization's cultural and ideological moments, examining everyday experiences of middle-class
life as well as claims to modernity, such as negotiating Indian and
global identities,[61] blending citizenship with entrepreneurship in
India,[62] and cultivating cosmopolitan attitudes and their boundary-
making effects in Egypt.[63] Drawing from histories of middle classes
around the world, Ricardo López and Barbara Weinstein argued that
the meaning of "middle class" is inherently transnational, describing "modernity [as] a process of constant translation, citation, and
contestation."[64] Lars Meier and Hellmuth Lange examined cultural
homogenization through convergent consumption patterns and
everyday practices in emerging middle-class lifestyles across the
Global South, where buying or owning Western imports often signifies that a consumer is "modern."[65]

Echoing the cultural turn in middle-class analysis championed by Bourdieu,[66] most scholarship on the middle classes in the

developing world has focused on consumerism and its impact.[67] For example, Steve Derne argued for basing transnational class analysis in India on "shared patterns of consumption more than shared positions in the economy," despite acknowledging that it is the Indians with "high incomes, college degrees, English-language skills, and global connections"—that is, with a highly specific set of marketable qualities—that actually comprise a "transnational middle class."[68] Thanks to globalized media consumption, principally the increasing availability of cable TV and magazines offering Western content at the turn of the millennium,[69] this group perceives itself as a *middle* class on a transnational scale in terms of consumption, still positioned below "consuming classes" of Western Europe and the United States but above the Indian poor and middle-class Indians who lack English skills and global connections.[70] Studies of the Turkish middle class have thus far followed suit, examining Turkish professional-managerial employees' strategies of distinction through consumption,[71] residential preferences,[72] and cosmopolitanism.[73] What we miss in these accounts, however, is an in-depth investigation into how employment plays into the transnational aspects of middle-class formation.

TOWARD AN EMPLOYMENT-CENTERED THEORY OF MIDDLE-CLASS FORMATION

How should we conceptualize the formation of this culturally convergent, emerging group of business professionals and managers who help make the global economy tick? Leslie Sklair proposed a "transnational capitalist class" including professional-managerial employees of TNCs,[74] but incorporating nonpropertied middle classes (most of my respondents) into a capitalist class poses several conceptual problems.[75] Other scholars of global capitalism have restricted the transnational capitalist class to the *owners* of TNCs and to corporate executives like CEOs or CFOs.[76] In fact, even most of the transnationally mobile European managers known as Eurostars are considered to participate in " 'middling' forms of transnationalism" instead of representing the global elite.[77]

I prefer conceptualizing these privileged, upper fractions of the middle classes populated by business professionals in the Global South as *transnational middle classes*. Occupying an "intermediate position between the national and the global,"[78] these individuals are defined by their *trans*national orientation with respect to consumption and lifestyle but even more by their employment trajectories. Put simply, their employment allows them to *transcend* their nation-state. While the concept of a "global middle class" allows us to analyze the dynamics of global inequality with a single unit of analysis,[79] I focus on the transnational and upper fractions of each country's middle class. Therefore, the term trans*national* better captures my methodology, attuned as it is to the lingering importance of nation-states in class formation.[80]

The term "middle class" emphasizes that the variegated life experiences and class identity of this group are shaped by the group's middling location in both the national class structure (however defined and despite the dynamic nature of this "structure") and the global stratification regime—as noted above, below the middle classes of the North but above those of the South.[81] Various theorizations of new middle classes, such as "professional-managerial class"[82] or "new petty bourgeoisie,"[83] while effectively capturing this group's ideological and political attitudes, miss the transnational dimensions of how this class is made. Although the concept of "transnational professional class" underscores the occupational aspect of this transnational emergence,[84] the conventional sociological understanding of "professionals" (e.g., doctors and lawyers) does not necessarily encompass "business professionals" like managers and consultants.[85] I do not purport to resolve the structural and consequential ambiguities of this emerging group; not only does it occupy what Wright identified as a "contradictory class location" within its national context, but it is also caught between national and global as well as between North and South. My use of the term "middle class" aims not to resolve but to highlight such generative ambiguities.

In my definition, I prioritize the transnational aspects of employment over lifestyle and consumption, including putting Bourdieusian insights on middle-class consumption to work in the world of employment. It is true that the mobility of commodities and culture outpaces that of both capital and labor, and most studies on the transnational processes of middle-class formation have looked at consumption behaviors and individuals' sense of modernity. But upscale consumption is not the sole defining attribute of this category. Occupational prestige—including working for prestigious, brand-name firms such as McKinsey and Google—provides an inimitable source of distinction, whereas lifestyle practices (e.g., traveling abroad for vacations) or conspicuous consumption patterns (e.g., consuming expensive Western imports) are available to anyone with access to consumer credit. Relying on the "primacy of work" thesis—that working conditions affect one's life and society regardless of returns[86]—I propose a reconstruction of middle-class analyses to better account for transnational middle-class formation in the Global South.

In addition to prioritizing an in-depth investigation of the transnationalization of white-collar jobs via TNCs,[87] I undertake this reconstruction by focusing on the organizational makings of inequality.[88] Focusing on firms reveals between-workplace earnings inequality as a crucial component of the contemporary rise of inequality.[89] Similarly, examining the sources of professional-managerial employment—whether the TNCs of the core economies or domestic employers in the Global South (including public and private firms)—highlights the economic underpinnings of transnational middle-class formation. Prestigious firms typically select based on certain cultural features in their hiring; thus, their recruitment practices shape the cultural makeup of middle classes in underappreciated ways. Unlike most domestic companies, TNCs often unequally reinforce international migration of high-skill labor, affording both intra- and intercompany transfers.[90] These are significant perks of TNCs for Southern elite workers.

Focusing on employment at TNCs illuminates transnational middle-class formations in the Global South because TNCs provide their business professionals and managers with the symbolic capital that distinguishes the Southern transnational middle classes from their domestic middle-class counterparts. The professional-managerial employees of prestigious domestic companies could also enjoy such symbolic capital—particularly if those companies are giant TNCs (e.g., Samsung and Hyundai for South Koreans)—insofar as the companies afford comparable prestige, life chances, and work cultures compared to their international counterparts. For instance, these firms often adopt Western corporate cultures and enact "isomorphism."[91] So too do their employees partake in the international field of business (albeit less so), similar labor processes, and workplace cultures such as high-performance work systems.[92] People engaged in other " 'middling' forms of transnationalism," like international nongovernmental organization (INGO) workers, those migrating to sustain mixed-nationality relationships, or small-scale entrepreneurs, could also be deemed part of the transnational middle classes.[93] Here, I focus on prestigious TNCs' professional-managerial employees in the interest of analytical clarity; such a focus helps me elucidate the crucial yet underappreciated role of TNCs in remaking the middle classes in the Global South.

THE EMERGENCE OF A TRANSNATIONAL
MIDDLE CLASS IN TURKEY

Turkey's political economic past could be seen as a pendulum swinging between the poles of free markets and heavy regulation[94]—something like what Karl Polanyi described as "double movement."[95] As in many other countries in the Global South,[96] the Turkish state—more than Turkish society—has been the main animator of that pendulum. Here, I outline a brief, Polanyian "double movement" account of the political economic history of Turkey, with a particular focus on the last two decades of the twentieth century, during which the transnational Turkish middle class was emerging.

After the end of the Ottoman Empire, the modern Turkish state was founded in 1923 on principles of secularism, nationalism, and republicanism. Fixated on catching up with the "West," Turkey had gone through a top-down attempt at modernization or, more accurately, Westernization. This top-to-bottom transformation deepened the *alafranga* versus *alaturca* (i.e., the modern/Western versus old-fashioned/Turkish) rift of the late Ottoman era. In the early years of the republic, when these social, cultural, legal, and political transformations were at their height, Turkey followed a liberal economic approach. With the Great Depression of 1929, however, this relatively relaxed approach gave way to a strongly protectionist and interventionist etatist period. Through the difficult era of the Great Depression and World War II, the Turkish state pushed for a national economy and prioritized its economic independence. State enterprises constituted the main conduit of industrialization.[97] This etatist era of the Turkish economy ended—along with single-party rule—with the 1950 elections when the Republican People's Party lost to the Democrat Party. This shift marked the beginning of a relatively economically liberal era. Bolstered in part by the considerable foreign aid received through the Marshall Plan, Turkey relaxed its emphasis on economic independence in favor of a more market-oriented approach that relied heavily on agricultural exports. However, this period ended with a coup d'état that forcefully pushed the pendulum toward heavy state participation in the economy, and a new constitution was drafted in 1961 that granted unforeseen opportunities for collective action and a stronger civil society.

Following the coup and in keeping with the era's dominant ideology of developmentalism, Turkey established the *Devlet Planlama Teşkilatı* (State Planning Organization) in 1960. It directed the industrialization process with a series of five-year plans organized around the principle of ISI. This period saw aggressive tariffs, capital controls, and a fixed currency regime, which protected the nascent Turkish bourgeoisie, as well as the expansion of large-scale, state-owned enterprises ranging from factories to infrastructure companies that employed the bulk of the Turkish middle class. Their production was mainly for the domestic market instead of exports and relied mostly on domestic supply chains.[98] From the late 1960s onward, as urbanization and industrialization accelerated, labor and other social movements began to play a more central role in Turkish politics. The escalation of violence among the Turkish state, socialist, ultranationalist, and Islamist movements throughout the 1970s, coupled with economic crises triggered by the dynamics of the global economy as well as the inherent difficulties of ISI, precipitated another coup d'état in 1980.[99]

The Turkish Transition from Developmentalism to Neoliberalism

As protectionist economic measures faded in the 1980s, these developmentalist trends changed as well. The 1980 coup was a watershed moment for Turkey, reorienting its social, economic, cultural, and political trajectories. The interim military council appointed

Turgut Özal as the deputy prime minister—another example of market-friendly technocrats rising to the commanding heights of state power in the developing world.[100] Özal's career path reflected Turkey's political economic transformation. An electrical engineer by training, he worked at the State Planning Organization in the 1960s, at the World Bank in the United States from 1971 to 1973, and at various business groups in Turkey from 1973 to 1980).[101] Following the IMF's prescriptions to stabilize the Turkish economy,[102] Özal authored the infamous austerity measures announced on January 24, 1980, and became known as the architect of Turkey's neoliberalization. Marking the shift from the state-led ISI to a business-led, export-oriented growth model, the Özal governments closely followed the Washington Consensus: liberalizing international trade, capital controls, and exchange rates; cutting public spending; and privatizing state-owned enterprises (SOEs).[103] These broad changes increased rates of FDI during Özal's reign (1980–1993); however, Turkey's FDI inflows remained consistently lower than those of comparable emerging economies, including those in Latin America and South Asia.[104]

The 2001 economic crisis again required Turkey to seek IMF aid, kicking off a second wave of neoliberalization. The nation adopted a range of structural adjustment programs such as further liberalization and new regulations in banking and finance, austerity policies, and an expansion of privatization.[105] Most notably, a 2003 capital controls law further reduced restraints on FDI. As figure 1.1 illustrates, Turkey aggressively lowered its restrictions on international capital flows in the early 2000s.

While FDI in Turkey increased considerably with the second wave of neoliberalization, figure 1.2 shows that Turkey still underperformed compared to many other middle-income countries, mainly because of foreign investors' concerns over its political and legal stability and the sustainability of its reforms.[106] When coupled

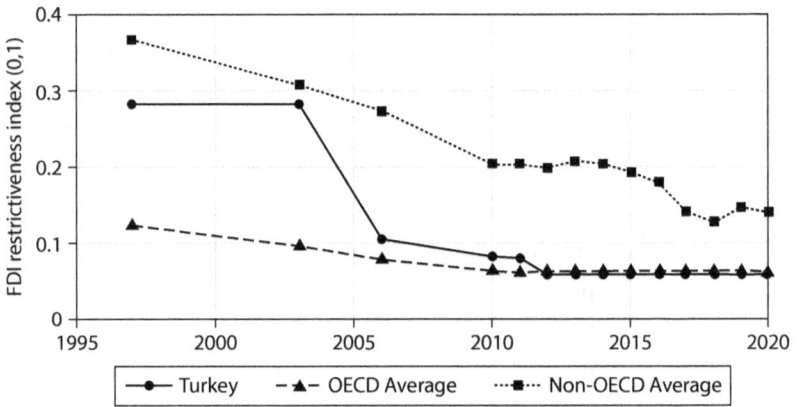

FIGURE 1.1 OECD's FDI Restrictiveness Index scores for Turkey since the 1990s, compared to OECD and non-OECD countries' average scores. OECD, "OECD FDI Regulatory Restrictiveness Index (Edition 2020)," OECD International Direct Investment Statistics (database), 2021, https://doi.org/10.1787/06c5b964-en.

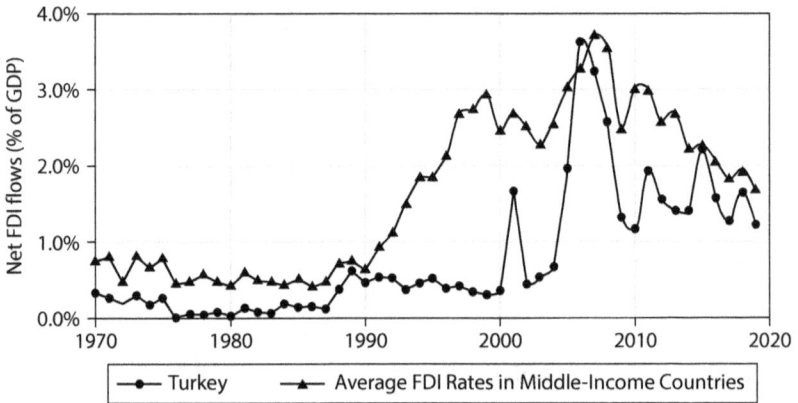

FIGURE 1.2 Foreign direct investment (FDI) in Turkey since the 1970s, compared to middle-income countries. World Bank, "Foreign Direct Investment, Net Inflows (% of GDP)—Turkey, Middle Income," World Development Indicators (database), 2022, https://data.worldbank.org/indicator/BX.KLT.DINV.WD.GD.ZS?locations=TR-XP.

with advances in communication technologies, however, even comparably lower levels of FDI brought the Turkish economy to a tight global integration. In particular, the increased prevalence of TNCs in the Turkish labor market, one of the most consequential outcomes of neoliberalization in Turkey, helped bifurcate the salaried middle class, encouraging its transnational fractions to ascend and grow vis-à-vis its state-employed, domestic fractions.

The Arrival of Transnational Corporations and the Bifurcation of the Turkish Salariat

The pre-1980s Turkish middle class consisted mainly of civil servants, shopkeepers and small employers (urban and rural), and white-collar workers.[107] In the previous decades in Turkey, as in other developing countries, state-led modernization projects had bolstered state-building intelligentsia as a key middle-class group.[108] Unlike advanced capitalist countries, where the middle class typically comprised entrepreneurial groups and salariat, the core of the pre-1980s Turkish middle class was the bureaucratic elite because "civil service . . . provided the most fertile field for employment, status, power, and prestige."[109]

During the mid-twentieth century, the ranks of white-collar workers and managers had been bolstered through nascent industrialization and rural flight.[110] In the ISI period, however, many of these individuals were employed at either SOEs or state-sponsored private firms. For example, in 1977, 63 percent of engineers (a key occupational group of middle classes across the world) enjoyed public employment,[111] and even the managers employed in the private sector—35 percent of all private-sector managers in 1965[112]—often had employment experience at SOEs.[113] In essence, the Turkish middle class relied on the state for employment, education, health care, status, and a sense of meaning before the 1980s, like its counter-parts in other countries of the Global South.[114]

While the role of industrialization and urbanization in flourishing middle classes became more pronounced with the global integration of the Turkish economy during the 1980s, this integration also fragmented the Turkish middle classes. The post-1980s class structure was characterized by "proletarianization with polarization": even as large numbers of farmers and farm workers migrated to cities and swelled the ranks of manual laborers and the unemployed, the proportion of business professionals and managers in the labor force almost doubled, jumping from 1.59 percent (294,000 people) in 1980 to 3.08 percent (800,000 people) in 2000.[115] This spike in the number of white-collar employees was, as I show below, partly because of increasing FDI flows and the transformation of Istanbul into a global city with the arrival of TNCs.[116]

As the Turkish salariat expanded, its internal composition changed dramatically. First, the privatization of large-scale SOEs steadily reduced the ratio of civil servants in the salaried middle class, and white-collar workers increasingly found employment at private firms. Figure 1.3 displays how the share of engineers employed at private firms rose at the expense of state enterprises.

Second, TNCs began to attract more high-skilled labor than both the Turkish state and Turkish companies. Although TNCs did operate in Turkey before the 1980s, their number and importance for the Turkish middle class was insignificant because of the unwelcoming conditions of ISI and third world developmentalism, which tended to favor domestic business.[117] Nevertheless, Turkey's neoliberalization, including its relaxation of restrictions on the activities of foreign-owned companies in the 1980s, as well as information technology (IT) advances beginning in the 1990s, increased the number of TNCs, especially in Istanbul.[118]

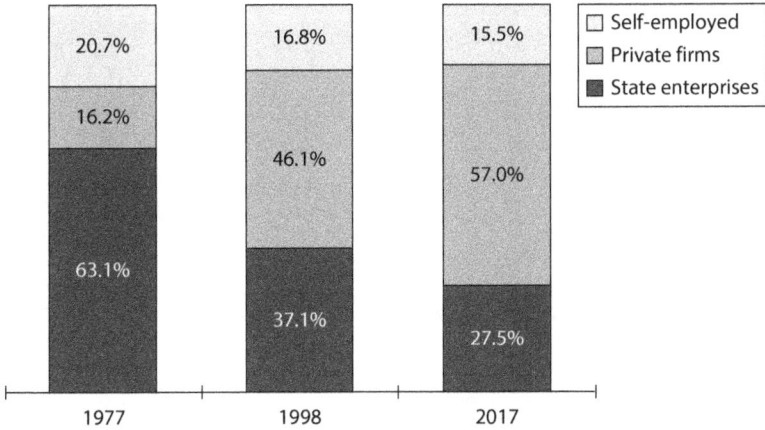

			Self-employed
20.7%	16.8%	15.5%	Private firms
16.2%			State enterprises
	46.1%	57.0%	
63.1%	37.1%	27.5%	
1977	1998	2017	

FIGURE 1.3 The share of Turkish engineers by employment in 1977, 1998, and 2017. Data for the 1977 statistics comes from Nilüfer Göle, *Mühendisler ve İdeoloji Öncü Devrimcilerden Yenilikçi Seçkinlere* (Metis Yayınları, 1986), 114–15. The 1998 statistics come from Ahmet Haşim Köse and Ahmet Öncü, "A Class Analysis of the Professional and Political Ideologies of Engineers in Turkey," in *The Ravages of Neo-Liberalism: Economy, Society, and Gender in Turkey*, ed. Nesecan Balkan and Sungur Savran (Nova Science, 2002), 148. The 2017 statistics come from Turkish Statistical Institute, "Labor Force Microdata Statistics 2017," 2017.

Note: The author recalculated the 1998 statistics by omitting unemployed and retired engineers from Köse and Öncü's sample for consistency with the 1977 statistics. The 2017 statistics are the author's own calculations from the Turkish Statistical Institute's 2017 microdata on the labor force.

Figure 1.4 shows the exponential rise in the number of TNCs operating in Turkey, from 78 in 1980 to approximately 74,000 in 2020. Turkey's economic growth alone cannot explain this increase because, as figure 1.2 indicates, the FDI net inflows climbed even when measured as a *percentage* of Turkey's gross domestic product (GDP).

As FDI inflows continued, TNCs became increasingly prevalent in the Turkish labor market. In manufacturing alone, for example,

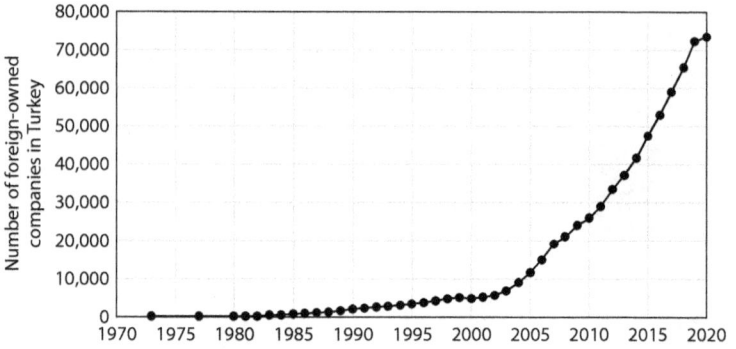

FIGURE 1.4 The number of foreign-owned companies operating in Turkey since the early 1970s. Data for the years 1973 to 1977 come from Devlet Planlama Teşkilatı, "Dördüncü Beş Yıllık Kalkınma Planı 1979–1983" (1979), 68. The data for 1980 to 1994 come from Sefer Şener, "Osmanlı'dan Günümüze Türkiye'de Yabancı Sermaye," *Bilgi Sosyal Bilimler Dergisi* 16, no. 1 (2008): 38, https://dergipark.org.tr/tr/pub/bilgisosyal /issue/29126/311561. The data for 1990 to 1999 come from Devlet Planlama Teşkilatı, "Doğrudan Yabancı Sermaye Yatırımları Özel İhtisas Komisyonu Raporu," *Sekizinci Beş Yılık Kalkınma Planı* (2000), 10. The data for 2000 to 2006 come from General Directorate of Foreign Investment, "Foreign Direct Investments in Turkey 2006" (2007), 19. The data for 2007 to 2017 come from Presidency of the Republic of Turkey Investment Office, "Business Services Sector in Turkey" (2018), 9, https://www .invest.gov.tr/tr/library/publications/lists/investpublications/is -hizmetleri-sektoru-raporu.pdf. The data for 2018 come from Presidency of the Republic of Turkey Investment Office, "Invest in Türkiye," *Invest in Türkiye*, February 2020, 7. The data for 2019 come from "İş Dünyası Katar'la İş Birliğini Güçlendirecek," *Milliyet*, September 26, 2020, https://www.milliyet.com.tr/ekonomi/is-dunyasi-katarla-is-birligini -guclendirecek-6315720. The data for 2020 come from Presidency of the Republic of Turkey Investment Office, "Why Invest in Turkey?" (2021), 21, https://www.invest.gov.tr/tr/library/publications/lists /investpublications/neden-turkiyeye-yatirim-yapmali.pdf.

the number of employees in foreign affiliates rose from 1.5 percent of the total number of employees in 1986 to 3.2 percent in 1990,[119] before jumping to 7 percent in 2001.[120] Confirmatory data are not available, but as FDI has continued to climb, we can presume that this trend has continued into the twenty-first century and that these ratios have increased further. In addition, the Turkish economy's global integration required a larger service sector, including management consulting, auditing, finance, insurance, and corporate law firms, to coordinate FDI flows and international trade. In Istanbul, employment in finance, insurance, and real-estate alone rose from 5.3 percent in 1980 to 7.1 percent in 1990.[121] The business-to-business professional services sector, dominated by TNCs, boomed as Istanbul became an emerging global city, suggesting that the number of white-collar employees of TNCs in Turkey and their overall labor force share has risen as well. In 1977, for example, there were four foreign-capital banks; whereas, in 1988, there were twenty-two,[122] and, by December 2024, foreign-capital banks constituted nearly half of the total (twenty-five of fifty-eight).[123] The share of foreign-capital banks among deposit banks averaged around 11 percent from 1960 to 1980, and then jumped to an average of 34 percent in the 1980s and 1990s and then to 55 percent in the 2000s and 2010s.[124] Note, too, that elite professional services firms such as McKinsey, one of the Big Three consulting firms, and Deloitte, one of the Big Four accounting firms,[125] opened their first branches in Istanbul (in 1995 and 1986, respectively).[126] All these factors suggest that the increasing presence of TNCs in Turkey has boosted the number of white-collar employees and their overall share in the labor force.

Providing professional-managerial employees with the premiums of higher income, prestige, and the chance of global upward mobility (including immigration to the Global North), TNCs emerged as the most desired employers for the highly educated

Turkish labor force. When I asked my interviewees, who were graduating seniors at an elite public university (n = 15) to name their top ten companies for employment, they offered a total of 111 answers with 58 unique responses—and only five SOEs and five Turkish companies made the list. (The five most-desired companies were McKinsey, BCG, Bain, Procter & Gamble, and Microsoft.) Put simply, Turkey's best and brightest entering the workforce hope to land at TNCs rather than at domestic employers.

Much of TNCs' appeal comes from the greater economic returns they offer. The 1994 UN World Investment Report found that, compared to domestic firms, "the increase in wage differentials in favour of foreign affiliates [TNC offices or branches in host countries] ranged from over 10 per cent in France, Ireland, Sweden and the United Kingdom to a peak of 134 per cent in Turkey."[127] More than twenty years later, this differential is still evident. Figure 1.5 displays the salary premium for white-collar employment at TNCs in Turkey from 2017 to 2018: on average, salaries for professional-managerial employees at TNCs were nearly double those offered at public-sector or other private-sector employers. And this premium is even higher for Turkish professionals working in New York City.

Against the backdrop of soaring inflation, reduced public expenditures, and lucrative TNC salaries during the 1990s, the altered composition of employers bifurcated the Turkish salariat. Purchasing power and overall quality of life for state employees and civil servants decayed compared to those enjoyed by professional-managerial workers at private firms.[128] Competition for high-quality education and markers of social capital became more intense and further polarized the middle class[129] as civil servants fell further out of favor and the number of TNC employees continued to rise.[130]

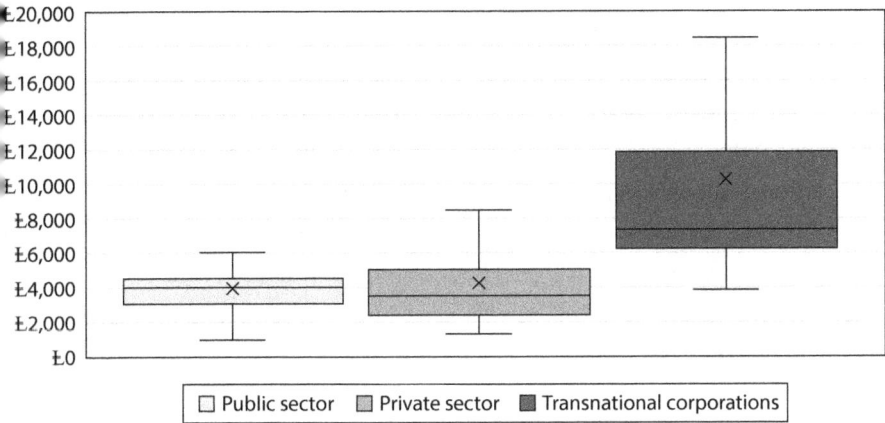

FIGURE 1.5 Box plot of professional-managerial salary distributions by workplace in Istanbul, 2017–2018. Data for the salaries of professional-managerial employees in the public and private sectors come from Turkish Statistical Institute, "Labor Force Microdata Statistics 2017," 2017.

Note: Although the best available, the Turkish Statistical Institute's 2017 microdata do not reveal the employer beyond the public-private dichotomy. Because the salary information at TNCs is unavailable, the author used his interview data to remedy this. Note that the author's sample consists only of prestigious TNCs and thus cannot be representative; nevertheless, considering their salary information in a comparative context is still instructive, if not conclusive. To enhance the validity of this comparison, the author excluded health and teaching professionals from the Turkish labor force microdata (i.e., ISCO-08 codes of 22 and 23, respectively) and selected full-time professional-managerial workers who were living in Istanbul, who were under forty years old, and who held college degrees or beyond—all of which were key features of the author's sample. Note that including health and teaching professionals reveals even a starker pay gap.

The Hegemonic Rise of a Turkish Yuppiedom and Success-Driven Habitus

As the economic prospects of young urban professionals were further buoyed by changes in the high-skill labor market, a high-status, transnational middle-class identity took shape, and it reveled in exclusive consumption behaviors. A strong and durable disposition of seeking success—what I call a success-driven habitus—underlay this identity (I delve deeper into this in chapter 2) and was inspired by TNCs' emergence and their encouragement of a high-achievement culture in the Turkish high-skill labor market.

The research on the Turkish middle classes in general and their differentiating transnational fractions in particular has defined the boundaries of this new middle class in terms of its consumption practices,[131] specifically its emphasis on "conspicuous consumption and connoisseurship,"[132] and on deployment of Western imports and global brands as status markers.[133] Thanks to its symbolic capital of achievement, this class emerged as trendsetters, "primary movers of consumption patterns, which are usually organized around global lifestyles."[134]

Beneath this account of "keeping up with the Joneses" via consumption lies a profound social transformation: the heightening of a competitive individualism that signifies this class's subjectivity and justifies its (self-)assessment as successful.[135] Hayri Kozanoğlu aptly observed that yuppies are those who have "*achieved* the desires and longings of a major part of society," and thereby become the "*symbols of success*" by winning every tournament of school and work.[136]

Turkish engineers—a core constituent of the Turkish middle classes before and after the 1980s—epitomize this competitive individualism by subscribing to the "ideology of the ladder."[137] Turkish engineers of the ISI era, mostly employed at SOEs, evinced a social justice–oriented attitude, unlike many of their counterparts in the core economies of the world.[138] As Ahmet Haşim Köse and Ahmet Öncü put it, they were "mostly perceived (and they also perceived themselves) as the actors responsible for the growth of social welfare."[139] But as developmentalism ended the association of engineering with social welfare, an individualistic valence blessed by neoliberalism came to dominate the profession. Rather than a path to serving the nation, an engineering major was increasingly seen as a means of getting ahead.[140] In fact, civil service even came to be looked down on compared to a career in the private sector, especially at a TNC. My interviewees used the popular Turkish phrase *memur kafası* ("civil servant mentality") to present this contrast. This phrase associates public employment with laziness, inefficiency, and lack of enthusiasm or passion—rather than a means to work-life balance, job security, welfare benefits, and working for the social good.

Turkey's increasing premium on white-collar employment at TNCs encouraged such competitive and individualistic attitudes, and these young workers had been groomed to seek success from their earliest years. Public education was broadly celebrated before the 1980s.[141] Nevertheless, the growth of the Turkish youth in numbers coupled with diminished public education expenditures and the privatization of education have made higher education increasingly selective. Exposed to high-stakes testing in their formative years, they experience intense anxiety around success and failure. Private tutoring and cram schools, which have been sine qua non to success in college and high school admission exams, emerged in this space.[142] Yet most Turkish citizens perceive high-stakes testing as fundamentally meritocratic, further enabling the hegemonic quality of the transnational Turkish middle class. The discourse of meritocracy encourages people to internalize their position as self-determined.[143] A prestigious college degree is, in this sense, the transnational Turkish middle class's badge of honor: an instantiation of grit and hard work.

My interviewees stressed that this badge begs for employment with a prestigious TNC because it is the ultimate symbol of postgraduate success. In the words of Hülya, a management senior set to work at a tech giant's office in Europe, "People typically follow the mainstream . . . get[ting] into a giant corporate firm. Because they also perceive that they can continue being successful that way." Her remark, which positions TNC employment as the "mainstream," captures TNC's hegemony among her peers, as well as the paramount importance of *continuing* to be successful. Similarly, Bülent, the senior we met at the beginning of the chapter who compared working at a Big Three firm to carrying "the key of a BMW car," equated the recognition and status conferred by his job to consuming high-end commodities and services (BMWs, a spontaneous trip to Paris) that signal distinction both within and beyond Turkey. To borrow from Bourdieu, through employment at TNCs, the members of the transnational Turkish middle class can exchange their cultural capital into economic, social, and symbolic capital at a very high rate.

For their part, prestigious TNCs prefer employees with ambition and determination, which are expressions of a success-driven habitus. But they also call for fluency in English, international experience, and cosmopolitan taste. While the latter two characteristics are never articulated as explicit requirements in hiring, they often function as elimination criteria. For example, discussions regarding extracurricular activities during interviews effectively provide the substance to assess whether a candidate might "fit" the company's culture—akin to professional services firms' practices of "hiring as cultural matching" in the United States.[144]

TNCs in Turkey have actively selected on such de facto criteria of employment, so these features have become defining cultural aspects of the transnational Turkish middle class. Employees at Istanbul offices of TNCs were expected to be capable of working with an international audience, including clients and colleagues in the other branches and headquarters. Bülent, for instance, who had done an internship in the Big Three firm that he was going to work, said, "[The Istanbul office] wants a new hire to be socially strong also because the Istanbul office wants to be liked in the global [occasions], [for example,] they want to be liked by the [a global city] office."

By "socially strong," Bülent meant the ability to fit better an international audience; "global [occasions]" are international annual or biannual events that bring together different branches of the company and employees of the company from around the world. In such circles, displaying a more "Western" lifestyle—demonstrating an Anglo-American, upper-middle-class taste in hobbies, activities, and cultural consumption—was seen as a mark of belonging by both other offices and the headquarters. The squash rackets protruding from Bülent's backpack squared with his account: the Turkish elite are less likely to play squash than are their American or British counterparts, but for those employed at TNCs, especially elite professional service firms, the game now has a certain cachet.

More broadly, the "social strength" Bülent invoked is the product of *transnational cultural capital*. If we follow Bourdieu's elaboration of capitals as field-specific entities, globalization and transnationalization of a field should engender its own forms of capital or transnationalization.[145] Considering that employees of TNCs function in a global business field, transnational cultural capital could be construed as a unique subset or form of cultural capital capable of boosting its holders' position within the field. In addition to top educational credentials, markers of transnational cultural capital include international exposure, such as studying abroad for a semester or having a summer internship beyond Turkey; extracurricular activities like participating in or organizing a model UN or case-study competitions; volunteering for international student organizations, and internships or employment at famous TNCs.

One important manifestation of transnational cultural capital is cosmopolitanism, or "an orientation of openness to foreign others and cultures."[146] This became an increasingly important form of cultural capital.[147] Cultivation of cosmopolitan dispositions and taste relies on familial upbringing and strategizing.[148] Thus, access to this form of transnational cultural capital is unequal and stratified. Cosmopolitanism in the context of neoliberalism's "Anglo-American centered transnationality"[149] takes the narrow form of a comfortable familiarity with North American and Western European societies and cultures.[150] As T. Deniz Erkmen put it: "For most of them [members of the transnational Turkish middle class] 'transnational' equals 'foreign,' which in turn means 'Western.'"[151] Turkish students can deepen such familiarity when they enroll in international student exchange programs or pursue internships in North America or Europe; those of means might also volunteer, take summer school courses, or even take elaborate summer vacations abroad (perhaps by enrolling in Work & Travel USA or traveling around Europe with an Interrail pass).

Transnational cultural capital emerges as one of the most distinctive features of the transnational Turkish middle-class culture mainly because, as I will demonstrate in chapter 2, candidates whose displays of it are insufficient are often eliminated from recruitment at TNCs. Furthermore, a display of international experience and cosmopolitan taste is among the most prevalent everyday distinction practices of the transnational middle class. Vacations abroad and stylish exhibitions of them on social media, most popularly Instagram, are a common way to mark oneself as a member of the transnational Turkish middle class. International travel is indeed one of the primary sources of aspirational consumption in Turkey.

Transcending Turkey via Labor Migration to the Global North

The members of the transnational Turkish middle class construct and enact their identities as world citizens, and their class positions and dispositions traverse both national boundaries and employ-ment.[152] Signifying their *transnational* career ambitions, many members of this class have emigrated from Turkey to the Global North—a phenomenon often referred to as brain drain. Among Turkish immigrants to Organisation for Economic Co-operation and Development (OECD) countries, the proportion of those with tertiary education nearly tripled, from 4.47 percent (66,000 people) in 1980, to 12.42 percent (260,000) in 2010.[153] These trends have increased over the last decade, especially with Turkey's increasing authoritarianism and economic instability: Turkey has been deemed the least attractive OECD country for high-skilled labor.[154] This has made international migration even more vital for those hoping to join the transnational Turkish middle class. It is also true that cross-border labor mobility is often hindered by visa and work permit requirements, especially for those migrating from the South to the North compared to those migrating within the Global North or South, or from the North to the South. In fact, birth tourism to the United States is increasingly popular among the members of the trans-national Turkish middle class to preempt such difficulties for their offspring.[155]

For most high-skilled Turkish labor, TNC employment can over-come the visa barriers of immigration to the North. For instance, expatriation, or intracompany transfers (e.g., moving from a TNC's Istanbul branch to its New York office), provide prestigious employ-ment in the North while simultaneously resolving the legal com-plexities of obtaining a visa or work permit. One of my respondents, Ahmet, a management consultant at a Big Three firm, told me that he ended up in the firm's New York City office with a short-term L-1 visa (specifically designed for intracompany transfers at man-agerial and executive level) and that he was waiting for an H-1B visa that would allow him to keep working there or another com-pany for a few additional years. Similarly, intercompany transfers (seeking employment at a firm in the North prior to moving there) offer another path of mobility through TNCs. For instance, Hakan, a manager at a Big Four firm in Istanbul, planned to immigrate to Europe and targeted Big Four firms' offices there via LinkedIn.

Pursuing higher education—a college degree or more commonly a master's degree—from a prestigious university in the United States or Western Europe and then entering the local labor market is also very common. Most Turkish H-1B visa holders in the United States have followed this path. For example, Ozan, the Wall Street investment banker we met in the introduction to this book, landed his job after earning an MBA from one of the most prominent business schools in the United States. He explained that he was able to enroll with some scholarship—which also brought him to the notice of potential employers—chiefly because of his prior employment at a world-renowned consulting firm in Istanbul. In sum, employment within TNCs affords international legitimacy to the skills and cultural capital of Turkish business professionals and presents them with various means of overcoming visa barriers to emigration from the Global South.

This chapter has used the Turkish case to examine middle-class formation in the Global South in the context of globalization. Turkey's profound shift from developmentalism to neoliberalism and its economy's global integration since the 1980s constitute the key macro-level processes undergirding the transnational Turkish middle class. Against this backdrop, including an overall reduction in state employment and privatization of welfare practices, TNCs in Turkey outpaced both the Turkish state and domestic companies in attracting high-skill labor and emerged as the primary employer of the country's most educated labor force. Providing these highly skilled workers with higher economic returns and global career opportunities, TNCs helped spawn a new Turkish yuppiedom, in sharp contrast to the nation's preexisting middle class that had been employed primarily by the state. This bifurcation in the middle class reveals the layering of a globally mobile, neoliberal subjectivity atop a nationally embedded, preexisting middle-class counterpart. The most distinctive characteristic of this ascendant middle-class culture has been a competitive individualism in the form of consumerism and careerism with a global orientation. In the developmentalist era of the mid-twentieth century public-sector doctors, lawyers, and engineers were popular role models, but the business professionals and managers of famous TNCs have become the new forebears of modernity, the champions of meritocracy, and the hegemonic symbols of success, thus redefining the good life for the masses.

The curious overlap of globalization with industrialization and urbanization in the Global South during the late twentieth century implies a more complex middle-class formation across developing economies, one that is best examined using a transnational lens. Prioritizing an employment-centered understanding of middle-class formation clarifies this phenomenon by emphasizing the role of TNCs in the reconstitution of middle classes in the Global South. Unlike one-sided accounts of cultural homogenization, which overstress global circulation and consumption of Western cultural goods by the middle classes, investigating employment at TNCs incorporates socioeconomic *and* cultural processes of class formation—influences that are simultaneously transnational and local. In the Turkish case, TNCs with deep pockets have transformed domestic labor markets for skilled labor and connected them to global ones, introducing new social mobility pathways by offering above-market rates of pay and higher status. TNCs' selective and homophilious recruitment practices have also a direct homogenizing impact on this class culture and create an impetus for new middle-class reproduction strategies. Considering these effects reveals TNCs as consequential agents of social change in the Global South, and their influence has heretofore been underappreciated. Since the dawn of the British East India Company in 1600, most large-scale private enterprises have been pushing for globalization, and by the late twentieth century, some TNCs had already evolved into behemoths that were consequential in shaping it.

From this discussion of the macro-level processes that structured the rise of the transnational Turkish middle class, the next chapter will turn to the meso-level processes of its formation through education and hiring. Specifically, I will examine the recruitment of senior undergraduates to entry-level, white-collar jobs at TNCs in Turkey.

2

BECOMING ELITE WORKERS

Who gets what kinds of jobs, and why? This question is a key inquiry of class formation and reproduction of social inequalities. College degrees, for instance, are important predictors of white-collar employment and therefore of membership in middle classes. Nevertheless, a college degree does not automatically bring a white-collar job. Job applicants compete with each other as they navigate the labor market, and they often have to pass through a series of filters, through which many are eliminated, before they are hired. Examining how college students are transformed into white-collar labor following their graduation— a critical moment of liminality in the life course—and are sorted in the labor market can illuminate "pathways to social class."[1]

Of course, some white-collar jobs are more competitive to attain; professional-managerial positions that populate the higher echelons of the labor market require certain educational credentials as well as skill sets. While college students compete for such high-salary and high-prestige entry-level jobs that provide them with steep social mobility, only a tiny fraction of them can join the elite labor force. It is true that hierarchies in schooling and the labor market are tightly linked, particularly in countries with high socioeconomic inequality.[2] Nevertheless, even attending an elite college cannot, by itself, guarantee elite employment.

A turning point in the life course, college graduation has been described as a transformation of "mediated class locations" into "direct class locations."[3] Before graduation, students often occupy an implied or "shadow class" location because they depend primarily on others (e.g., their parents) who already are in the paid workforce; these ties suggest but do not determine students' future or actualized direct class locations. Because of the temporal character of class locations and their inherently indeterminant nature thanks to intragenerational social mobility, examining such moments of actualization, such as being in the job market in the senior year of college, is a fruitful field for social inquiry into class formation.[4]

In the Turkish context, where college students' most desired employers came to be world-renowned transnational corporations, examining who can get prestigious entry-level jobs at transnational corporations can help us understand the making of the transnational Turkish middle class. I argue that the hiring practices of transnational corporations directly influence the socioeconomic and cultural composition of the transnational middle class because they systematically filter job applicants and select individuals with certain qualities. Such qualities contribute to the definition of the transnational middle class-ness, which makes it crucial to unpack the logics behind such filtering.

In this chapter, I examine the organizational and institutional, meso-level aspects of the formation of Turkey's transnational middle class by focusing on university-to-work transitions. Considering hiring as a moment of gatekeeping and transnational corporations as gatekeepers of transnational middle classes, the main question I ask is: How do the recruitment practices of transnational corporations influence the formation of the transnational middle class in Turkey? In dealing with this key question, I break it up into three interrelated sets of questions: What are the practiced elimination criteria for the prestigious entry-level white-collar jobs at transnational corporations? Who can land these jobs, and how? What do these criteria imply for the emerging transnational middle class-ness? To answer these questions, I cover both the supply and demand side of the elite labor market, triangulating interviews with: (1) human resources (HR) professionals who recruit candidates for entry-level jobs at transnational corporations, (2) senior undergraduates from an elite public university—one of Turkey's top-six universities—who have been in the job market, and (3) elite business professionals and managers who have been on both sides of the hiring process. In my interviews, my questions to the HR professionals and managers mainly revolved around their practices of hiring and their views on what desirable and undesirable white-collar workers look like. I supplement this account with the elite business professionals and managers' own accounts of what successful hiring requires and how their own hiring processes went. Finally, my questions to senior undergraduates mainly revolved around their experiences of navigating the labor market, including job search, hiring, and internship experiences, and their thoughts on potential postcollege trajectories.

With an inspiration from Paul Willis's *Learning to Labor*,[5] I use my interview data to shed light on what kinds of credentials, skills, experiences, and dispositions as well as tastes and lifestyles are rewarded and eventually become markers of transnational middle class-ness; how individuals cultivate and signal and/or fake these attributes during hiring processes, and what this implies for class identity; how recruitment processes contribute to a feeling of distinction in the very beginning of their careers; how their recruitment experiences shape their view of meritocracy; and what mediates the reproduction of class and social mobility and, more important, how so.

In her comprehensive study of hiring in elite labor markets, Lauren Rivera examined elite professional service firms in New York,[6] some of which are also active in Istanbul. Rivera found that hiring in the highest echelon of entry-level corporate jobs requires more than being competent because recruitment relies on "a process of cultural matching between candidates, evaluators, and firms."[7] Casting hiring as an emotional process, Rivera showed how interpersonal evaluation determines whether a candidate is found "fit" or not.[8] While this account provides convincing arguments on how these firms contribute to the reproduction of elites, we do not know whether similar dynamics are at play in other prestigious corporations and in other national contexts. If we think of hiring mainly as cultural matching, rooted in interpersonal evaluation and emotional dynamics, we would expect to find similar, if not necessarily stronger, findings for other prestigious corporations such as Big Tech and consumer goods giants. By taking such a broader range of corporations into account, we can then consider hiring as a meso-level, organizational aspect of middle-class formation.

My interviews reveal a layered process of reproduction of inequality in the formation of the transnational middle class in Turkey. The first phase begins with curriculum vitae (CV) screening and university targeting that frequently—and sometimes exclusively—targets the students from Turkey's top six universities. Successfully running the gauntlet of job interviews and obtaining employment at a prestigious transnational corporation and, by extension, a spot in the transnational middle class, require candidates to display certain personality traits convincingly, such as being ambitious and result-oriented, as well as high-quality transnational cultural capital—fluency in English, international experience, and cosmopolitan taste. Thus, these features emerge as the most distinctive and defining aspects of the transnational Turkish middle class.

Evaluation of these attributes is where a key tension in hiring practices and approaches takes place: while HR professionals are more attuned to assessing merit and competence via regimented practices, revenue-generating managers often act as tiebreakers and rely on more subjective evaluation practices. Nevertheless, both groups usually assess not only a candidate's competence for the position but also their fit with the current pool of employees (be it at the team, department, or corporation level). As the majority of the employees of transnational corporations are upper-middle-class individuals, such homophilous evaluation practices, or what I call *class homophily* in hiring, help facilitate social closure and reproduction of inequality writ large. This is most explicitly seen in the recruitment processes of elite professional service firms.

By focusing on transnational corporations' hiring processes for entry-level jobs, we can also gain insight into the processes through which new members of the transnational middle class form their expectations. By expectations, I mean the hopes and projections that inform and shape these individuals' future well-being: the benchmarks they use to compare and contrast themselves with others on the grounds of work and career as well as life. Interviews with students of an elite public university, who were soon-to-be elite business professionals at transnational corporations, demonstrate that they considered only a narrow range of careers to be worthy. Amy Binder and colleagues found that a large ratio of elite college students in the United States (e.g., around 50 percent of Harvard's 2014 graduates) are funneled into only a narrow range of careers.[9] Similarly, for many of my respondents, employment *only* at prestigious corporations was deemed a credible sign of continued success—anything less was falling short. My research suggests that similar dynamics are at play in the context of Turkey's elite undergraduates. Like their American counterparts, they *learn* to desire employment at elite professional service firms, consumer goods behemoths, and big tech companies during their time on campus.

My interviews also show how they formed high expectations for their corporate careers. Getting a job at a prestigious transnational corporation is usually a long and cumbersome process full of a variety of tests, and companies often advertise how selective they are and how few people can actually get their jobs. The demanding education that my respondents had passed through, which armed them with high levels of skills, also raised their expectations around the kinds of work they would do upon graduation and the quality of life they should enjoy. Thus, they desired global career trajectories that promised to satisfy such high hopes: intellectually challenging work with considerable impact, and a solidly upper- or upper-middle-class income and lifestyle.

EDUCATIONAL BACKGROUND OF THE TRANSNATIONAL MIDDLE CLASS

What makes an individual a potential member of the transnational middle class is to have prestigious educational credentials. Obtaining these credentials, however, has become extremely competitive since the 1980s. Before that time, in keeping with the era's developmentalist ideology and economy, public education was the name of the game, and a high school degree was sufficient to achieve middle-class status.[10] With the 1980s, the demographic pushes of an increasing youth population, coupled with reductions in public spending on education and an increase in private education, made entry into higher education ever more selective.[11] Success in high-stakes testing became the new condition of middle class-ness, and this change had biographical impacts on the post-1980s Turkish cohorts because they began to be exposed to such high-stakes testing as early as age eleven. "The Selective Middle School Exams," for example, which determine entry to elite middle and high schools, were first offered in 1983.[12] Similar tests for high school and university admissions became the major educational focus, while the importance and value of education for a student was reduced to their rankings in these exams, which are still taken by millions of students each year.

As the socioeconomic polarization even within the middle classes increased in the past decades, the stakes in these exams followed suit. Following the state's economic incentives for investment in private schools,[13] including private universities,[14] a secondary market for private tutoring and cram schools emerged,[15] and they have been essential for success in these exams. Thus, the reproduction of middle class in Turkey has been contingent upon a "within class competition among families for [high] quality education and the accumulation of cultural and social capital in general."[16]

Primary and Secondary Education in Turkey

Although the education system in Turkey has been in constant change since the 1980s, its overall structure has stayed intact: students attend four to five years of primary school, followed by three to four years of middle school and four years of high school, adding up to twelve years of mandatory education. There is a hierarchy among the schools at all levels, established via students' performance on centralized nationwide exams that are sponsored and facilitated by the Ministry of Education. For middle school and high school students in particular, rankings on these exams determine whether they can attend certain schools or not.

The various kinds of high schools include *Anadolu* (Anatolia), science, private, social sciences, *İmam Hatip* (provides Islamic education in addition to the general high school curriculum), vocational, fine arts, and sports high schools. The first three of these—*Anadolu*, science, and private high schools—have the highest rate of success in college entry. Therefore, they are powerful engines for sorting students into a track to the middle class and better lives. Unlike other high schools, these three kinds of schools often offer one year of mandatory English-language preparation followed by three years of high school education. At some of these schools, English is also the language of instruction. Gaining better English-language skills is one of the key advantages of attending these schools because it enables these students to develop their "transnational cultural capital," which I will describe in more detail later in this chapter. Of course, the quality of education is also stratified across these schools; the science high schools often attract the top-ranked students in sciences, followed by *Anadolu* high schools. This is often paralleled by these high schools' rate of success in placing their students in the best colleges. Private high schools cover the whole gamut of educational quality and resulting success rates.

Being successful in these exams requires diligent preparation and often the support of tutors or cram schools. This is one of the most important ways in which class and wealth influence social mobility chances: the wealthier a family, the higher chance for a student to access such extra preparation and be successful in these exams.

The other significant way in which wealth affects a student's future is whether they can afford to attend private school. Private schools' competitive advantage vis-à-vis public schools is that they typically provide their students with better English-language skills as well as richer extracurricular activities. The most prestigious private schools were founded as foreign private high schools in the late Ottoman era, catering to the citizens of foreign nationals living in the Ottoman territories. These elite institutions—four American, six French, two Italian, one German, and one Austrian—are mostly concentrated in Istanbul with a few in other large cities such as Izmir and Ankara. Following the increasing globalization and economic liberalization of Turkey in the 1980s, demand for these schools increased because they equip their students with especially high-quality transnational cultural capital. For instance, rather than teaching foreign languages in a language learning class, these schools offer all instruction in English, French, German, or Italian. In addition, these schools' richer extracurricular repertoire and history of cosmopolitan institutional culture usually help their students develop a comfortable familiarity with global culture and a global orientation to their lives and careers. In fact, to date, attendance at these high schools might be one of the most important predictors of joining the Turkish elite (that is, the economic and cultural but not necessarily political elite): these schools serve as elite institutions, educating the students of elite families. Students wishing to attend private foreign high schools must be ranked competitively in the national high school entrance exams, which determine their eligibility as well as the scholarships and the amount of financial help that they can get.

To illustrate, one of the best high schools in Turkey, Robert College (its official full name is *Özel Amerikan Robert Lisesi*), typically accepts the most successful students whose families can also afford an expensive annual tuition, which was 100,000 Turkish liras in 2019, almost quadruple the annual net minimum wage. Its graduates are remarkably successful: in 2019, 53 percent of Robert College graduates went on to enroll in prestigious universities in Europe, Canada, the United Kingdom, and the United States. The remaining 47 percent enrolled in universities in Turkey, half of them in one of the top six universities that I will turn to next.

Higher Education in Turkey

Tuition at public universities in Turkey is heavily subsidized (as of 2019, per-semester tuition was around 15 to 20 percent of the net monthly minimum wage). Nevertheless, admission is selective, and it is facilitated by a competitive national exam conducted by the Council of Higher Education of Turkey. In 2019, around 2.5 million students took this exam, vying for one of about 800,000 spots at Turkish universities—about one spot for every three test takers. The students are assessed in three areas, which can be roughly classified as science, social sciences, and humanities. Their scores in each area also depend on their choice of track in high schools; for example, the humanities score of a student who opted for the science track at high school will be compromised. Students' performance on this exam not only determines which university they can attend but also which major they can pursue; college students commit to majors before they begin their university education, and while it is possible to change majors or pursue double majors, it is often difficult. Such rigidity and early tracking into a major (students typically choose one of the three tracks at the end of the first year of high school) are among the most pronounced structural reasons of occupational regret in Turkey, an issue that I discuss in more detail in chapters 3 and 4.

After the students receive their scores and rankings, they submit their lists of preferred university-major combinations to the Council of Higher Education. The higher their ranking, the higher the chance that they will be admitted to their top choices. As is the case with the entrance exam of high schools, tutors and cram schools are deemed vital to success in the university admission tests and are expensive even for middle-class families. Unlike U.S. college admissions, extracurricular activities have no impact at all in students' placement; it depends solely on their grades in high school and their rankings in the university entrance exam.

The top majors for university students in Turkey are engineering, medicine, economics, management, and law; economics and management joined this list at the turn of the new millennium.[17] This addition could be seen a consequence of transition from developmentalism to neoliberalism and the global integration of the Turkish economy. While most graduates of medicine and law majors pursue noncorporate careers in Turkey (either self- or state-employed),[18] engineering, economics, and management form the backbone of the transnational Turkish middle class because these majors are highly preferred by transnational corporations. As I will show in more detail below, if a Turkish student aims for the transnational middle class, they would do well to pursue one of the above majors at one of the top six universities: Koç University, Sabancı University, Bilkent University, Boğaziçi University, Middle East Technical University, and Istanbul Technical University.[19] The first three of these are private universities, founded by the richest conglomerates of Turkey; they are expensive to attend, and scholarships depend on students' rankings in the entrance exam.

While the national ranking of these universities is renewed annually, these six universities historically have been noted as distinctively better than the rest. One important source of differentiation is that they were among the first colleges to offer English as the language of instruction,[20] contributing to a vital piece of their students' transnational cultural capital. Degrees from these institutions are taken as legitimate signs of high-quality education, and they are essential for employment at prestigious transnational corporations. They are also badges of honor for the transnational Turkish middle class, signaling their grit and hard work in their upward mobility.

SELECTION INTO THE TRANSNATIONAL MIDDLE CLASS

At prestigious transnational corporations, recruitment processes for entry-level jobs typically take recent college graduates or senior undergraduates through a multistep process of funneling and elimination. These steps fall into four categories: (1) CV screening based on colleges; (2) standardized tests measuring quantitative and qualitative aptitude, as well as English-language skills; (3) interviews with HR professionals and prospective immediate managers, and sometimes with executive-level managers; and (4) case studies and on-the-job assessments. In addition, candidates' references are contacted to screen for any last-minute issues. Except for this final stage of reference checks, the ordering, the number, and the actual content of these steps of elimination varies across companies and positions to be filled. My interviews suggest that the number of distinct steps of elimination ranges from three to eight.

The largest cut usually occurs in the CV screening phase. Here, the alma mater serves as the clearest criterion; my respondents confirmed that the transnational corporations focus almost exclusively on Turkey's six top universities. Few, if any, candidates from other universities pass beyond this first stage. While some of my HR respondents disclosed that they eliminate candidates right off the bat with such CV screening, many appeared reluctant to state that they focus solely on these six universities (and sometimes just a couple of them), although some mentioned later in the interviews that they filtered with respect to colleges. They usually qualified their stance by saying that, even if they do not filter as such, after selecting candidates based on a series of other criteria such as English-language skills, the candidate pool turns out to be heavily skewed toward these six schools anyway. For instance, Ülkü, an HR professional from one of the leading finance firms, stated, "We don't filter schools. But when we eliminate candidates based on their English [language skills] and internship experience, we always end up with the best schools." Lila, a marketing manager at a consumer goods giant, confirmed these observations by telling me, "Whenever I walk in the corridor, all I see is Boğaziçi people, graduated either one year earlier or later than me."

Many employers use standardized tests that are akin to the university entrance exam as a basis for further winnowing the candidate pool. Prizing high qualitative and quantitative aptitude, much like the university entrance exam, this stage reinforces the advantage of the top six university students. Such an effect is more pronounced when these tests measure directly or rely on English-language skills, which turns out to be one of the most defining aspects of the cultural capital of the transnational Turkish middle class.

The interviews are another crucial step of elimination and arguably the one that involves the most subjective evaluation as to whether a candidate should get the job. Initial interviews are most often done by HR professionals. Revenue-generating managers (not to be confused with HR managers) come into the picture later, often to pick from an already very select pool of applicants to their own teams. Interviews, of course, include questions aiming to gauge the candidate's position-related competencies, such as working knowledge of software or proficiency in some area of business. But the most important part of these interviews is to understand and evaluate the candidate with respect to the enigmatic notion of fit. These later interviews usually start with an open-ended question like "Could you tell us a bit about yourself?" or "Why do you want to work in this position at this corporation?" The answers reveal a lot about a candidate's personality, communication and other skills, and class background.

Elimination via case studies blends interviews and standardized tests in a social context because it involves solving predetermined business cases with a team of other candidates. The evaluation considers both the solution process and the presentation of results. While the teams are working on their cases, HR professionals often wander around the teams and observe candidates. There is a tacit understanding of the ideal behavior and approaches to solving case studies that is gained through specific kinds of social learning (e.g., being active members of student clubs, closely following and attending career events, and absorbing the corporate language and style of communication from these). We can think of these moments, such as interviews and case studies, as micro fields in Bourdieusian sense in that the display of certain dispositions and attitudes, such as the language that is used during presentation and one's demeanor while interacting with team members, usually influence one's perceived value and fitness.

Taken together, these eliminations suggest an ideal Turkish white-collar job applicant from the perspective of a prestigious transnational corporation.[21]

The Ideal White Collar

First, an ideal white-collar employee of TNCs gets their degree from one of the six top Turkish universities (or other elite colleges in the United States or Europe), and they are preferably also a graduate of one of Turkey's elite private high schools. They major in engineering, economics, or management, although other majors may be acceptable as long as the applicant displays other characteristics of a desirable white-collar worker. They are fluent in English, and they may also have some skills in other European languages such as Spanish, French, German, and Italian. They have lived abroad for a while, usually somewhere in Europe or North America, for example, through student exchange programs, summer schools, or internships. In other words, they have some experience of surviving and thriving in international contexts. They have internship experience at prestigious corporations; because they have, in a sense, already begun working as white-collar workers, they display familiarity with the corporate world's norms and manners. They are well rounded: not only are they successful in terms of grade point average (GPA), but they also have been engaged in and ideally gained recognition for extracurricular activities, such as athletics, case studies, or other competitions. They have experience working in organizations like student clubs—some of which are colloquially known as "career clubs" to highlight the instrumental use of engagement with these mini-organizations—and preferably have occupied leadership positions in these. They have clear-cut stories of achievement in their organizational past, having run clubs and organizations or run events like career fairs, sports competitions, fundraising drives, or parties. Overall, they can be simply noted as overachievers, displaying an overarching disposition to be successful in whatever field they are.

REQUIRED HABITUS INSTEAD OF SKILL SETS

Most of these desirable features—including college degree, major, internship experience, extracurricular activities, and awards—are visible from an applicant's CV. Nevertheless, they are insufficient on their own because there are additional and more subtle properties that the transnational corporations look for in desirable candidates that cannot be directly read from their CVs alone. Such qualities could be best thought of as habitus, personality, or soft skills (as opposed to hard skills, such as proficiency in a method or software). The properties that I heard frequently in my interviews were, "competitive," "ambitious," "eager to rise up in the corporate life," "proactive," "curious," "active," "has an appetite for learning," "communicates concisely and clearly," "good at multitasking," "detail oriented," "result oriented," "does not crack under stress," "open to collaboration," "extravert," "has leadership spirit," and "team player." The HR professionals and managers try to understand whether candidates have these traits through interviews and personality inventories. In effect, what they look for is not candidates who have job-related know-how but rather certain personalities or a set of dispositions; in Bourdieusian terms, these companies search for the right habitus that is in harmony with the field of (international) business in general and the field of industry in which these companies operate in particular. In effect, personality is the new skill.

Such a shift in hiring patterns, hiring for habitus instead of certain skill sets, is usually attributed to the rise of post-Fordism.[22] The principles of lean manufacturing demanded workers who are agile, flexible, and swift to adapt to ever-changing business and work conditions.[23] Indeed, most transnational corporations expect they will need to provide the necessary hard skills, and most have mandatory job-specific training for each cohort of their new hires. Ayse, a senior auditor at a Big Four company, went through initial training in Amsterdam with her cohort, along with hundreds of their peers from a wide range of European countries. She added that almost none of the training materials were familiar to her. In other words, she did not have the job-specific know-how before her recruitment.

TRANSNATIONAL CULTURAL CAPITAL

One of the most important criteria of elimination that transnational corporations use in hiring white-collar candidates could be thought of along the lines of transnational cultural capital. As I detail below, attaining transnational cultural capital is expensive, and thus its acquisition and deployment play into the reproduction of inequality.[24] English-language skills, the amount and quality of international experience, and an accompanying cosmopolitan taste emerged from my interviews as especially consequential in securing employment at transnational corporations.

Fluency in English is a fundamental component of transnational cultural capital. This is almost taken for granted today because English has emerged from the globalization of the late twentieth century as the global lingua franca. My interviewees reported that companies eliminate many job applicants based on their insufficient English-language skills. One respondent, an HR professional at a fast-moving consumption goods (FMCG) giant, mentioned that many candidates are eliminated based simply on how they describe their English-language abilities on their CVs: "Because even the candidates who write 'advanced' [for their English skills in their CVs] can turn out inarticulate, I immediately eliminate applicants who write 'intermediate.' "

Speaking English fluently is positively correlated with class background for various reasons. First, private schools in Turkey usually provide higher-quality English-language education than public schools do. As noted earlier, English-language instruction is arguably the competitive advantage of private schools. Part of the cachet of a college degree from one of the top six universities stems from the fact that the instructional language at these schools is English, and these graduates often have better English-language skills. Obtaining bachelor's degrees from colleges in the United States and Europe is an immediate boost to transnational cultural capital in the Turkish context. One of the best ways to perfect one's English-language skills is through immersion, for example, by living abroad.[25] However, living abroad is an expensive proposition for many Turkish families and students.

Another important aspect of accumulating transnational cultural capital is having international experience. Here, international experience could be simply thought of as a set of experiences that includes interacting with people from different nationalities on a project or even, more simply, working, living, and surviving in an international context (such as in a country other than one's own). The most frequent ways that Turkish students gain such international experience include internships, volunteer work, and summer schools abroad; student exchange programs; or prolonged summer vacations abroad such as traveling around Europe with Interrail pass or Work & Travel USA.

Respondents suggested that having international experience per se has become almost a tacit precondition of employment in transnational corporations. For instance, Sibel, a senior engineering major who secured a job at a consumer goods giant, noted that everyone in her cohort had some sort of international experience. "I don't think [having international experience] is a criterion of elimination," she said, "but I think [companies] find it important." Fatma, another senior engineering major who got a job at a Big Three consulting firm, likewise remembered that, during her recruitment, she had a long chat with an interviewer about Denmark, where she had spent a semester as an exchange student and where her interviewer had been several times. She also had answered a job interview question about overcoming difficulties by describing her travel experiences with the Interrail pass, and she believed that these answers also had a positive effect. She described such instances of overlaps as important moments in her interview.

Displaying international experience matters in job interviews at transnational corporations, even though it is not necessarily an explicit criterion of elimination, insofar as it serves as a chance to engender emotional resonance and thereby increase the chances of being selected from among other applicants. Melodi, an HR professional at a Big Four company, described asking candidates open-ended questions as icebreakers, such as asking them to comment on one of the pictures on the wall in the interview room. One candidate chose a picture with bikes in it and commented that it reminded of him of Amsterdam, which happened to be a city she also loved and where they each had lived for a while. She reported that that candidate eventually got the job and that experiencing such overlap and resonance helped him stand out from the other candidates as a better fit for the position.

The importance of international experience is not just a matter of overlap in cosmopolitan taste and life experience; it is sometimes required explicitly for the transnational nature of the business field. Signaling that one is "globally competent" not only provides a boost to the careers of business professionals and managers,[26] it also sometimes emerges as a precondition for even entry-level jobs at transnational corporations. For example, Ferhat, an engineering senior who got a job at a major investment bank in London, disclosed that he sought advice for the job interviews from one of the alumni of his university already working at that company. He recalled that the insider advice was to signal that he was a "world citizen." British citizens, he was told, constituted only a tiny fraction of the employees of that investment bank, and he needed to be able to signal that he would be comfortable working in a such diverse multinational context. He told me his strategy for sending that signal was to share that he had been to Germany several times during high school, traveled around Europe with the Interrail pass, and pursued an exchange semester in East Asia. After recounting how he convincingly communicated his world citizenry in these job interviews, he immediately reflected a bit shyly, "Of course, I was able to do all of these because my family's financial situation could afford it, and there is such an inequality of opportunity."

As Ferhat noted, most of these ways of gaining international experience require extensive resources that may be difficult for even middle-class Turkish families to marshal. Hence, deconstruction of the recruitment processes of transnational corporations enables us to see how selection into the transnational middle class reproduces existing inequality. This is the case even for the most meritocratic and egalitarian way of obtaining international experience for college students: student exchange programs. First, the top six universities have more bilateral agreements for providing their students with international exchange semesters than other schools do. Getting into one of these six universities is correlated with class background, which means that the most advantaged students have greatest access to this benefit.

Second, there are two kinds of exchange programs that Turkish students pursue most frequently, but both are out of reach for students of modest means. The first one relies on bilateral agreements among universities, which mostly covers universities in the United States. This route does not provide students with scholarships and hence requires a good deal of money provided by the students' families. The second route is the EU-funded Erasmus Exchange Program, which covers most of the European countries. Although the Erasmus Exchange Program provides its exchange students with some financial scholarships, these are usually insufficient and must be supplemented by students or their families. Tuğrul, an engineering senior who would go on to work at a consumer goods giant, told me that some of his friends did not apply for the Erasmus Exchange Program knowing that they would not be able to afford it even with the scholarship. The cost of exchange semesters abroad has risen even more out of reach in recent years with the devaluation of the Turkish lira vis-à-vis the euro and the dollar.

Third, there is a great demand for exchange semesters abroad, and the competition is fierce. Foreign study opportunities are very popular among students because of the opportunities for career gains, personal growth, and fun. My interviewees reported that the formal selection procedure for the Erasmus Exchange Program in their university ranks applicants according to a composite score based on a student's English test score on the Test of English as a Foreign Language (TOEFL), International English Language Testing System (IELTS), or the university's own proficiency exam; GPA; national ranking on the university entrance exam; and proficiency level in another language (such as French or German) if required by the host university. Given the importance of English and other language skills in even the most meritocratic path to international experience, preferring international experience for selection into prestigious jobs at transnational corporations becomes another systematic reproduction of inequality.[27]

Merit Versus Bias: Conflicting Assessments of Fitness

One of the tensions frequently raised by HR professionals in my interviews was about their conflicts with revenue-generating managers (i.e., not HR managers) over "objective versus subjective" evaluation of job candidates. HR professionals viewed themselves as objective evaluators of the candidates thanks to their specialization and professionalization and felt that managers tended to tilt the evaluations toward their subjective feelings based on their resonance with the candidates. Such was the potential for bias—what Duygu, an HR professional at a consumer goods company, described as the halo effect—that HR departments usually provided trainings for managers participating in job interviews, and HR professionals usually accompanied managers during the interviews. For instance, Asena, an HR professional at another consumer goods giant, disclosed that to prevent what they called likability bias, the HR department provided the managers with training and warned them of the blind spots that could be created by strong personal overlaps between themselves and candidates and that this could push them away from properly evaluating the candidates' competence. Nevertheless, she said, managers often act as tiebreakers and make the final call, which usually results in homophilous outcomes.

Along the continuum from objective to subjective, or more starkly put, from merit to bias, HR professionals and managers both invoked the sweet spot of "fit." In the interviews, it was usually difficult to unpack what respondents meant by a candidate's fitness, although it generally seemed to prioritize feelings over the objective evaluation of competence. Respondents used phrases like: "*enerjinin uyması*" ("whether our energies fit"), "*sinerjilerimiz uydu*" ("our synergies resonated"), "*buradaki dokuya uygun olmalı*" ("[candidate] should fit the [company] fabric here"), "*kanım kaynadı*" ("we hit it off"), "*içim ısındı*" ("felt warm with them"), "*aynı dili konuşmak*" ("speaking the same language"). Duygu literally said: "*kültürel uyuma bakıyoruz*" ("we look at the cultural matching"). Asena shared that, in interviews, she often told job applicants: "I have a shirt and we are looking at whether it fits you or not. If it fits, perfect! If not, that is fine, too." The idea that it is "fine" for a candidate not to fit the shirt, that is, not to fit the job and the company, is based on the assumption that the candidate would be unhappy in the long run with a poorly fitting shirt.

I identified four different, albeit intertwined, notions of cultural matching and fit: how well the candidate fits with (1) the current employees of the company in general, (2) the members of the team with whom the candidate will start working specifically, (3) the job and the position, and (4) the company's purported values and culture.

WHY ARE CULTURAL MATCHING AND FIT IMPORTANT IN HIRING?

The importance of cultural matching and fit stems partly from the fact that teamwork is an important part of the labor process at these prestigious corporations. Kübra, an HR professional at a Big Four company, mentioned that her firm examined candidates' "both business or technical, and people or non-technical aspects," where the latter is the area in which cultural matching takes place more explicitly. She emphasized the importance of the latter part by highlighting the teamwork-based labor process, noting, "nobody works individually here." The manager, as someone who oversees a team, has a direct interest in a new candidate's fit with the team members and their personal fit with the manager themself. These companies and managers can afford cultural matching in hiring because of the abundance of competent labor supply, thanks to the expansion of college education. Ülkü told me that the HR department usually selected and suggested a number of qualified candidates for a single position, and the managers made the final choice from that shortlist.

Such tiebreaking moments are prone to favoritism through managers' concerns over team harmony. Ülkü observed that managers usually preferred candidates who went to the same college or high school as they did. In addition, the pursuit of fit and subjective evaluations during interviews sometimes took the shape of parental transference between managers and candidates. Duygu, the HR professional we met earlier, noted that her HR department warned the managers to be watchful when they like a certain candidate in an interview because they may "want to behave parentally" toward that candidate. Melodi, an HR professional at a Big Four company, disclosed that in her own recruitment she felt some emotional resonance with the interviewing manager, to the extent that she felt that "she [the manager] was like my mom." She shared that her manager indeed took care of her not only during her recruitment but also after she began to work at that company.

Fitness has been portrayed as a positive quality in and of itself by both managers and HR professionals as well as senior undergraduates. In other words, both hiring and hired parties view cultural matching as something both beneficial and desirable. Duygu explained the importance of getting along with colleagues, which is often the justification for cultural matching, by giving examples from her own department: "You don't want to work with someone who is angry or someone with whom you have little in common. It is very natural [to look for cultural matching]." Nedim, an economics senior who got a job at a fintech startup, agreed: "If I were an employer or manager, I would do the same [seek cultural matching]. . . . After all, you are going to work face-to-face at least eight hours every day. You don't want to work with someone you don't like."

Bülent, the engineering senior who got a job at a Big Three firm who we met in chapter 1, portrayed this issue more starkly: "Imagine: You are working with five people, in a tiny meeting room, and seventy hours per week, and you cannot even chat with them for five minutes. . . . It is not sustainable." As I will discuss in chapter 3, the overwork that characterizes many of these firms narrows down the elite business professionals' social circles to their work colleagues only, making cultural matching important for job applicants in their nonwork spheres of life. Aras, another Big Three-bound engineering senior, exemplified this: "I play tennis, and it is important for me to find a coworker who plays tennis as well."

HOW ARE CULTURAL MATCHING AND FIT ASSESSED?

As Aras put it, a job applicant's hobbies matter in hiring decisions. It was likely that Aras would be on the other side of the hiring desk in a few years and that he would also be interested in overlaps between his hobbies and those of a potential team member. Extracurriculars came up frequently in my interviews with elite business professionals, senior undergraduates, and HR professionals, highlighting the way that they signal certain competences, incite excitement and further interest, and display certain personality traits and habitus. Hülya, a senior majoring in management who got a job at a tech giant in the United Kingdom, highlighted extracurriculars as the bread and butter of interviews because "otherwise you have no stories to tell." Ülkü stated that hobbies "tell us something about the personality of a candidate." Kübra, the HR professional who said that her firm assesses both technical and nontechnical competencies in hiring, acknowledged that overlap between the hobbies of a manager and a candidate matters in hiring decisions. However, she emphasized that this is not a purely subjective matter: managers "probably do not think that 'oh, my team members also do windsurfing, so I should hire this person.' Rather, doing windsurfing points toward a competence." A frequent theme around extracurriculars is that they usually signal a candidate's ability to multitask (e.g., taking classes and being successful while also engaging in a number of extracurriculars), as well as their curiosity, initiative, and persistence.

For certain positions, however, such as client-facing jobs at elite professional service firms (e.g., management consulting or investment banking), having certain hobbies and displaying a more upper-middle-class lifestyle rise to the level of tacit requirement. Melodi admitted that management consultants often interact with their clients, who are usually upper-level managers of the companies for whom they are consulting. As I will explore in the next section, these professional service firms want such interactions to go smoothly; thus, they prefer candidates who can display upper-middle-class lifestyles comfortably. She exemplified "being presentable" as "having no accent [while they speak Turkish]." A very similar point was raised by Güneş, an HR professional from a tech company, for sales positions: "For people who are going to face the clients, who could be seen as the ambassador of [the name of the tech company], such as sales positions . . . of course, speaking with an accent, their looks, etc. come to the fore [in evaluating a job candidate]."

Shared extracurricular interests also engender excitement and further interest and conversation between the interviewer and interviewee. Nedim remembered an interview in which he had hit it off with his prospective manager because both of them enjoyed paragliding. He expressed the overlap as a source of excitement,

"You meet with someone who played with the same toy. Isn't it very exciting?" I heard some exceptions, too; a few HR professionals told me they warned managers to be cautious about disclosing their expensive hobbies. İrem, an HR professional at a consumer goods giant, stated that her firm reminded managers not to disclose such personal details as they may complicate the interview: "Don't tell the candidates that you like sailing on the weekends because it might intimidate them."

Such overlaps in taste do not happen exclusively at the higher end of the socioeconomic scale's preferences and lifestyles. Demir, a management senior who would go on to work at a tech giant in Europe, mentioned that a manager in one of his interviews was from the same hometown as he was (not Istanbul) and this created an emotional resonance. He also recalled a similar incident in which it turned out that he and the interviewer had played the same online game for years. He had heard similar stories from his friends based on having attended the same high schools, particularly elite private high schools.

İrem provided another illustrative example. Her HR department assessed candidates' fit with the pool of current employees by gamifying the whole recruitment process. As she told it, candidates literally played specially designed video games that measured certain cognitive skills as well as decision making under stress, ability to cooperate, and pace of learning from mistakes. What was most striking in her account was that the HR team made the current employees of the company play these games first and took their average scores as the *benchmark* in assessing prospective employees. The ideal candidate, she said, was someone who was not too distant from these averages, whether above or below. In other words, Irem's firm did not rank the job applicants with respect to their performance and pick the best ones but rather checked whether candidates *fit* with the current pool of employees.

The rise of team-based labor processes with post-Fordism and prestigious transnational corporations' increasing adoption of them have made the question of whether the white-collar workers fit with each other more important than before.[28] Such a strong emphasis on fit reproduces the distribution of existing class backgrounds within the company. Of course, when most employees in a company are from elite backgrounds, such emphasis on fitness serves as social closure and systematically preserves the current level of inequality by reproducing the elites only from elite backgrounds.

Reproduction of the "Elite of the Elite"

There is further stratification within prestigious transnational corporations and the corresponding elite labor market. Most respondents agreed that the highest echelons of the elite labor market consist of tech giants and elite professional service firms, including management consulting, investment banking, and corporate law firms.[29] Kaan, a management consultant working in Istanbul, mentioned that the business professionals working in such elite professional service firms, including his own, referred to themselves as the "elite of the elite" in campus recruitment events. Ülkü noted that, when her team deemed a candidate not good enough for an investment banking position, they usually directed the candidate toward available commercial banking positions within the same firm. For my interviewees, phrases such as the "elite of the elite" were not solely self-referential. Kübra, who worked for a Big Four firm, referred to the employees of the Big Three consulting firms as the crème de la crème.

Getting a job at these firms is also widely considered the best possible postcollege career outcome. In my interviews with the

senior undergraduates, for example, I asked them to list ten companies that they would be "thrilled to work at" upon graduation,
and these elite firms were usually at the top of their lists. It was not
just an issue of desiring to work at such companies—getting a job at
these firms was a symbolically charged outcome pointing toward
a specific definition of *success*. For example, when I probed Ferhat
about his criteria for postcollege success and whether Big Three
consulting firms were part of it, he enthusiastically responded:
"Exactly! [Landing] one of the three."

Considering the various rewards reaped by being part of this
subsection of the elite labor force, phrases like "crème de la crème"
capture part of the reality: these firms provide their employees
with, among other things, the highest salaries, a prestigious identity of being among the most select group of business professionals,
and the steepest career ladders that lead all the way up to C-level
executive positions. Some of these firms pay their employees in U.S.
dollars instead of Turkish liras, which makes a huge difference for
workers in Turkey because of the increasingly disadvantaged position of Turkish lira against the euro and dollar. Such a difference
truly makes them part of the global elite labor force; after all, they
are getting more or less the same salaries as their peers in other
countries. The employees of these firms also have a higher rate of
international mobility via their intracompany networks; a management consultant at a Big Three firm working in Istanbul can ask for
a relocation to, say, London for family reasons. While this is also
possible for workers at other prestigious transnational corporations, I learned from my interviews that the rate is higher in elite
professional service firms.

The hiring mentality of elite professional service firms relies
more on *shortcuts* and the notion of fit than the HR-driven process described in the previous sections. The Big Three consulting
firms, for example, are known to target only a couple of schools in

Turkey's top six, sometimes complementing them with the best U.S. colleges. They hold invitation-only dinners at exclusive restaurants with only the most successful students of certain majors, such as the top five senior students majoring in industrial engineering. While these firms publicly advertise their job posts, they do not do so as widely as the other firms, and their campus recruitment events also target a very select group of candidates. Bülent, who was going on to work at a Big Three consulting firm, referred to these events as "hi-po dinners," meaning meeting with the high-potential candidates.

WHAT DOES CULTURAL MATCHING LOOK LIKE AT THE HIGHEST ECHELONS OF THE LABOR MARKET?

If fit with the current pool of employees is an important hiring criterion at elite professional service firms, then the first step of our examination should be to look a bit more deeply at the benchmark of cultural matching in hiring at these firms—in other words, to account for what a typical employee of these firms looks like. Based on my fieldwork and interviews, I suggest that a typical Turkish business professional working at these firms is usually from an upper- and upper-middle-class family; is "well rounded," that is, successful both in terms of coursework and extracurriculars; and is a graduate of an elite high school such as one of the foreign private high schools.

Being "well rounded" requires a lot of effort and resources as well as constant juggling between competing goals and objectives, such as keeping a high GPA, accumulating transnational cultural capital via pursuing exchange semesters abroad, holding internships at transnational corporations, engaging with highbrow and relatively expensive hobbies, and networking with career clubs. Ferhat described the sort of candidates who appeal to elite professional service firms: "[Getting a job in] consulting is very difficult. You should have both a really high GPA and a good social life. . . . When I look at the people who get these jobs, I generally see that they are the children of rich families, and they have done something [elite], such as traveling around the world, windsurfing, etc."

Fatma, the senior bound for a Big Three firm mentioned in chapter 1, told me, "They check your GPA. But in addition, they want to hear success stories in many other things." These "other things" usually function as the source of cultural matching in hiring, and as I discussed in the previous sections, extracurricular activities and hobbies are correlated with class backgrounds. Class homophily, then, also turns out to explain some part of why cultural matching operates more emphatically in the elite professional service firms' recruitment processes. As Bülent put it: "The first thing that they check out is whether they can be friends with you or not. . . . I think it is important for me, too. I want to hang out with people like me, I want to hear different things." When he said he wanted to hear "different things," Bülent was not calling for a more diverse work cohort. Quite the opposite: from Bülent's perspective, it was only "well rounded," cultured people—people "like me"—who could talk about a range of interesting things. These firms, with their exclusive employees from mostly upper-middle-class backgrounds, seem to satisfy such class homophily among the elite.

It is remarkable that in the United States too the symbolic boundary that sets the elite of the elite apart from the elite is articulated through a discourse of well rounded-ness: Amy Binder and Andrea Abel found that Harvard and Stanford students, a majority of whom pursue careers in this narrow band of firms, think that what elevates their institutions to the top of the Ivy League was that the former two provide its students with "well-rounded education."[30]

Students who do not come from wealthy backgrounds may find becoming well rounded challenging if they lack the resources to advance on all fronts at once. For example, Tuğrul, who came from a lower-middle-class family, lamented the way he spent his freshman and sophomore years, which he thought as the reason why he was sorted into a somewhat less prestigious niche: "I strove for career [*kariyer kastım*], and my GPA went down. Because of that, I could not apply for the Erasmus [exchange program]." This colloquial phrase *kariyer kasmak* means an intense effort to build up careerwise, which in practice means devotion to student clubs or career events instead of academics and personal life. While his efforts were not necessarily in vain—after all, he found a "good job" at a famous consumer goods company, Tuğrul framed this outcome as his own shortcoming. He regretted that he missed out on an exchange experience and thus he lost an important chance to find even higher prestige employment.

The cultivation of a well-rounded persona depends a lot on class background and familial upbringing, which creates visible stratification patterns even within firms. Melodi shared her observation of the social class contrast between consultants and auditors that work at the same Big Four company (consultants earn more than auditors and have higher occupational prestige): "The consultants' families are a bit more upper middle class. . . . They are more cultured people." By "more cultured," she meant not only a highbrow taste and lifestyle but also a global one—and, of course, "global" here is actually shorthand for the Global North. As I noted above, one of the most distinctive features of the transnational middle class is its transnational cultural capital, and this capital is especially important among elite professional service firms. The current pool of employees and new hires at these firms typically enjoy the highest quality transnational cultural capital: flawless English-language skills and a good deal of international experience.

Even more important than the amount of experience is the *quality* of that experience and the ease of the candidate in displaying it.

As we have seen in the advice Ferhat received about how to present himself in interviews, his international experience was sufficient as long as he could signal that he could exist and thrive *comfortably* in an international workplace and labor process. Bülent, who noted the difficulty of working in close quarters with coworkers with whom one has nothing in common, told me that, in an interview, when he mentioned his exchange semester in East Asia, the conversation led to him and his interviewer discussing the quality of food at a famous restaurant in Bali.

Part of the reason that these firms especially prize strong English-language skills and deeper international experience is that their labor process involves more international interactions than that of other prestigious transnational corporations. Respondents told me that business professionals in elite professional service firms engage with international business travel more frequently. This, of course, creates a greater need for perfected English and familiarity with a cosmopolitan culture. Kaan, the Istanbul-based management consultant, recalled a case in which his firm eliminated a candidate who had been born and raised in Kayseri, a much smaller and more provincial city than metropolitan Istanbul. Kaan remembered his manager asking rhetorically, "How can I send a guy from Kayseri to talk business with our client in Italy?" Here, the manager was using the candidate's hometown as a proxy to talk about his lack of fit with the company and job. Kaan noted that the manager's caution was based on the fact that the candidate did not have much international experience; hence, he might perform poorly if he were sent on an international mission. Arda, who had formerly worked as a consultant at a Big Three firm, shared a similar point about the center-versus-periphery hierarchy in terms of speaking Turkish with an accent: "If a candidate has an accent, it is an interesting case. I personally like it and find it really endearing. But I am pretty sure the office is not looking for someone with an accent. They want to see people with a higher socioeconomic status among themselves."

Speaking Turkish with an accent can signal either peripheral origins or a non-Turkish ethnic background—in other words, people not described by the popular term "White Turks."[31] This intersectional term refers to being ethnically Turkish, upper middle class, and secular, much like most members of the transnational Turkish middle class. As cultural matching unfolds in the hiring practices of transnational corporations, candidates who do not seem to fit this bill of White Turkishness are at a higher chance of being eliminated. For instance, some of my respondents (including one HR professional) disclosed to me that their firms directly eliminate women who wear headscarves, which may signal not only piousness but also political affiliation or sympathy with the conservative ruling party, the AKP (Adalet ve Kalkınma Partisi, the Justice and Development Party). Being vocal about one's Kurdish or Armenian descent could easily endanger a candidate's prospects of being hired. Being openly transgender would also seriously reduce the chance of being recruited as well.[32]

I was taken aback to learn that sometimes interviewers ask directly about candidates' class background. Ülkü described how this worked in her finance firm: "We [HR professionals] do not, but I know that some managers ask about the occupations of the candidates' parents. [By doing so,] they are trying to understand the character of a candidate, or whether they have any dysfunction in their family." As HR professionals are not the final arbiters of hiring in these firms, it is not difficult to assume that such cases of classism occur more frequently at elite professional services firms. Some students are well aware of these firms' conspicuous emphasis on elite backgrounds, and sometimes it even leads them to rule themselves out from applying to these firms in the first place. Sibel, the engineering senior that we met earlier, told me that she did not apply to the Big Three consulting firms because she anticipated that she would not get an offer: "I did not apply to save my self-esteem." Of course, ruling oneself out in this way arises not only from the perceived elitism in these firms' hiring decisions but also from the high standards these firms reputedly uphold, which applicants can find intimidating. Some respondents also suggested that these firms search for "alpha-type people."

One of the most striking distinctions of these firms' employees compared to those at other prestigious transnational corporations is that a very high ratio of them attended elite private high schools. Ebru, a management consultant at a Big Three firm who did not attend such a high school, shared her surprise when she found out that a majority of her teammates had attended Robert College: "I have never seen so many Robert alumni in a room," she said. Bülent observed the same pattern, stating: "Almost all the people who can get a job at these firms are from Robert College, Üsküdar American College, etc. And I don't think this is a coincidence." Such a consistent and obvious pattern could easily be interpreted as elitism.

Such preferential treatment can often take the form of favoritism. When I probed whether the high school matters in hiring, Ülkü replied: "The managers always pick graduates of Robert College, et cetera." Typical social closure processes, such as information hoarding, also take place in the recruitment processes of these firms. Fatma, who did not attend such an elite private high school, was part of a WhatsApp group with her classmates from the same cohort, sharing job posts, application deadlines, and tips. However, she did not see any information about jobs at elite firms in that group, and she speculated that "such posts were probably circulating among [elite] high school WhatsApp groups."

WHY IS CULTURAL MATCHING MORE PREVALENT AMONG ELITE PROFESSIONAL SERVICE FIRMS?

Cultural matching seems especially entrenched as a hiring norm in elite professional service firms for several reasons. First, many elite professional service firms have very small HR departments, if any; as a result, it is mostly the revenue-generating employees and managers, not HR professionals, who make the hiring decisions.[33] Therefore, these firms usually fall prey to what Asena called likability bias or what Duygu called halo effects.

Second, elite professional service firms justify their short-cuts of solely focusing on a couple of universities' top students as a means of prioritizing efficiency in hiring. In keeping with their role as efficiency experts optimizing the business processes of their clients, it seems that they have streamlined their own processes of recruitment along such lines. Much as HR professionals justify CV screening by noting that other elimination approaches would yield a similar candidate pool anyway, the managers of these firms who engage with hiring justify their targeted searches as a means of economizing their time and effort based on their experience of which universities offer top talent. As revenue-generating professionals who could generate higher revenues working for clients instead of engaging with hiring, they needed to make the best possible use of their time. Arda, who had formerly worked as a consultant at a Big Three firm, explained it this way: "Of course, the man [manager who is responsible for hiring] heads toward where the fruits are. . . . For example, they hired someone from X University in the previous years, and it turned out to be a poor hire. So, knowing that the graduates of Y University are always good hires, why would he bother trying to hire from X University again?"

Third, the average workweek in these firms is seventy hours, and team-based labor processes are the norm. Considering Bülent's remarks on the difficulty of working seventy hours a week in a small room with people you can't have a conversation with, getting along well is paramount in professional service sector jobs.

Fourth, professional service firms are client-facing businesses, and the clients are often C-level executives of prestigious corporations. In other words, the employees of these firms are interacting with the business elite every day. Hence, there is also an aesthetic labor that goes into their service such that the greater the overlap in lifestyles and tastes, the smoother such interactions are. Arda explained this as follows:

> We are doing business with bosses, senior clients. A client I worked with . . . you are twenty-five years old, the client is a senior guy, thirty-five years old. He has ten years of experience in this sector, and you are telling him, "You are doing it the wrong way, you should do it this way instead." To be able to say that, you need to have high IQ. First, you need to talk with him as a friend. You need to use the correct language.

These firms need to signal authority and sharp intelligence consistently to their clients, and hiring graduates of elite colleges and high schools also serves this end. The team of consultants that works to improve a clients' business are the most successful graduates of the best colleges, the "elite of the elite." The business models of these firms, through such targeted recruitments and selecting the cream of the crop of each cohort, rely on such monopolization of "intelligence" and its marketing.

HIGH HOPES OF THE TRANSNATIONAL MIDDLE CLASS

When these elite college students describe their desired postcollege trajectories, we see how the imperative of being successful in their postcollege lives shapes their notion of conceivable and desirable career paths, how global trajectories come into this picture, and how their high expectations regarding quality of working life influences their early career decisions.

Postcollege Trajectories

When I asked respondents about typical trajectories upon graduation, their responses could be grouped as follows: going corporate, working for startups, pursuing a graduate degree, or (rarely) taking a gap year or working for a nongovernmental organization (NGO). Fatma thought out loud about her postgraduation plans by detailing a handful of prestigious companies and a ranked set of alternative options:

> If I could not get into one of these companies, then I would pursue a master's degree or try to take a gap year. . . . People in good financial standing can take a gap year. . . . People who opt for startups are usually more secure people. And if you do not want an academic career, then you are left with nothing but corporate jobs. I would have wanted to work at an NGO, and I thought about it for a little while, but then I considered that it would be better if I first worked at a global company and then found a job at a global NGO. That way, I can do better things. If I start working for an NGO here [in Turkey], anyone can do what I am supposed to do, and I do not want to do work below my capacity.

Fatma's thoughts outline a widely shared hierarchy of worthy career paths. Working for prestigious transnational corporations is by far the most preferred option, in large part because of its tight connection to being successful. Working for NGOs, on the other hand, is not completely off the table but is less often pursued because NGOs in Turkey do not pay well—and because they have significantly less prestige than corporate jobs. For most of the students I interviewed, working for prestigious corporations was the way to go. As Hülya put it: "People typically follow the mainstream and that is to get into a giant corporate firm. Because they also perceive that they can continue being successful that way. For example, many people want tech [firms] mainly because it is cool and growing fast, and etc. . . . Consulting, tech, FMCG. . . . That is all there is."

Sibel, who was headed for a consumer goods firm, mentioned consulting and FMCG companies as the only career options. Demir, who would go on to work at a tech giant in Europe, cited the same list plus tech companies, qualifying his addition by noting, "There is only Google and Microsoft [in Turkey] and they only hire a couple of people." (In addition, these positions are not software but marketing jobs, an issue that I will explore further in chapter 3.) As a result, most students who want to work at tech corporations are forced to pursue careers in the Global North, mainly via pursuing graduate degrees from the well-known universities there.

Success-Driven Habitus and Globalization of Career Paths

The Turkish students who are the potential members of the transnational Turkish middle class and who have been successful throughout their education have a strong drive to continue being successful in their postcollege lives. That is a crucial reason why they aim for the most prestigious positions.

The tight coupling between success and employment at prestigious transnational corporations provides elite college students with an important path for their early career decisions, as we have heard from Fatma and Hülya. While many young people have high expectations, the expectations held by these elite college students are far beyond that of their peers. The difference, I argue, stems first from an ability to envision a brighter future and to consider it plausible given their milieus and backgrounds. Elite students regularly hear success stories about the alumni of their alma mater—for example, hearing about the CEOs who once sat in the same seats as they are—making such bright futures seem possible for them as well. Their own histories bear this out: throughout their adolescence, they have consistently ranked at the top levels in national exams, attended the best schools, and outperformed their peers. In the previous chapter, I labeled this a success-driven habitus mainly because these individuals' major disposition is to be successful in whatever field they choose. And as my respondents' stories show, the hiring processes in the elite labor market strongly prefer such habitus, which keeps driving these individuals to be overachievers in their postcollege lives.

When I asked Ferhat whether being successful was important for him, he laughed hard and answered, "Success is *really* important for me. . . . I can't get enough of it!" At the same time, his stated definition of postcollege success was quite narrow: getting a job at a Big Three consulting firm. Fatma said, "If it was not [a specific Big Three company], I would feel bad about myself." Sibel told me that she felt "proud" when she got a job at one of the most famous FMCG firms. Securing a job at a prestigious transnational corporation—as opposed to a Turkish firm (recall Ezgi's comparison of Coca-Cola with Uludağ in chapter 1)—was taken as the ultimate sign of the continuation of their success, something that defined who they have been all along.

These corporations also offer possibilities of immigration to global cities such as New York and London, which comes with many benefits. Gökçe, a chemistry major who would go on to work at a famous tobacco company, said she chose that firm because of its global network and the opportunity to live in New York, where she believed she would enjoy participating in the rich cultural scene. Similarly, Tuğrul expressed envy of one of his classmates who was going to work in the United Kingdom and would be paid in British pounds and not Turkish lira: "It hurts that my salary will be equal to 20 percent of his salary." It is noteworthy how Tuğrul's envy is conditional primarily on the Turkish lira's devaluation.

Money and standard of living are not the only benchmarks, however. Yasin, a computer science major, was motivated to find a job in Europe mainly because of nonmaterial aspects of quality of working life. Not only did he feel that he was overqualified for the few available jobs in his area of expertise in Turkey, but he was also impressed with the strong welfare practices in Germany, where his brother was working: "Work-life balance always has the top priority [in Germany]. Working dedicatedly for a company is absurd and while there are thirty days of annually paid vacation in Germany, we have zero days in the first year, and fourteen later on! . . . Besides, there are not many options [in Turkey] to earn a living by working in research and development."

High Hopes

As Yasin's reasoning illustrates, the available array of jobs in Istanbul is not intrinsically satisfying for many highly educated elite college students. Cemre, a senior computer science major who was going to work at a tech startup while pursuing her master's degree, summarized her expectation of having an intellectually exciting and challenging job with a popular phrase, "*o kadar okuduk yani!* [after all, we have studied this much!]," emphasizing that she had invested years of effort in her demanding education. She said that many of the available jobs in her area of expertise in Turkey, based on her internship experiences, were just too simple for her:

"I mean, I could perform the tasks required in these jobs after I graduated from high school." This theme—"I would not need a college degree to do that"—frequently surfaced in my interviews with elite business professionals as well, highlighting a significant discrepancy between their demanding college education, which had armed them with high-level skills (and expectations to match), and the actual content of their jobs, which required a minimal use of those skills, if any.

Some of the students who experienced underemployment during their internships at transnational corporations before graduation opted for startups instead of "going corporate," thinking that they could put their skills and creativity to work more at a startup. This is a relatively new trend, and some respondents attributed it to the culture of generations Y and Z. Ezgi, who interned at a transnational bank, thought that most corporate jobs, even in prestigious transnational corporations, were nothing but "Excel *ameleliği* [drudgery]"— *amele* is used in Turkish as a derogatory term for a day laborer. For Ezgi, office work that revolved around spreadsheets was menial, no different than manual labor, except that one does the same repetitive jobs with a computer.

Nedim, the paragliding student who majored in economics and was about to start work at a fintech startup, was crystal clear in his job preferences: "I am a highly qualified person, I want to like the daily occupations I'll have in my job." He elaborated that he had identified a benchmark wage that would guarantee for him a comfortably middle-class life; beyond that, he only cared about his colleagues and the actual content of the job. When I asked how he'd feel about a boring job that paid him a 50 percent higher salary, he responded that he would not accept it even if it paid 100 percent more. In contrast to Nedim, however, Ezgi made the case for accepting less interesting work by drawing a parallel between university and working life: "At [name of the bank she used to work as an intern], I realized that it is actually like school; you have classes, but you have breaks, and during the breaks, you hang out with friends [and classes become bearable]. So, as I have to earn a living, if I can get along with my colleagues, I could survive corporate jobs, too." This illustrates that part of the reason why these students prefer prestigious firms is to continue living in their social milieus. Note that when these students climb the career ladders and ascend to managerial positions, as I have discussed in the recruitment processes in the previous sections, their rather benign preference of "getting along" culminates in class homophily in hiring.

In addition to a familiar social circle, success, prestige, and high salaries, work at transnational corporations offers the opportunity to make a mark on the world. Sibel offered a glimpse of this when she described her daydreams: "I see myself, having made it to good positions, high-status positions, and I am influencing people." She believed that her current job, working at a consumer goods giant whose products sell all over the world, put her on the right track. Ferhat also emphasized the importance of prestige and impact: "Prestige and name [of the company] is important for me because, like . . . I want to do work that will have large impacts." The impacts that he desired to make were on the world scale, and working for transnational corporations was the path to that goal.

Having such ambitions of "making a difference" or "having large impacts" can be at odds with prioritizing work-life balance. In our interview, Tuğrul brought up the phrase "*memur kafası*," which roughly translates as "civil servant mentality" or "clerk mentality." This phrase refers to those working at state institutions, who are often characterized as lazy, inefficient, and lacking enthusiasm (although one might just as easily say that these jobs offer good work-life balance, job security, and welfare benefits). One important contrast with the old middle class in Turkey, which is often associated with such a "clerk mentality," is that, although they are part of the transnational middle class in Turkey—the most privileged fraction of the new middle class—and value work-life balance, they are usually willing to forgo it for the sake of prestige and upward mobility. While pointing to "clerk mentality" as an undesirable benchmark, Tuğrul also lamented the pattern of overwork and limited paid leave that came with work at a prestigious company:

> Although this [prioritizing work-life balance] brings you toward *memur kafası*. I mean, it is important, too. People work that much and buy giant TVs and Netflix, but come home and watch TV for an hour. Aren't we working to live? Dude, you can't live to work! Yes, they earn a lot and spend a lot, but they can only spend that much for three days in a year [due to lack of free time and vacations].

Nevertheless, he had decided to continue working at the consumer goods giant where he had interned because having an impact was paramount for him: "I didn't like consultancy. It is very theoretical. But in sales, at the end of the day, I check the numbers to see what worked and what did not. I like to make a difference." Note that, although phrases such as "making a difference" or "having an impact" often carry a meaning of "changing the world for the better," many of my respondents used them in a much more modest way to indicate that something in the world had changed as a result of their efforts (for better or worse). I will delve deeper into this topic in chapter 3.

These students' expectations regarding their future class positions were understandably high because they studied hard throughout their teenage years and ended up at the best universities. Only three out of the fifteen senior undergraduates I interviewed estimated that they would be in the middle class when they started their careers; the rest thought they would start as upper middle or upper class from the start. They also envisioned further upward mobility, and all the respondents except one estimated that, by age thirty, they would be either upper middle or upper class. Discovering that they may not land high-salary jobs can produce profound anxiety, even anger. After sharing a few failure stories from his job search, Demir vividly remembered a job interview at a transnational corporation that proposed to him a poorly compensated management trainee position with long work hours:

> Because I have already interned at [a top-notch consumer goods giant], I thought I could find a job in all the other companies. However, it was not the case. . . . In the final stage [of recruitment], I was being interviewed by the CEO and a couple of managers, and everything was going well, but at the very last minute of the meeting, the CEO asked me, "Are you ready to work a lot and earn little?" I answered, "Which one are you asking? Working a lot or earning little?" and the meeting room went ice cold. F*ck this, man! I mean, yeah, of course, I will work a lot! Why are you still showing off?

Although failing to secure that job, Demir was feeling lucky because he was able to get a dream job at a famous tech company in Europe.

While the privatization of education in Turkey from the 1980s onward put nonwealthy families at a disadvantage, selective high-stakes testing is still the chief means of upward mobility. Although the particulars of the education system and of the nationwide selection exams have changed frequently since then (only becoming much more competitive), the nature of them is still the same; the cultural legacy of these exams and their burning influence on the future of Turkish youth are arguably even more powerful today.

Students' rankings in these exams determine their life chances by limiting what subject they can major in and at which university, which, in the final analysis, determine whether they will be able to join the ranks of the middle classes or, better yet, the transnational middle class. Anxiety about such placement runs deep: as Henry J. Rutz and Erol M. Balkan aptly put it, "The new middle class is envied and admired, but it is never [feeling] secure."[34] As I will discuss in more detail in chapter 4, a deep status anxiety underlies the psyche of the new middle class, shaping the quality of their working lives.

The stages of hiring at TNCs that come after CV screening are marked by conflicting logics and practices of elimination: HR professionals usually intend to assess competence by pursuing a relatively more objective and accountable way, whereas revenue-generating managers operate as tiebreakers among a pool of more or less equal candidates, and they often rely on their subjective ways of evaluating whether a candidate would fit in, which is justified by seeking harmony in teamwork. However, both parties prioritize, sometimes overtly but mostly in subtle ways, the fitness of a candidate with the current pool of employees. Because a good deal of the employees of transnational corporations consist of upper-middle-class individuals, such assessments of fitness often end up in class homophily and social closure and thereby reproduction of inequality writ large. The recruitment processes of elite professional service firms are particularly filled with the most obvious examples of such social closure practices that almost guarantees the continuing success of elites. This could be attributed to these firms' lack of HR professionals and their priority of efficiency in recruitment efforts by revenue-generating business professionals, and to the tacit requirements of working with upper-class clientele in their daily businesses.

These findings imply that transnational corporations, by holding similar practices of recruitment around the globe, yield similar repertoires for reproducing inequality. When we compare the

United States and Turkey, for example, we see striking parallels in both recruitment practices of transnational corporations, particularly elite professional service firms, and their outcomes of elite social closure. The production of social inequalities long precedes graduation from college, but examining the transition to adulthood and the transformation of successful students into the elite labor force reveals another layer to the resilience of inequality facilitated by the hiring practices of prestigious transnational corporations.

Transnational corporations have favored post-Fordist labor processes and prize teamwork, which puts a strong emphasis on fit. It is also important to note that these firms can place this level of emphasis on "cultural matching" in hiring only when there is an abundance of skilled labor. In other words, firms can afford to select only people with a certain set of dispositions because there are many people capable of doing these jobs. Thanks to the expansion of college education, the labor supply for elite corporate positions has expanded as well. Some HR professionals of major consumer goods companies reported that they were seeing declining interest in corporate jobs as a result of increased immigration to European and North American countries as well as the popularity of working at startups. As a result, they have recently begun to recruit from universities other than the top six. They also commented that their new hires from nonelite universities were also pretty good and accomplished, which highlights the abundance of sufficiently skilled labor in the job market.

The interviews with graduating seniors from an elite public university also illustrate that they considered only a very narrow range of careers to be worthy because employment at prestigious corporations is often seen as the ultimate sign of the success that is a cornerstone of their perceived self-worth. These students have gone through a very demanding education since their childhoods, and that investment, hand in hand with their sense of having obtained a high-level skill set, gives them high expectations for their future employment and careers. Such high expectations provide part of their impetus for pursuing global career trajectories, which they expect will yield intellectually challenging jobs with large-scale impacts. Surveys with these students show that they predict they will end up in the upper or upper middle classes with regard to future incomes and lifestyles.

In chapter 3, I will turn to what happens next for these winners in the global labor market. Once successful college students turn into elite workers, does achieving that admired goal bring a contented career and a happy life?

3

DISAPPOINTED AND EXHAUSTED

Desiring to exercise the skills that one has cultivated during college is an understandable expectation. Tuğba, who was working as a process engineer at a prestigious engineering consulting company, told me proudly, "Only chemical engineers can design these processes." But Tuğba's attitude that "not everyone can do what I am doing at work" was surprisingly uncommon in my interviews. Far more respondents told me something along the lines of "a college degree is unnecessary for my job." Erman's case is an illuminating example. As a sales manager in the baby care unit of one of the largest consumer goods companies in the world, he was earning a high salary for his age (especially compared to his parents' meager teacher salaries). But his job was not living up to his expectations: "I won awards in physics competitions when I was in high school, and I studied electronics engineering in college and nowadays, in the last analysis, I am selling diapers! . . . I learn nothing new in my job. I feel that my learning speed slowed down significantly, I feel I am becoming a dull person."

Many respondents sounded much more like Erman than like Tugba. In addition to feeling disappointed with what they have been doing every day at work, they were also typically feeling exhausted, physically and mentally. Lila, a marketing manager at another consumer goods giant, shared with me that one day she fell asleep and snored loudly during a yoga session she joined after work because she was so drained. She had felt "so humiliated" that she had to change her yoga studio.

What happened to all that optimism and high expectations that we saw in chapter 2? What made things go sour at work for the best and brightest of Turkish youth? Why and how can these elite workers—salaried employees with high-income, high-prestige corporate jobs—be discontented with their work, and eventually, their lives?

In *Good Jobs, Bad Jobs*, a trendsetting book in job quality research, Arne Kalleberg argued that the quality gap between good jobs— well-paying jobs that offer relative autonomy and control over labor and some level of job security—and bad jobs has been on the rise.[1] The literature on job quality reflects this lopsidedness. There have been numerous studies concerning poor quality manual labor, service work, and rising precarity, but there are not many in-depth inquiries into the so-called good jobs. Focusing on what are arguably the best corporate jobs, this chapter "studies up."[2] My interviews with Turkish elite workers reveal the whole range between content and discontent. However, two themes of discontent— unfulfilling work and overwork—loom surprisingly large. In addition, even contented workers show considerable status anxiety in their working lives, which partly explains why elite business professionals continue to put up with overwork and unfulfilling work. (In chapter 4, I will examine what happens when status anxiety and other factors keeping these workers at their jobs no longer suffice and workers opt out.)

What is the importance of studying the contents and discontents of elite labor? The "good job, bad job" distinction has traditionally been used to distinguish between secure white-collar versus precarious blue-collar and service-sector jobs. Applying this distinction within the higher echelons of corporate jobs seems somewhat counterintuitive: after all, these jobs are widely viewed as the paradigmatic "good" jobs. As I discussed in the introduction to this book, however, white-collar blues are prevalent among Turkish elite business professionals, nor are these feelings confined to the transnational Turkish middle class. The *New York Times Magazine*'s February 2019 special issue, devoted to the theme of the future of work, featured a lead article on American elite business professionals titled: "Wealthy, Successful and Miserable."[3]

Such surprising moments are fertile grounds for theory generation and extension when bolstered by an abductive analysis.[4] In terms of extant theories of alienation, for instance, the discouraging experience of a blue-collar worker constitutes relatively low-hanging fruit; it would not be surprising to find an alienated member of the proletariat on the shop floor.[5] However, elite business professionals are virtually the opposite of the typical blue-collar worker—their jobs are relatively challenging and nonrepetitive and offer high pay and benefits, although they still have to sell their labor to keep earning a middle-class living. It is much more surprising to find systematic dissatisfaction and alienation in that context.

Work is one of the most assiduously studied spheres of life in the social sciences, particularly in sociology. The vexed relationship between individuals and the divisions of labor they inhabit has been a core preoccupation of classical sociology, such as Karl Marx's treatment of alienation and Émile Durkheim's anomie. The literature on work and its consequential effects on our well-being has multiplied significantly since then. What follows is a brief review of the major lenses that shed light on the quality of white-collar working life.

JOB QUALITY AND JOB SATISFACTION

Job quality research usually focuses on the entire labor force and strives to generate a comprehensive, multidimensional, multilevel, and multicontextual understanding of job quality.[6] Such research is often motivated by the need for a broad understanding of the macro level dynamics of the workforce to better serve the policymaking of organizations such as the International Labour Organization (ILO), the Organisation for Economic Co-operation and Development (OECD), and the European Union (EU).[7] Examining the entire landscape of labor, this research has highlighted the expansion of low-wage jobs and rising precarity as the most urgent problems.[8] This virtue of examining the labor force holistically, however, leads to prioritizing the study of "bad jobs." Such research ends up focusing primarily on the economic aspects of job quality, mainly relying on the assumption that higher pay is usually positively related to noneconomic aspects of job quality.[9] Hence, the macro lens of this research is unfit for my in-depth investigation into smaller segments of the labor market,[10] including so-called good jobs. Nevertheless, job quality research is a useful model insofar as it details an array of measures and indexes for tapping into noneconomic aspects of job quality as well, including autonomy and control over labor, schedule and work hours, meaningful work, and workplace relations.

Job satisfaction is another widely used concept in studies of the quality of working life. Unlike job quality research, research into job satisfaction adopts a micro focus on individuals' subjective understanding of their quality of working life. Its ease of use— usually only a couple of carefully crafted questions suffice—and its accuracy in predicting absenteeism and employee turnover have made it a standard component of multidimensional inquiries of job quality research.[11] It is comprehensive insofar as it inquires about a worker's affective assessment of the totality of job quality, which includes almost everything from pay to relations with colleagues in the workplace. The main problem of using the job satisfaction lens is just that, however: although both global and specific aspects of job satisfaction have long been a subject of study, these still have to be reinforced with a qualitative, in-depth investigation of why workers perceive their job satisfaction the way they do.[12]

LABOR PROCESS AND ALIENATION

The labor process school of thought seems to lie somewhere between these two main lines of research. With its emphasis on meso-level dynamics, this approach attempts to assess quality of working life by focusing on the workplace and the social organization of work there.[13] Typical work in this vein of research is a workplace ethnography, which provides nitty-gritty details of everyday working life. Especially when focused on "bad jobs," such analysis usually centers around how objective working conditions underpin managerial control, worker consent, and alienation.

The twentieth century, and particularly the 1960s–1980s, was a hotbed of alienation research.[14] It is instructive for my analysis to cover its two main debates, which will help us better understand how alienation is in fact a useful lens to examine the quality of white-collar working life as well. The first debate concerns whether alienation should be studied as an objective phenomenon at the level of societies or a subjective phenomenon at the level of individuals. Marxists have typically argued that alienation springs from objective conditions of labor under capitalism and that the study of alienation research should focus on the objective conditions of labor. Contrary to this view, social psychological perspectives posit that, because the same objective conditions can be experienced differently at the subjective level, alienation is intrinsically social-psychological.[15] Each of these perspectives has its own merit, but as with most subjective/objective dichotomies in social theory, it is more fruitful to take a holistic approach. This is particularly the case for alienation because Marx's account of alienation is certainly interpretable as a synthesis of objective and subjective.[16] When we stop seeing alienation as merely a "state of mind" or a purely "objective condition" and take a more dynamic, social, and processual perspective, the synthesis becomes unavoidable.[17]

The second debate concerns the ambiguous impact of technology on the alienation of labor. Robert Blauner famously argued, on the one hand, that the alienation of labor follows a reverse U-shaped curve, first increasing then declining so that the most advanced technology minimizes repetitive and boring labor and unleashes more free time.[18] Thus, arguably, the problem of alienation stems from not capitalism per se but from industrialization and bureaucratization and is thus a temporary problem. Harry Braverman argued on the other hand that, as technology advances following Frederick Taylor's scientific management principles in production, the bifurcation between conception (i.e., design) and execution in labor takes off as well, and hence we expect deskilling of workers coterminous with the concentration of managerial jobs in the very few, and higher rates of proletarianization and degradation of labor.[19]

Blauner's work has been criticized for its interpretation, measurement, and design inconsistencies; Braverman's work has been criticized for being too deterministic and pessimistic.[20] Both highlight how important it is to be on the design side of the labor processes for a higher quality of working life insofar as it yields higher worker autonomy and more free time (and not to mention the bigger paycheck). Michael Burawoy's influential ethnographies enriched this debate further by illustrating how social organization of work intertwines with worker agency in eliciting workers' consent to working harder than necessary and in dealing with boredom on the shop floor.[21]

Alienation Beyond Manual Labor

In the light of these key debates on alienation, if we approach its original description by Marx pragmatically, alienation can be mostly understood through its effects:

> First, the fact that labour is *external* to the worker . . . that in his work, therefore, he does not affirm himself but denies himself, does not feel content but unhappy, does not develop freely his physical and mental energy but mortifies his body and ruins his mind. The worker therefore only feels himself outside his work, and in his work feels outside himself. . . . His labour is therefore not voluntary, but coerced; it is *forced labour*. It is therefore not the satisfaction of a need; it is merely a *means* to satisfy needs external to it. Its alien character emerges clearly in the fact that as soon as no physical or other compulsion exists, labour is shunned like the plague.[22]

Here I see four different deficits that together constitute the alienation of labor. First, there is the loss of workers' satisfaction of seeing their productive/creative powers reflected in the end product (i.e., loss of authorship). Second, there is the loss of human freedom and autonomy to determine when, how long, how to, and on what to work. Third, there is the loss of living up to one's (human) potential through engaging with creative and intrinsically satisfying activity at work, and fourth, there is the loss of energy, time, and (eventually) capacity to engage with creative and intrinsically satisfying activity at *nonworking times* as well.

If we conceptualize alienation in this way, then there is no reason to limit the experience of separation or feeling distant from
one's laboring activity, the gist of alienation experience, to manual
labor. Even if very few studies tackle the question of alienation of
elite, professional-managerial labor head on,[23] we can still use the
studies that focus on various nonfactory work environments from
the lens of alienation. An excellent example can be found in Arlie
Hochschild's groundbreaking study of "emotional labor" and alienation of workers in the American service sector.[24] Hochschild can
be said to have developed an alienation theory for service-sector
workers, focusing on how workers in these sectors discipline their
emotions to earn a living and how in return they feel distant from
their own feelings in nonwork contexts. While the concept of "emotional labor" aimed to capture the experience of alienation in the
public-facing service sector, it is illuminating for white-collar workers in office settings—in which how one seems and sounds can be
consequential—as well as to the business-to-business consulting
sector, in which the elite workers interact face to face with their clients on a daily basis.[25] Management consultants, for instance, must
face their client (another business), and must satisfy this client by
not only delivering effective solutions but also convincing the client that their solutions will in fact work out as they intend.[26] This
includes different kinds of emotional labor, such as demonstrating
a high level of self-confidence (appearing sharp and smart, both
visually with their clothing and verbally with their quick wits) and
personableness (smiling and comforting the client despite how the
client reacts)—both very similar to service-sector workers.

Another great and more recent example of examining nonfactory labor from the alienation perspective is Michael Siciliano's
meticulous ethnography of precarious "creative labor" in the culture industries.[27] Much like emotional labor creating a unique taste
of alienation, Siciliano shows how even creative labor, which is

almost antithetical to backbreaking and boring manual labor, can be pregnant with "alienated judgment" under the whims of capitalist control over labor. His ethnography details how sound engineers and YouTube content creators with their "cool jobs" may still feel alienated from the end product they themselves had helped create and sometimes even from related leisure activities writ large, such as listening to music.[28] While deeply engaged with their labor and deriving intrinsic satisfaction from it, lacking the final authority in decision making with regard to the aesthetics of their creative work, they typically end up disidentifying themselves from the end product (i.e., losing authorship).[29] Siciliano's work is instructive in showing how worker control over labor is paramount for our understanding of alienation.

When it comes to elite, professional-managerial workers, however, in-depth research on the quality of their working life experience has been rather scarce because their job quality is usually taken for granted; after all, they are the top of the labor markets. The one issue, however, about elite white-collar workers that was not scarcely studied is their poor work-life balance.[30] Exemplary in this vein of research is Gideon Kunda's ethnography of a high-tech firm, which holds that the modern corporation has been a "greedy institution" and "engineering culture" to control professional labor by eliciting consent to an undivided commitment to the workplace.[31] High-status business professionals are subject to a "work devotion schema," a prevalent cultural set of expectations and norms *engineered* by the higher echelons of corporate management across industries, demanding that occupants of these jobs dedicate themselves to their work even at the expense of their families.[32] The work devotion schema, combined with elite business professionals' relatively higher levels of autonomy over their labor, can lead to the "stress of higher status" in which the line between work and nonwork is blurred, but to the detriment of the workers.[33] Other researchers have found evidence supporting the "stress of higher status" thesis and have also examined how elite business professionals engage with "time work" to cope with the contemporary discontents of overwork.[34]

Nevertheless, overworked professionals have been predominantly studied in terms of how their overwork negatively influences family life.[35] Sociologists' emphasis on work-family conflict as the most important nonwork concern, however, has limited the description of alienating outcomes of overwork to the domestic domain and to married couples with children[36]—at the expense of other losses such as time for creative activity, social gatherings, civic engagement, and personal well-being. A more comprehensive understanding of work/nonwork interference requires further empirical research into how single and young adults experience and cope with overwork.

Overall, there are striking similarities between the effects of overwork in so-called good jobs and Marx's original description of alienation from one's labor quoted above (including damage to mind and body, an aversion toward work, and reduced time for nonwork activities). This overlap encourages exploring the quality of working life experience of elite business professionals from the alienation perspective.

John Goldthorpe and colleagues' "embourgeoisement thesis" represents the conventional wisdom that has countered this point, arguing that the material returns from work are very important insofar as workers become more affluent, working conditions become less important.[37] True, alienation theory could be critiqued for eliding the material returns of work in assessing quality of working life. Nevertheless, I argue that such a "shortcoming" (rather counterintuitively) makes alienation theory particularly suitable for studying the lived experience of elite workers and their well-being. Drawing on a survey of Americans in 2008 and 2009, Nobel laureates Daniel Kahneman and Angus Deaton found that while higher income does contribute to a positive evaluation of life and emotional well-being, its marginal returns on the emotional well-being begin to diminish beyond $75,000.[38] (Note that the salaries of the business professionals I am covering here are considerably above this threshold although they also live in New York City, which is much more expensive than an average city in the United States.) It makes one wonder, if we momentarily disregard the high salaries of elite white-collar workers, what would be left of their job satisfaction?

Job Satisfaction Versus Alienation

Arne Kalleberg has offered a rich theory of job satisfaction that conceptualizes it as a unitary measure, determined by the discrepancy between an array of work values (i.e., a personal benchmark) and job rewards.[39] Superior to most uncritical job satisfaction perspectives with its emphasis on worker autonomy, Kalleberg argued that job rewards are strongly influenced by workers' control over their work; for example, if unemployment is high, then workers have fewer job options to find the right fit for themselves as well as little bargaining power to secure financial benefits. Kalleberg also found some evidence that a worker's degree of control over employment situations has an independent effect on their job satisfaction, although most of the impact on satisfaction is still mediated by the rewards.

My respondents' assessment of their own job satisfaction seems to follow this pattern to a point. Halfway through each interview, I asked my respondents to rank their current job satisfaction on a scale from 1 to 10, and their scores were not particularly low; the average job satisfaction of my sample (excluding opt-outs) was 6.7 out of 10 (see the appendix for the job satisfaction levels of my elite workers sample). Very few rated their satisfaction lower than 5; that is, most of my respondents rated their satisfaction as positive overall. Yet their responses also reveal how relying only on standard job satisfaction measures fail to tap into the discontent of elite labor. Even as my respondents reported average or sometimes even high job satisfaction values, many of them were offering negative answers to open-ended questions regarding the quality of their work lives. For example, when I asked Erman, the sales manager we met at the beginning of this chapter, to rank his job satisfaction from 1 to 10, he thought for a while and responded this way:

ERMAN: Six . . .

MUSTAFA (THE AUTHOR): Not six and a half or seven?

ERMAN: I was in between five and a half. But I said six because, first, it pays well, and second, because it is a prestigious position, I could still catapult myself out of the system. . . . I mean . . . I think I was actually generous when I said six. [laughs uneasily] This is because, from time to time . . . even [partner's name] told me that I am being ungrateful. I mean, I am earning well, you know. Even when I was thinking of my [job satisfaction] score, I probably thought "don't be ungrateful" in the back of my mind. Dude, you change this into five. Five, it is. [laughing uneasily] I've been cursing and complaining for an hour now, it'd be inaccurate to say six.

Many respondents who gave higher job satisfaction scores than Erman were often surprised that their scores were so high. Like Erman, they usually thought out loud, surmising that the high salary and prestige of their jobs were discouraging them from reporting lower scores.

Alienation theory may shed some light on this paradox. While there are important overlaps between alienation theory and job satisfaction perspective, the main distinction between the two is that alienation theory considers the productive and creative activity of humans to be an end in itself; as a result, increasing the material rewards of work cannot solve the basic problem of the instrumentalization of labor. In other words, alienation theory holds that no amount of money or other material benefits can ultimately compensate for the alienating work experience. The theory of job satisfaction, on the other hand, is utilitarian in its essence. By considering job satisfaction as an overall measure, it posits that some negative aspects of the work can be compensated for by positive aspects. The focus is on a quantifiable assessment of values versus rewards, or benchmark expectations versus actual conditions. In alienation theory, the comparison between benchmark and actual is more implicit and qualitative (e.g., in Marx, original human nature versus actual state of humanity or, more precisely, the craftspeople of precapitalism versus the proletariat), and there is little discussion of external rewards, particularly because the only reward (external and internal) of the proletariat is a tendential drift toward subsistence. Hence, alienation has long been perceived as a theory appropriate for studying blue-collar laborers, the working class, who live only by subsistence; once a worker becomes affluent or white collar, a job satisfaction optic seems to be more appropriate—and even more so for elite workers whose compensation is so high that some of them can even be considered part of the so-called 1 percent (although only in terms of income and not wealth—a key consideration that often escapes the commonsensical understanding of social class, which is also partly why I prefer the term "middle class" for elite workers). However, a close examination of the lived experience of elite workers shows the applicability of the alienation perspective.

THE DISCONTENTS OF TURKISH ELITE LABOR

My interviews with Turkish elite business professionals reveal a great deal about their quality of working life experience at prestigious transnational corporations in Istanbul and New York. Table 3.1

Table 3.1 Descriptive data on the characteristics of the professional-managerial employee sample

	Elite workers	Corporate dropouts
N	48	17
Age		
Median	31	30
Range	[25, 44]	[27, 37]
Gender		
Female	21	9
Male	27	8
Marital status		
Single	38	12
Married	10	5
Has children	5	2
Educational attainment		
College degree	24	11
Graduate degree	24	6
Class background		
Working poor	0	0
Lower middle class	0	0
Middle class	20	4
Upper middle class	25	11
Upper class	3	2
Parental class background		
Working poor	1	0
Lower middle class	9	1
Middle class	18	6
Upper middle class	20	9
Upper class	0	1
Workplace authority		
Expert	26	10
Manager	22	7
Industry		
Professional services	27	7
Production and manufacturing	13	8
Technology	8	2

details the aggregate demographic and socioeconomic character-istics of my elite worker sample (see the appendix for the anony-mized details of each interviewee).[40]

In my analysis of these interviews, I do not treat the concept of alienation as a binary indicator and label people accordingly to produce a frequentist answer to whether my sample of elite labor is alienated or not. Instead, I examine respondents' experiences around quality of working life that are congruent with a processual understanding of alienation. Rather than treating human flourish-ing and alienation as abstract humanistic concepts, I ground my benchmarks in my empirical material, complementing discussion of respondents' negative experiences with other respondents' posi-tive experiences on the same issue.

My interviews suggest two key dimensions of the lived experi-ence of quality of working life among Turkish elite white-collar workers, which are outlined in figure 3.1. On the horizontal axis, we have perceived work-life balance, with the poles of feeling overworked versus balanced. On the vertical axis, we have per-ceived fulfillment with one's job, with the poles of fulfilled versus unfulfilled.

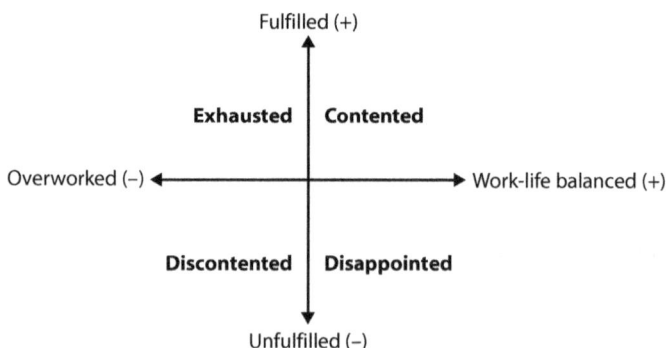

FIGURE 3.1 A typology of the lived experience of quality of working life

These two axes yield four ideal typical work experiences: in the upper-right quadrant are *contented* professionals, who feel fulfilled with a reasonable work-life balance. In my sample, these were mostly software engineers. Diametrically opposite are *discontented* professionals, who are overworked and unfulfilled; these were chiefly investment bankers and finance professionals. In the upper-left quadrant are the *exhausted*; in my sample, these were mainly management consultants and corporate lawyers, who felt fulfilled in their jobs but severely overworked. In the bottom right quadrant are *disappointed* professionals. In my sample, these were mostly mid-level managers at consumer goods companies who, while they had a reasonable work-life balance, lacked fulfillment from their jobs.

Although it may sound appealing to allocate my interviewees to these various categories, these ideal types should serve us better as a logical map, illuminating the dynamics of quality of working life. Note that the experiences that I portray are dynamic; that is, a professional's location in this Cartesian space can change as the individual changes jobs, positions, and companies; this is particularly the case for elite business professionals, who change employers rather frequently. I learned from my interviews, however, that such moves typically involve a trade-off between fulfillment and work-life balance and rarely lead them to a contented quality of working life.

Unfulfilling Work: A Lost Potential

One of the most surprising and striking things I learned from my interviews was just how alien the idea of fulfilling work was for the majority of the elite business professionals I spoke with. For example, halfway through each interview, I used a vignette instrument (see the appendix) to further explore and understand people's work orientations. The vignette differentiates among three kinds of work orientations—considering one's work a job, a career, or a calling—represented by the narratives of Person A, Person B, and Person C, respectively.[41] I asked each respondent to read the vignette text on the front side of the page, then turn the page over and think aloud while answering a set of questions written on the back. After respondents read the description of Person C—someone who loves their job, derives great satisfaction from it, and sees it as a calling—many characterized Person C as a workaholic, even when they were provided with examples that encouraged people to imagine Person's C job as different from their own. The idea that Person C might actually be content in their job simply did not occur to them. If I reminded the respondent that Person C finds work satisfying and believes their work makes the world a better place, they were dismissive, replying with something along the lines of, "Yeah, there are some strange people like that." This suggests that the majority of these elite business professionals cannot even conceive of the possibility of a fulfilling working life: they do not think the top-right quadrant in the quality of working life typology even exists. They instead think of people who express job satisfaction as strange or inauthentic to the point that they are lying about their happiness.[42]

Erman, the sales manager in the baby care unit of a consumer goods behemoth whom we met earlier, grew up in a small city, and through his hard work and talent, he ended up first at one of Turkey's best universities and, upon graduation, at one of the most prestigious companies in the world. He thought that working at a job that one is "passionate" about was the peak of a happy life, but he had gradually lost hope that he could achieve this himself:

First, you think that, "Okay, I will spend at least eight hours every weekday working, so it should better be something [intrinsically] satisfying." This is Phase I. Then, you realize that it is not really possible, so you say "Okay, then I should manage my work better so that *at least* I should not let my work intervene in my leisure and private life." After this second phase, comes Phase III. You are fed up with your job, and also you realize and accept that you will not be a CEO when you are forty or something, so you say "f*ck work!" You start saying *no* to your manager's demands. You just want a mediocre yet secure position in the company. It does not give you a chance to climb up the career ladder but also is not so demanding because you become an expert at that position.

At the start of his career, Erman believed that satisfying work and living a happy life were one and the same, but we see in his account the emergence of a separation between his work and his life—a creeping alienation—beginning with his unfulfilling work experience. The very concept of work-life balance suggests alienation to begin with, implying that work eats away at life and is poised on the opposite pole of life; it is something that should be balanced. Erman's description of the gradual decay of his hopes represents a battle that is lost inch by inch as he retreats from a potentially higher level of happiness to a lower level.

Such a processual understanding of alienation also highlights the way that work is rationalized as an instrument rather than as an end in itself. Once someone realizes that their own work cannot be inherently fulfilling, the next thing they hold onto is the returns from the work. Someone with a career orientation (like Person B) could still be somewhat more engaged than someone with a job orientation (like Person A) if the career orientation justifies working as a means toward something beyond simply earning a living—for example, a means to a higher status position. Such an orientation might help create a game-like understanding of working over the long run, similar to Burawoy's famous account of "making out" on the shop floor.[43] For instance, Nazım, who was working at a world-renowned American bank, defined himself as a "gamer" and told me how he framed his efforts at work as a game in which he was seeking to "level up." Trying to rise on the career ladder became an end in itself that kept him working hard.

Someone with a purely transactional job orientation like Person A, on the other hand, usually experiences work as toil; the less of it there is, the merrier one is. Some of my respondents experienced their work this way. Gökhan, a manager at a world-renowned insurance giant, thought of work as "an exchange, a contract. And nothing more." For Gökhan, the only reason for working was to get paid and "nothing more." And in fact, over time, this attitude can turn into a belief that it cannot be otherwise: as Gökhan put it, "If work was something pleasant, then they would not pay us for it, right?"

But what makes the working experience unfulfilling for elite labor? Two prevalent themes emerged from my interview data: lack of intrinsic satisfaction with one's work and lack of meaning attached to one's job.

UNDEREMPLOYMENT AND OCCUPATIONAL REGRET

One way a person can get intrinsic satisfaction from a job is if that job offers challenges such as problem solving or skill deployment instead of being easy, routine, and repetitive. It is common-sensical to expect that jobs involving elite labor require certain expertise and skill sets that not everyone possesses. Even for people with such credentials, these jobs should still involve active intellectual challenges. Nevertheless, skill mismatch—more precisely, the experience of underemployment qua overqualification—is an important aspect of discontent among Turkish elite labor.

Serkan and Evren, who both worked as financial controllers at a well-known consumer goods company, told me that they were bored using spreadsheets all the time (recall Ezgi called it "Excel *ameleliği* [drudgery]" in chapter 2). Serkan said: "The only times that I have a positive experience using Excel is when I write a new formula that shortens the amount of time that I spend in Excel." On the other hand, Soner, a management consultant at a Big Three firm, told me that he loved his job mainly because he thought "consulting is somewhere between academia and business" because it required research and problem solving on a daily basis. Ebru, a Big Three management consultant whom we met in chapter 2, transitioned to that job from the telecommunications sector and said that she was happier after the switch because "I started to use my brain again."

The discourse of a job's being intellectually challenging or not overlaps with Braverman's deskilling thesis and his account of Taylor's "scientific management," which suggests separation of design of tasks from their execution.[44] Minimizing worker autonomy and the respective room for creativity, play, or exercising judgment at work, the design and execution separation has been mostly used to account for the alienation of repetitive manual labor. But I argue that a version of this is key to understanding the discontent of elite white-collar workers as well.

One of the key parallels between blue- and white-collar alienation is the issue of skill mismatch.[45] In fact, the Marxian account of alienation, which was originally formulated to account for the experiences of blue-collar workers with shop-floor jobs, can be thought of more broadly as a case of skill mismatch and underemployment.[46] The experience of a worker like Serkan conducting repetitive spreadsheet calculations versus coding a program to automate such repetitive tasks[47] is not so different from the Marxian example of an artisan, such as a shoemaker, becoming a proletarian on the assembly line. In both cases, the worker experiences underemployment—what differentiates white-collar from blue-collar alienation is not skill mismatch but *where* that mismatch occurs on a skills spectrum from low- to high-skilled labor, typically manual labor considered at one end and knowledge work at the other. And when such a mismatch occurs at the higher echelons on a skills spectrum (skills that take more time and resources to achieve and that command greater social respect), workers' high expectations create the perfect recipe for resentment.

Note that getting intrinsic satisfaction from one's labor is also a subjective issue. Although many of my interviewees reported that management consulting involves problem solving and skill use and development, Berk—a former management consultant—eventually found the work quite repetitive and boring; the content of the problems kept changing, but the form of consulting work stayed the same for him. "I began to feel like Sisyphus," he said. Contrary to Albert Camus's advice of finding a way look at the boulder anew—to smile and enjoy the grind—he decided to quit and now runs a startup.

The gap between design and execution that we see at the micro level is also present at a macro level when we look at the relationship between the headquarters of transnational corporations (TNCs) and their branches. The television show *The Office*, for example, shows Dunder Mifflin's New York headquarters as the place where strategic decisions are made; the Scranton branch consists only of sales and accounting departments and a warehouse. Respondents who worked at Google's New York and Istanbul offices told me a similar story: there are no software engineering jobs in Istanbul, just marketing and sales jobs. In other words, headquarters are the places where the global design of business processes take place; the branches are tasked with local or regional execution of those global designs.

I argue that TNCs amplify the design versus execution gap, further entrenching the global core versus periphery divide. This separation creates structural conditions for underemployment and alienation of not only blue-collar but also white-collar labor in periphery countries, including semiperiphery ones such as Turkey.[48] For example, Ece and Nisa, who had both been marketing professionals at a consumer goods company but eventually quit their jobs, complained that there was not much room for creativity in their jobs. Even when preparing TV commercials for the Turkish audience, they were often asked to follow the scripts provided by the headquarters in the United States.[49]

The New York versus Istanbul comparison is very telling about the design versus execution gap at a macro level. Turkish elite workers in New York were more likely than their counterparts in Istanbul to have a graduate degree. Having a graduate degree boosts people's skills as well as their expectations for intellectually challenging work—so it would seem that those who attain them would likely experience underemployment. Nevertheless, respondents in New York reported fewer experiences of underemployment than their peers in Istanbul did. This suggests that New York boasts a richer job array that can satisfy elite labor in terms of skills required and challenges that come with these jobs. In Istanbul, even though there is a smaller portion of elite workers with graduate degrees, respondents reported more cases of underemployment, which implies that the array of high-skilled jobs in Istanbul is insufficient for the elite labor pool there.

Another reflection of this gap at a global scale can be seen from a comparison of the potential prestigious career paths after graduation from top colleges in the United States and Turkey. When we examine Ivy League universities in the United States, the most prestigious postgraduation options generally entail employment in the elite professional services sector, including investment banking, management consulting, law, and recently the technology industry.[50] In Turkey, however, as I discussed in chapter 2, senior undergraduates told me that the most prestigious options were either (1) going to a global city such as New York or London to be employed at one of the aforementioned sectors, (2) seeking graduate degrees there to be able to land in such sectors eventually, or (3) staying in Turkey and going for elite professional services or prestigious consumer good companies. Compared to the United States, Turkey's lack of a tech sector and the prominence of the consumer goods sector as one of the most prestigious postcollege employment opportunities is a clear example of how a country's or region's economic development and the positions it occupies in the global division of labor can directly affect the quality of working life for its elite labor pool via offering a wider or narrower range of jobs at the higher-skilled end of the jobs spectrum.

Those who lacked intrinsic satisfaction from their jobs also often framed their experiences with stories of occupational regret. As I described in detail in chapter 2, Turkey's system of higher education and the ways in which students are distributed to majors in college push graduating senior high school students to make premature career choices. For example, Erman, who had won awards in physics competitions in high school, ended up studying electronics engineering (a more prestigious major) instead of physics:

> I was already in the science track, and my university exam results came in really good. Now, the results were stellar . . . I was actually considering studying arts and sciences, I was really into physics and math, and if I were to choose that path, I was considering being an academic. But I could not gather my courage to major in physics because my ranking was pretty good. I was hitting high scores in preparatory exams, and I knew all along that I could be placed in a good engineering major. I was relying on my idealism, that I would choose arts and sciences when the time came. I just could not.

Erman's story of forgoing a physics major over electronics engineering is not unique. Tunç, a graduating senior who was already working at a world-renowned car manufacturer, shared that he had wanted to be a pilot ever since he was a child but chose electronics engineering instead of joining the air force academy, partly because he was told "not to waste" his high ranking. A non-negligible number of high-ranking students who choose electronics engineering majors do so mainly because it has been one of the most prestigious majors that admits only the top-scoring students.[51] Even if they are in love with sciences, like Erman, and get great scores on the university entrance exam, they do not choose physics majors because of the huge status and financial gap between physics and electronics engineering.[52] Considering their success-driven habitus, it is more important for them to be in what is recognized as the top tier, even if the content of the work is less appealing. Many such people experience dissonance through years in college and then try to reconcile it by pursuing double majors in physics, and some of them study for PhDs in physics instead of electronics engineering. The perceived status and financial gap between physics—or, more precisely, studying science for science's sake—and engineering among families and students is a typical case of occupational regret in Turkey. Other similar cases I came across in my interviews included majoring in management and economics instead of psychology, sociology, history, or philosophy.

JUSTIFICATION FAILURES

Elite workers also experience separation from their labor when their jobs seem to lack meaning and purpose. This usually appears in one of two ways: recognition deficits that are accompanied by a feeling of worthlessness and a value mismatch between elite workers and their jobs that engenders inner conflicts. In both cases, workers fail to find meaning in what they are doing at work or cannot justify why they keep doing what they are doing.

Many of the elite workers I interviewed complained about recognition deficits, expressing some variation of the phrase "I am replaceable." By this, they meant both that their jobs were not secure and that their individuality and uniqueness, and the importance of their contributions to their work, went unrecognized. Ayşe, a senior auditor working in New York, put it this way: "The company would lose nothing and go on as is if I am gone." Canan, a corporate lawyer working in New York, disclosed her feelings with a classic phrase: "I am just a cog in a machine." Many of these workers held up working at startups as an alternative and compared their work experiences to those of startup workers. Even interviewees who did not have any first-degree contacts working in startups made such a comparison, which suggests that the image of startup workers is becoming an important cultural benchmark of today's postindustrial times.

Alper, who was working as a consultant in New York, made a very telling comparison of large corporate bodies with startups: "Well, since the [startup] company is only ten people, if you are gone, then the company loses at least 10 percent of its workforce." He also suspected that one would probably feel more "ownership" in a startup job, even though these often involve more stress as well as longer and erratic working hours. Still, such a trade-off seemed desirable to him and to many other interviewees who saw it as a comparison between a giant corporate bureaucracy crushing human souls and "a small team of friends."

Several of my respondents, especially the management consultants, explicitly emphasized the significance of feeling important and recognized. When I asked about the things that they liked most about their jobs, many offered replies along the lines of "being impactful." Management consulting projects usually consist of

taking a client's issue or problem and improving or resolving it—
something that consultants saw as leading to concrete changes in
the world. They saw this kind of work as quite different from the
cyclical tasks of typical industrial companies, which they felt simply reproduced a business as is. "You make a real change. After your
involvement, things happen differently somewhere in the world,"
said Muhsin, who had a PhD in life sciences but had become disil-
lusioned with academia's "horribly long" delayed gratification and
was working as a consultant at a Big Three firm. Ahmet, another Big
Three management consultant whom we met in chapter 1, highlighted the importance of recognition: "When you see the project
that you led [written up] in the *Wall Street Journal* as having saved
X million dollars, you feel good." Another management consultant,
Tolga, related how having had a direct influence on top-level management gave him the feeling that his labor was not in vain: "You
present your own solutions to CEOs, not to midlevel management,
and you convince upper management, and you soon see that your
suggestions are implemented."

As I discussed in chapter 2, elite workers have been deemed the
smartest and most skilled in their cohort throughout their edu-
cations, and they have been accultured to have a high expectation that their work will be intellectually challenging and that
they will change the world. The frustration of these hopes creates
cases of relative deprivation, which often leads to disillusionment
over time.

Some experiences of alienation from one's labor also stem from
value mismatches, including a failure to fit in with the corporate
work culture of elite labor. Ömer, a data scientist working for a Wall
Street firm, spoke about the culture of competition and attention
scarcity in his workplace, noting that he received feedback from
his immediate manager that he should talk more in team meetings. He found this criticism meaningless: "I don't talk because

there is nothing that I should add," he said. "And I hear people talking bullsh*t, only for the sake of seeming that they are interested and contributing. But they are not." He was also told to "show off his contributions," which Ömer felt was "immoral." "You don't brag about what you brought to the table," he said, "It is your job to [contribute] in the first place, it is not something extra." However, his manager told him that unless he did more to advertise his accomplishments, it would be very difficult for him to get a promotion because "what the upper management wants to see is 'engagement and excitement,'" and his manager would find it easier "to defend my promotion if the upper management sees my contributions themselves." He didn't think he could muster engagement and excitement. "I can only fake them," he said. But he added that at least his coworkers are "okay people" and that "if I had gone with investment banking [instead of commercial banking], I would have ended up among alpha-male type people, which would make me very unhappy."

Another major source of separation from one's labor is the mismatch between people's desire to contribute to some kind of social good and what they are actually doing at work. Melih, a software engineer working at a tech company, said that he felt good about his company's motto: "Don't be evil." In his case, there was no discrepancy between his perception of his company's actions, its stated values, and his own. In strong contrast, Ömer made his discontent on this front very clear:

> What I do at work is to find ways to charge higher interest to middle-class families' debts. . . . I would be a lot happier if I could use my statistics skills for cancer research or analysis of political polls instead of trying to charge higher interest for indebted families. . . . [referring to the mission statement of his company] "Our Values" . . . you don't have any values!

Ömer's disgust with his company's "hypocrisy" took such an extreme form that one day he secretly unplugged a screen on his floor that constantly replayed a video clip articulating the mission statement of the company. Ömer's resistance to giving in had so far saved him from what Jana Costas and Peter Fleming identified as "self-alienation": that his "true" self is not his corporate self, he is not a "sell-out."[53] Yet this resistance had also been wearing him down emotionally.

On this front, some elite workers try to carve out meaning from their employment by exploring corporate social responsibility projects. Evren, for example, told me that he felt morally compensated when he used the company's social responsibility budget for animal shelters. While he was critical of corporate social responsibility in general, he also said, "It is better to have such projects than having none." Lila, the marketing manager at a consumer goods giant we met at the beginning of this chapter, explained how she felt contented with her job, not because of what she did at work but because of her work on sustainability and gender equity projects within the company. Working on these projects cost her a lot of extra hours, which were not paid as overtime compensation, but she still felt satisfied with her job overall.

The importance of values in the experience of alienation sometimes takes the form of an ideological mismatch. Başak, an engineer at a pharmaceutical company, demonstrated what could be thought of as class consciousness. Although she was not part of any labor movement or unions, she perceived her employment relation from a conflictual point of view: if she was not on guard, she said, the company would try to exploit more and more of her labor. When she and her coworkers were asked to take turns coming to work on the weekends with no extra compensation, for instance, she openly refused to participate. However, to her displeasure, her peers complied.

I mean, are you idiots? Why do you accept [working on the weekends]? Let's suppose you were afraid [to step up on your own], fair enough. But after I deserted, why haven't you joined me? You see that I don't work at the weekends because I refused. But you are angry at *me* [instead of the manager], because I don't share this burden with you? Bullsh*t!

Her story of resistance is illustrative of how such ideological mismatches can create alienation from work as well as social isolation. Although she saved herself extra work, her colleagues stopped talking to her.

Gökhan, who saw his employment as a straightforward exchange of time for money, described how his antagonistic relationship with his company exhausted him emotionally:

I always need to be alert that they comply with our contract. Any expense that I make for the company, I should be paid back. If you break our contract, make me work overtime and don't pay me back, then I have no problem with charging extra expenses that I have not actually done. Tit for tat! I don't let them f*ck with me, but this is exhausting. Emotionally, it is very exhausting. . . . My contractual understanding of my employment is the only meaningful thing about my work. The only meaningful thing . . . I work for them and they pay me as we agreed upon. When you defect on that too, I go crazy.

Overwork and Colonization of Life by Work

If unfulfilling work points to a certain distance between work and the rest of life, overwork widens it to a chasm—and not in the interest of the worker. Overwork forces work to become the most central aspect of one's life. Overwork can be seen as a process through which work monopolizes one's life at the expense of other spheres that are vital for a meaningful life, including family, friends, leisure and hobbies, civic engagement, and community. The issue of overwork and its discontents can be considered separately from unfulfilling work because even if work is fulfilling, overwork can still damage an individual, independent of the content of the job. Overwork is not just a problem of working extended hours but also one of work intensification. Working more hours directly reduces the amount of time for nonwork activities; intensification of work plagues the quality of nonwork activities by letting work seep into leisure pursuits.

Five themes of overwork emerged from my interviews: (1) overwork aggravates work-family conflict, (2) overwork eats away at the worker's physical and mental health, (3) overwork either diminishes leisure or makes it unfulfilling, (4) overwork narrows the worker's social network and weakens their existing social ties, and (5) elite labor's consent to overwork brings about the additional grievance of self-blame.

WORK-FAMILY CONFLICT

Work-family conflict was a serious problem for my respondents. When I was trying to schedule our interviews, respondents often had difficulty finding a proper time. This was especially true for parents, who also had to adhere to stricter time limits. For example, when I asked Leyla, a consultant at a Big Three firm, when we could meet, she thought aloud on the phone about the times during the weekend when her daughter would probably be asleep. During our interview, she shared the difficulties of work-family conflict:

> Before I had my daughter, I divided the whole week into five days of work, two days of fun. Nowadays I have to bend this scheme.

I really want to be able to manage [my work-life balance] as it was, and whenever I cannot, I feel inadequate, I feel remorse. I am constantly trying to solve optimization problems during the day. "When can I leave [work] today? How many minutes can I see her? Can I leave now and come back to the office later?" Every single moment of every day . . . and I am tired of this. And the weekend, I already could not spend enough time with her, so I have to maximize the time we spend together, and this is why I told you that we can only meet at 2:00 because she's asleep now. Only when she sleeps, I can do other things, you know, socializing. I mean, sometimes I even cannot satisfy my basic needs. So, I'm having a very difficult life, or I mean, a life that is made difficult and I am unhappy about it.

Hakan, a manager at a Big Four company who we met in chapter 1, quite angrily told me how he ended up drawing strict lines between time spent at work and home:

The very first vacation with my daughter, back then a fourteen-month-old baby . . . seven days of vacation . . . I worked full-time for six of them. There was an important business deal, and I was preparing a proposal. The last day, my boss called me to tell me, "There is a disagreement, so we are not going to propose to them." Why did I work this much? From that day on, I never worked on a holiday. After that day, I never worked at home in the evenings, neither checked my phone nor replied to a single email. For example, when I arrive home, I check my phone before I get off my car and reply to all the important emails. Then I turn off my phone. Even if a partner calls me, he cannot reach me; it's off! I don't care anymore. Enough is enough!

Consistent with the findings of the sociology of work literature on elite labor, work-family conflict was a huge issue to many elite white-collar parents in my sample. As we will see in chapter 4, this is often a key reason that elite business professionals opt out of their corporate careers. Nevertheless, other issues with overwork hurt elite white-collar workers, parents and nonparents alike.

DECAY OF HEALTH AND WELL-BEING

One of the most important of these issues is the impact of overwork on physical health. Yasemin, an auditor, told me that her job took a major toll: "My hair turned white and I am twenty-three years old! And I gained nine kilos because of poor sleep and eating habits." Lila, whom we met at the beginning of this chapter, shared that she developed gastrointestinal disorders such as acid reflux after prolonged periods of overwork and the resulting stress.

Several respondents pointed to these sorts of bodily ailments as a warning signal that work had come to dominate their lives excessively. Erman described how work had invaded his nonworking life in terms of both time and intensity—and his body was in a sense the last line of defense:

> There is always something that you are missing and there are always things that you should be prepared for the close future and so, even when you try to shut your brain down in your spare time, work pops up . . . "Oh damn, I should prepare that report." I start reading a novel, and five minutes later I think, "No sh*t, I didn't reply to that email." Constant juggling! Work is *always* on my mind. *Always!* The only time that I can shut my brain off [from work] is when I play soccer because my body knows that if I don't, I can get severely injured.

Several respondents offered similar reflections on the body's role as the last line of defense. Olcay, a corporate lawyer, provided me with almost the same story as Erman; the only difference was that he played tennis instead of soccer. These accounts are very similar to Alexandra Michel's nine-year ethnography of Wall Street invest-ment bankers.[54] Michel found that the human body at work remains autonomous of organizational control, but unfortunately mani-fests this autonomy only through breaking down, which among her respondents started to happen after four years. Through later years, the cases of body breakdowns intensified so much so that the investment bankers in her study began to think of their bodies as authoritative subjects, separate from themselves, telling them to modify their work behavior to the extent of quitting the corporate world altogether. Erman and Olcay's accounts resonate with this finding because they both refer to their bodies as distinct entities.

The exhaustion resulting from overwork can also cause severe psychological distress. It is very common among elite business pro-fessionals to see a therapist to cope with overwork and its psychic costs. Berk, the former management consultant who went on to run a startup, told me that half of his cohort at the Big Three firm were using antidepressants to cope with the stress and tempo of overwork. It was disheartening for me to hear similar themes from different people regarding their negative experience of overwork, which colored their days from start to end: "I was getting up sad every day," "I was crying every night."

DIMINISHED AND UNFULFILLING LEISURE TIME

Another negative effect of overwork is a reduction in both the quan-tity and quality of leisure. Overwork, by definition, shortens non-work hours and leaves the overworked with less sleep, less leisure, or both. It can also undermine the quality of leisure, leaving work-ers with nominal time for leisure activities but not the vital energy as a result of exhaustion. Ayşe, the auditor, stated that after work-ing so intensely: "You can only end up with having nice dinners or going to chic cafes and gossiping or shopping. . . . I missed having an intellectually satisfying conversation. I was an intellectual person, but I feel that is not the case anymore." Several respondents' stories echoed Max Horkheimer and Theodor W. Adorno's "culture industry" argument that overwork exploits a worker's vitality so that they can engage only in passive entertainment.[55] Olcay, a corporate lawyer, showed me the magazine he was reading before I arrived at our interview, noting, "I can only read magazine articles because they are just a couple of pages. I am exhausted after work, and even on the weekends, I cannot focus. I miss reading a novel." Over time, one's intellectual and cultural appetite as well as the ability to engage with active leisure diminishes. Erman shared angrily that whenever he tried to watch a movie or read a novel, he fell asleep in the middle because of exhaustion.

Faced with intense overwork, some workers opted out altogether. Yasemin, who complained that her hair had gone prematurely white, quit her exhausting job and settled down to a nine-to-five job with lower prestige and pay but that rarely demanded overtime. She described how much thought she had put into her decision to quit, but also how happy the move had made her:

> You know, you feel that *you are losing your privilege* by such a move. You think, "Should I try to hold on?" But I could not tolerate anymore. I mean, my hair was turning white! What more tolerance? And I had chosen this company because it was giving additional vacation instead of paying for overtime, and even under these conditions . . . I decided that I could not take it anymore. And now, I am doing a lot of things outside work: I started cooking, swimming, going to the gym almost every day, following a class on how to knit, reading novels again . . . I am happy.

WEAKENING SOCIAL TIES AND SOCIAL DEPRIVATION
Another negative consequence of overwork is that it weakens workers' social relations by both making it more difficult to maintain

their existing social ties and preventing workers from forming new ties outside the workplace. Canan, the corporate lawyer, sadly stated, "I constantly miss my friends' and family's birthdays. Over time, it hurts them and me as well, which strains our relationships." Evren stated, "It sucks to work on a Sunday, particularly more so if it is your birthday, a day in which you come together with your family and friends." He added that, although his colleagues celebrated his birthday with a cake at work, "it is not the same thing." Such strains can lead to tie dissolution. Selin, a marketing manager, described how she had lost track of her old friends from college: "At first, they were calling and inviting me to their gatherings. But over time, as I missed the majority of these gatherings, they stopped even informing me. In one of the meetings, I was able to join by chance, a friend of mine told me that she has not invited me because she knew that I would answer: 'I am sorry but I will be working.'"

Workers' narrowing circles of social connection most clearly show up in the patterns of romantic relations (which could in fact partly explain why assortative mating—marriage between couples that are similar to each other in terms of socioeconomic background and cultural traits—has been on the rise).[56] Ayşe, who said she was missing out on intellectual conversations because she was "hanging out with white-collars like her all the time," said that at first, she had frowned on her coworkers flirting with each other in the workplace. But later she realized that "they have neither time nor social circles apart from work. It is all work. What can you expect? Of course, they are going to flirt with each other at the workplace!"

CONSENT TO OVERWORK BRINGS SELF-BLAME

This ambition to endure intense working conditions in spite of the significant strain on workers' bodies, psyches, and social relationships to ascend the career ladder is the most distinctive feature of elite workers. My interviews offer insight into how overwork is

negotiated and justified in the elite labor market and how this nego-
tiation itself causes elite workers additional distress and discontent.
In sum, the burden and blame of working overtime is shifted from
companies to workers so that elite workers feel that whether or not
they overwork is fundamentally up to them. The result, for most of
these workers, is not a critique of the system but additional cycles
of self-blaming and feelings of incompetence.[57]

Many of my interviews that included discussion of overwork
employed a discourse of efficiency. This frame posits that if someone is working overtime, then the first thing to do is not to decrease
the amount of work but instead to increase efficiency. For instance,
when I asked Erman whether he ever pushed back at his manager
about his workload, he responded:

> When you complain about your workload, they [management]
> point toward efficiency. It is not the huge amount of workload;
> it is *you* who fail to meet the demands. And management uses
> hypocritical language; they call this "opportunity." "Oh Erman,
> maybe you have some missed opportunities here." I hate this
> corporate language! They think that it is a polite and posi-
> tive way to tell you that you suck, but I can read between the
> lines. . . . The work never finishes. Even if you can work twenty-
> four hours a day, you will still have incomplete tasks.

The importance of efficiency as a value emerges more strikingly
when we compare the daily routines of business professionals in
New York and Istanbul. A huge contrast appears at lunch time: in
Istanbul, elite business professionals usually go out for an hour-
long, relatively luxurious lunch; the norm in New York is to eat at
your desk with your team while still working. Some of my New York
interviewees were critical of this practice because it eliminated
their only chance to socialize and take an actual break during the

intense workday. However, a majority internalized the efficiency discourse: inefficiency became the sole explanation for working overtime, and they pointed to the Turkish work culture as the reason people worked overtime in Istanbul.[58]

When I asked respondents whether and how much they overworked, in terms of both time and intensity, some noted that they did have the option not to. For instance, some management consulting firms offered what was known as "the 80 percent opportunity": work four days a week instead of five, and receive 80 percent of the full-time salary. To my question if they or their colleagues ever used this scheme, the immediate answer was that only pregnant women and mothers did, although the accommodation was available for anyone. Soner, a consultant, was uncertain why this was: "I have not given enough thought to it, why we don't really do it." However, Ahmet, another consultant, admitted, "I think there is some stigma to the 80 percent rule," noting that taking advantage of the opportunity would imply to management that you do not want to work as "passionately" as you used to or as much as your peers. "Seeming passionate" about one's job is a contemporary phenomenon, and it is much more prevalent in the consultancy world. Alper stated, "Yeah, passion is one of the buzzwords that industry [management consultancy] likes to hear." While elite workers noted a stigma attached to seeming "not passionate enough"—which meant a lesser chance of being promoted—they still felt that the choice to avoid overwork was theirs to make.

Thanks to their overachieving habits, the elite business professionals sometimes signed up for overwork voluntarily, justifying this via a discourse of responsibility. Ayşe, the auditor, stated, "I like to have responsibility. But it is also exhausting." Selin, a marketing manager, shared a story of exploitation wrapped in a veneer of responsibility and "impactfulness": "I like our company because as a general management practice, as long as I can carry it, they give me more responsibility," even as she described taking over tasks that had previously been handled by others.

Onur, a marketing manager, noted the social dimensions that made it difficult to avoid overwork: "You know, it is like, when you run with a group, the pace is set by others around you as well. Of course, you don't have to fit in with them, but you usually do. And if everyone around you is running fast, you cannot drag them down. Otherwise, you stick out." In this "keeping up with the Joneses" account regarding work performance and success, there is still room to take action, but it would "drag the team down." Onur was much more concerned with "sticking out," which overlaps with the stigma of seeming "not passionate enough." What these stories boil down to is that, although the elite workers suffer from overwork, and either implicitly or explicitly know that the negative consequences of avoiding overwork are dictated by the companies, they still put the blame of overwork on themselves instead of framing more structural accounts, such as blaming corporate culture, managerial regimes, or overwork culture in general, or pointing to lack of or failure to implement labor market regulations.

My interviews with elite workers challenge the widespread implicit assumption that high-salary, high-status corporate positions provide their occupants with a happy life. Although a fraction of the workers I spoke with felt content with their jobs at TNCs, many felt disappointed or exhausted or both. Despite having the best corporate jobs, these members of the transnational Turkish middle class centered themes of overwork and lack of intrinsic satisfaction and meaning from work, inviting us to reconsider the good jobs versus bad jobs debate and to revisit the question, What makes a good job good in the first place?

My empirical analysis suggests the importance of bringing meaningful and intrinsically satisfying jobs back to the center of the quality of working life debates. Moreover, the analysis shows that many single young adults suffer from overwork and that the issue of overwork extends beyond its role in work-family conflict. Overwork should be considered more generally as work's interference with the nonwork portion of life, including the quality and quantity of leisure. Through these two dimensions of fulfillment and work-life balance, I derived a typology that can capture various overall experiences of the quality of working life.

Having covered the moments of selective entry into high-prestige, high-salary transnational corporate jobs in chapter 2, and the experience of working at them in this chapter, I next turn to the moment when some respondents decided to escape alienation by quitting. Chapter 4 will focus on the tales of opting out from corporate careers and the aftermath of these decisions.

4

WHITE-COLLAR OPT-OUT

This is the dream: for a typical middle-class family with children, the zenith of a desirable future for their children includes a prestigious college and landing a high-salary, high-prestige job upon graduation. Many people consider this the only path to a happy life; the ubiquitous prescription of occupational success and high salaries shapes the aspirations of middle classes around the globe. But as we have seen, those who have achieved that dream of membership in the transnational Turkish middle class, many holders of the so-called good jobs, do not report contentment. In chapter 3, I examined the quality of working life narratives and experience of Turkish elite business professionals and managers "who made it." Now I turn to the ones who, having made it, end up opting out of corporate careers. How do people end up abandoning such hard-earned, privileged positions?

White-collar opt-out encompasses a broader resignation from fast-track careers composed of professional-managerial employment.[1] As we saw in chapter 2, landing such sought-after, highly selective jobs requires enormous sacrifices early in life. Everything these business professionals have done in the early part of their lives has set them on a trajectory to have one of these coveted professional positions, and yet some of them decide to give them up. More so than being a professional decision, white-collar opt-out involves a huge *life* decision. Thus, white-collar workers who opt out experience their resignations as profound biographical changes, often accompanied by an existential question of "What am I doing with my life?" and epiphanies of memento mori and carpe diem.

Anchored in ambitious professional-managerial careers, the yuppie lifestyle revolves around the vicious cycle of overwork and overspending.[2] Such a life is often characterized as elegant, but it is also fast-paced, extremely busy, and exhausting, especially for parents, and mothers in particular. Sociologists have mostly considered those leaving these careers for stay-at-home motherhood.[3] However, such research captures only one aspect of white-collar opt-out. My research shows that those who opt out comprise a broader demographic, including nonparenting young men as well as a wide range of postresignation trajectories, including occupational changes that require attaining new skill sets.

How do these opt-out processes begin and unfold? I argue that opt-out decisions are often triggered by alienation, the crux of which is the depressing experience of feeling ever more separated from one's labor because of disappointment with and exhaustion from work. As we have seen, elite workers sometimes complain of boredom and overqualification, and they do not get intrinsic satisfaction from their daily tasks at work. Others experience value mismatches and recognition deficits at their workplace, which makes it more difficult to attach meaning to their work. This disappointment is often intensified by the contrast with their high hopes and expectations, which have been structured by their continuous hard work and success throughout their schooling. Narratives of burnout also loomed large in my interviews. Many respondents reported exhaustion due to long and intense work schedules, which led to a range of serious problems. Not only did my respondents report work-family conflict, they also complained of worsening physical and mental health, increasingly scarce and unsatisfying leisure time, and social deprivation because of limited nonwork social interactions with friends and family—all of which add up to an impoverished life experience.

Even with these intense push factors inciting the impulse to opt out, I found that business professionals' consent is deeply entrenched; few take the plunge unless the push factors are complemented by pull factors, many of which revolve around a quest for self-realization or a yearning for "positive freedom."[4] Following their resignations, they may take time off for soul searching (e.g., going on long and elaborate vacations, such as backpacking around the world), engaging with family (e.g., spending high-quality time with family or significant others and friends), changing their mode of earning a living (e.g., pursuing entrepreneurship, becoming a freelancer, or cultivating new skill sets for an occupational change), and/or leaving the city for provincial or rural areas.

Even when push and pull factors are aligned, white-collar opt-outs are not straightforward phenomena. Comparing my respondents who opted out with those who did not, it becomes clear that such alignment is a necessary but insufficient condition for actually opting out. The ultimate outcome also depends on activating *safety nets*—the economic and social supports that ease concerns over opting out—as well as loosening *golden handcuffs*—the various privileges that bind these individuals to their careers. Safety nets and golden handcuffs inform business professionals' career decisions such that the degree of their presence or absence influences professionals' *capacity* to quit. Put differently, even if push and pull factors drive some professionals to the edge of resigning from a corporate career, the lack of a safety net or the tight grasp of golden handcuffs may keep these individuals from actually calling it quits.

Compared with their corporate employment before their opt-out, the business professionals who go on to pursue noncorporate jobs typically earn less but work fewer hours and report more fulfillment from their new jobs; they find their jobs more meaningful and get more intrinsic satisfaction from their labor. Overall, they report a higher quality of working life and greater content-ment, which has broader implications for debates on inequality, the future of work, and our individual and collective well-being.

OPTING OUT?

Defined as voluntary severance of employment ties by workers, turnover—of which opting out can be thought of as a case—has been studied extensively, especially by management and organiza-tions scholars. The main question turnover literature poses is how to best predict turnover. There is a well-established consensus that job dissatisfaction—which is often conceptualized as an overall measure, assuming that negative aspects of a job can be compensated for by its positive aspects—is among the strongest drivers of resignation.[5] Turnover is often treated mainly as a managerial issue, a cost to the employer, the tacit assumption being that people who leave their jobs are quitting to work for another similar employer rather than mak-ing a dramatic change or leaving the workforce altogether.[6] However, this assumption can conceal broader trends in the world of work, such as the increasing prevalence of burnout across employers and even industries. It also downplays the importance of the safety nets that are essential to the resignation decision. Thus, viewing white-collar opt-out—which does not involve taking a job with another corporate employer or sometimes even continued employment—as a job change/turnover issue leaves much out of the picture.

Gender and Work-Family Conflict

The phrase "opt-out," as it relates to the world of corporate work, was in fact first popularized in 2003 with a *New York Times Magazine* article, "The Opt-Out Revolution."[7] The article explored how and why well-educated women were apparently forgoing the fruits of decades-long feminist struggles over work, leaving their corporate jobs, and instead going back to the traditional role of stay-at-home motherhood. This account of women's corporate flight inspired a stream of academic inquiries, especially focusing on gender and work-family conflict, because of sitting at the center of gender equality debates in the context of education, work, and family.[8]

Researchers of work-family conflict in the United States could not find statistical evidence that opting out for family was so widespread as to be termed a revolution.[9] Nevertheless, there is evidence that it is more prevalent among the upper middle class compared to the lower classes—there is even a considerable difference between graduates of elite and nonelite colleges.[10] One precondition of the opt-outs by such women was being married to high-earner partners because opting out for family makes it difficult to secure full-time employment again.[11] Parents who are temporarily unemployed to take care of their children are seen as less desirable employees than those who have been unemployed because of job loss; such opt-outs, Mary Blair-Loy argued, violate the ideal worker norm, which envisions a dedicated worker who prioritizes work over all else.[12] Pamela Stone and Meg Lovejoy found that when upper-middle-class women were able to opt back in, the process was long and complicated, and the resulting jobs were often traditionally female ones with lower pay.[13] Given all these factors, why were these well-educated mothers choosing to opt out?

Drawing from in-depth interviews with elite women professionals, Stone argued that—contrary to media depictions and even her subjects' own framing of their opt-out as a choice—opting out is a reactive decision that stems from "a choice gap"; it represents more of a push from the workplace than a pull toward domestic life.[14] Opting out, Stone argued, is a last-resort response to the double bind of work and family that emanates from a professional culture that rejects flexibility and part-time work. In a follow-up study, Stone and Lovejoy qualified this argument further, asserting that the main driver of these upper-middle-class women's opting out, as well as the difficulties of opting back in, follow from what they called a "paradox of privilege" in which gender interests (such as professional accomplishment and gender equality) and class interests (such as intensive parenting for the purpose of status keeping) are incompatible.[15]

The opt-out studies from the gender and family perspective powerfully illuminate how the motherhood penalty pushes mothers to opt out.[16] However, this constitutes only one aspect of the broader opt-out phenomenon. The nonfamilial, gendered aspects of opting out, such as women who opt out for alternative careers and not to care for children, has received little attention.[17] Nonparenting men who opt out are unaccounted for by the gender and family perspective. Indeed, even the prominent sociologists of work-family conflict have begun to argue for a focus on work-life balance, calling on us to adopt a wider lens that considers the main problem with work not as work-family conflict but as "overload."[18]

Neoliberalization and the Rise of Boundaryless Careers

White-collar opt-out may also be examined in terms of career change or transition. Such an approach is valuable because it can encompass both work-family conflict and turnover perspectives while also putting opting out in a broader historical context. Careers have long been conceptualized as linear sequences of jobs or positions,[19] vertical upward mobility through a predictable organizational path that comes with an increase in status and economic rewards at each stage.[20] Most commonly used for professionals, it is tightly associated with intragenerational mobility.[21] It is often accompanied by a metaphor of ladders, suggesting a predictable ascent in socioeconomic status. Nevertheless, career progressions have been increasingly unstable since the 1980s.[22] This increase in precarity has been attributed to a pervasive and consequential change in the mode of production, a shift from Fordism to post-Fordism.[23] This change manifested itself in the white-collar world of work as an expansion of "high-performance work systems" and the "work devotion schema."[24] In tandem with the respective broader social change, often described as a transition from modernity to postmodernity or late modernity,[25] or the rise of neoliberalism and a "new spirit of capitalism,"[26] this prevalent shift in the organization of work and employment has been put forward to understand how linear career paths gave way to nonlinear ones,[27] such as "boundaryless careers" or "kaleidoscope careers."[28]

All these new conceptions highlight the way that, contrary to the implications of the traditional notion of a career, modern work organizations have lost their ability to anchor their employees' lives.[29] This is partly because of the collapse of internal labor markets, a phenomenon known as "broken ladders."[30] Michael B. Arthur and Denise M. Rousseau have described employees' increasing independence from their firms in their career progressions as a "boundaryless career."[31] The predictable, upward mobility within a firm (the so-called normal career that entails a rise in status and income) has been noted as a "nostalgic" construct in today's new economy.[32] Increasing precarity in the labor markets has even prompted scholars to postulate that workers now engage in a sustained effort to remain employed, such as "employment management work," "personal branding," and "entrepreneurial self."[33] Gianpiero Petriglieri, Jennifer Louise Petriglieri, and Jack Denfeld Wood argued that contemporary careers require "portable selves" that can be forged in "identity workspaces," such as MBA programs.[34] Studies such as these aptly expose the ideological aspects of neoliberalism that pre-scribes self-reliance and privatization of risk instead of social secu-rity measures.

An alternative account of boundarylessness examines the demand side, emphasizing workers' increasing demand for "protean careers" that prioritize freedom, self-directedness, and intrinsic work values, which are posited as "basic elements of human needs for growth and meaning."[35] Maury Peiperl and Yehuda Baruch integrated the protean and boundaryless concepts in their examination of "post-corporate careers," in which workers quit large organizations for self-employment or startup ventures while continuing to work in more or less the same line of occupation—for example, a management consultant or an accountant exiting their firm and becoming self-employed or founding their own firm with some colleagues.[36] Lisa A. Mainiero and Sherry E. Sullivan argued that business professionals increasingly seek authenticity, work-life balance, and challenge and that their differential priorities, partly shaped by the life course, give rise to "kaleidoscope careers" in which workers switch companies, industries, countries, and even occupations at a higher rate.[37] In such studies, opting out from corporate careers is often presented as part of a cultural push toward individualization or reinvention of the self as a response to globalization,[38] for example, seeking occupational change as a self-curation process.[39]

Careers as Life Histories, Opt-Outs as Turning Points

While "modern career theory and common parlance" have mostly thought of career as vertical mobility, Stephen Barley insisted on the broader meaning of careers, describing them as "abstracts of an individual's history of participation in a social collective."[40] Fol-lowing the Chicago school, Sullivan and Baruch defined career as "an individual's work-related and other relevant experiences, both inside and outside of organizations, that form a unique pattern over the individual's life span."[41] When we approach careers in such a historical fashion, we can think of white-collar opt-out as a "turning point," a significant moment of change from one trajectory to another in the life course.[42] A turning point is, by definition, a historical construct because the path that follows the turning point is a new trajectory in comparison to the old one; if it is not, that moment is better described as a perturbation.[43]

Turning points are marked by great anxiety whether they involve quitting a religious order[44] or resigning from an executive position to become a stay-at-home mother.[45] They are experienced as biographical events because they constitute changes in core identity narratives that define the self. White-collar opt-out, including occupational change, becoming a stay-at-home parent, and urban flight, represents another such drastic change in life trajectory, whereas finding a comparable job at another corporation or landing a higher position at a more prestigious company does not. Much more than just quitting a job, opting out involves stepping out of a larger life trajectory that these workers have followed since a very early age.

Figure 4.1 summarizes business professionals' common postresignation pathways and delineates the ideal types of white-collar opt-out in relation to other forms of voluntary employment change.

Exploring the "how" of transitions from corporate careers to self-employment, entrepreneurship, and different occupations, Herminia Ibarra suggested that people seldom know what they want from their careers.[46] Ibarra argued that career change is accompanied by experimentation, shifting social connections, and sense making. Being deeply unhappy with one's job or occupation alone does not necessarily result in career change; rather, business professionals begin to consider career change only when both good

Workforce exit   **Opt out**   **Job change**

Business degrees (e.g., seeking an MBA, LLM)

Early retirement (e.g., FIRE [financial independence, retire early] movement)

Stay-at-home parenting

Soul-searching (e.g., backpacking)

Urban flight (e.g., leaving cities for ecofarming)

Occupational change (e.g., acquiring new degree or a skill set)

Self-employment (e.g., freelancing)

Entrepreneurship (e.g., kicking off a startup or a café)

Downward mobility (e.g., a lower pay and status position for work-life balance and fulfillment)

Upward mobility (e.g., a higher-level position at a better firm)

Horizontal mobility (e.g., a comparable position at a comparable firm)

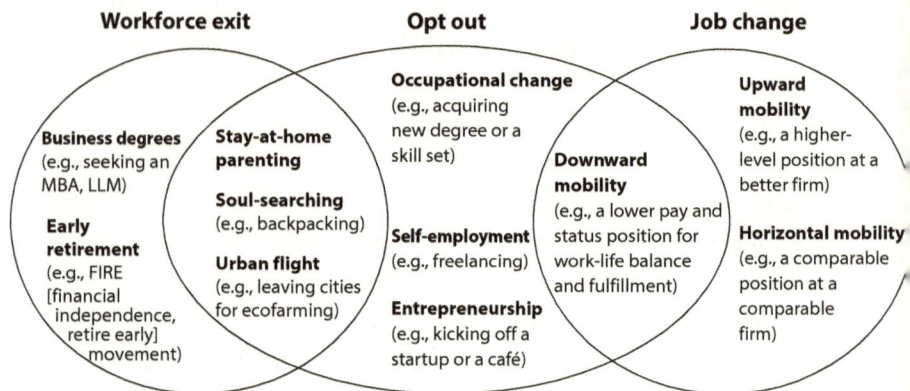

FIGURE 4.1 Common pathways that elite workers follow upon their resignation

and bad potential selves become more visible to them.[47] Helen Rose Fuchs Ebaugh's general theory of role exit, "the process of disengagement from a role that is central to one's self-identity and the reestablishment of an identity in a new role," highlights the contingent nature of turning points and how positive reactions from others and positive experiences of "role rehearsal" are paramount to successful role exits.[48]

These identity-based approaches to career changes illuminate the social and cultural aspects of opting out while downplaying its political and economic dimensions. For example, Ibarra left "the real question" to the end of her book: "Under what conditions are people able to break with the past and plunge into a new and happier future?"[49] This important yet unanswered question invites us to explore further why some business professionals end up breaking with their careers while others either do not consider opting out in the first place or want to resign but cannot.

Alienation from Labor and Worker Consent

Overall, role exit theory and new career literature alike underappreciate the significance of social class in the making of nontraditional careers.[50] Some perspectives of social class, especially that of the middle classes, can help us arrive at a more complete theory of white-collar opt-out, one that can incorporate the key insights of the research on work-family conflict, turnover, boundaryless careers, and identity work. I take my cue from Erik Olin Wright, who instructively attributes an inherent ambivalence to professional-managerial employees because they occupy a "contradictory class location" between well-off property owners and suffering proletariat.[51] Professional-managerial employees occupy a space that is full of tension—to outside observers, these people may seem like they have "made it" or "have it all," but people in these positions may lament the boredom, meaninglessness, and intense stress and pressure of their workplace. Unlike executive-level managers (e.g., CEOs or high-level directors), most professional-managerial employees do not occupy the commanding heights of the corporations they work for and could be most aptly defined as "elite workers."[52] As such, they are not *the* elites who own or rule; they are the elite of *workers* who occupy the high echelons of labor markets thanks to their prestigious educational credentials and skill sets. And they are susceptible to alienating work conditions akin to those experienced by their working-class counterparts.

Nicos Poulantzas captured this elusive nature of "the salariat" or "the new petite bourgeoisie" by linking them with careers. Compared to the working class and traditional petite bourgeoisie (shopkeepers and self-employed artisans), professional-managerial employees have an intragenerational, upward mobility throughout their life courses.[53] Weberian definitions of middle classes also rely heavily on career; for example, John Goldthorpe argues that among employees, what matters most in distinguishing one class from another is whether they enter a "service relationship" with their employers that is characterized by a career ladder with progressive incomes.[54] Adhering to "the ideology of the ladder,"[55] professional-managerial employees are marked by the ambition of climbing up the corporate hierarchy or "white-collar pyramids" for a better life.[56] Poulantzas observed, "Afraid of proletarianization below, attracted to the bourgeoisie above, the new petty bourgeoisie often aspires to 'promotion,' to a 'career,' to 'upward social mobility,' . . . it does not want to break the ladders by which it imagines it can climb."[57] White-collar opt-out thus entails abandoning those ladders, which implies a change of direction in the class-based trajectory of upward mobility. Opting out of corporate careers points toward a loss of faith in the *illusio*[58] or, to use Michael Burawoy's gaming metaphor, quitting the white-collar game of climbing up the career ladders.[59]

I conceptualize white-collar opt-out as a withdrawal of consent that constitutes a turning point in which a worker attempts to reclaim control over their life and future by abandoning the career ladders that purport to be the established pathway to happiness. I argue that this turning point is precipitated by the alienation of labor, the gist of which is the experience of feeling disconnected from labor activity—be it manual, emotional, aesthetic, or intellectual labor—and an accompanying impoverished life experience.

Structured by taxing and unfulfilling everyday work experience in the corporate workplace, alienation from white-collar labor is generally characterized by a lack of intrinsic satisfaction with and meaning derived from work and by burnout because overwork tends to suffocate nonwork spheres of life such as family, friends, hobbies and leisure activities, and civic engagement. However, there are additional elements to what could be called middle-class alienation, such as "relative deprivation," which captures the middle-class experience of "a discrepancy between the 'ought' and the 'is.'"[60] The core premise of relative deprivation is that "people may be subjectively deprived with reference to their expectations even though an objective observer might not judge them to be in want."[61] In chapter 2, I traced elite workers' high hopes for corporate careers to the costly emotional and financial investments in their competitive education, which is supposedly required to attain the necessary skills to land coveted jobs.[62] Thus, the discontents of elite workers, who earn high salaries and yet feel broadly disappointed, can indeed be articulated as expressions of their relative deprivation. Objectively speaking, they are financially better off than the working poor and are living not as precariously; nevertheless, as I showed in chapter 3 and will delve deeper in this chapter, this does not automatically translate into experiencing even the best corporate jobs as "good jobs." Instead, middle-class alienation is often accompanied by a sense of a "deficient relationship to the future," both in the world of work and beyond.[63] Resigning from the corporate world of work is usually also motivated by a broader resignation from the hegemonic middle-class script and its binding practice of the "work-and-spend cycle."[64] Faced with relative deprivation and an impoverished life experience—in short, with middle-class alienation—elite workers withdraw their consent to corporate work and to many of the imperatives of prevalent middle-class notion of success.

The concept of consent—workers' voluntary compliance to their domination—has been used mostly in the realm of "bad jobs" to examine why workers participate in their own exploitation by pushing themselves to work harder or for free.[65] Examining white-collar opt-out through the lens of consent is useful because it brings autonomy and worker agency to the fore while also revealing the structural underpinnings of opting out.

THE WITHDRAWAL OF
WHITE-COLLAR CONSENT

Quitting a corporate career is seldom an impulsive decision. After all, having a high-salary position in a world-renowned transnational corporation is a dream for many people, and the rewards are considerable; the average earnings of my interviewees, for example, put them in the top earnings decile of Turkey and the United States, and some were already in the top 1 percent. In addition to high salaries and prestige, their hard-earned professional identities are central to who they are. As we have seen, the (college) education system in Turkey provides its students with less scope for self-exploration in terms of potential postcollege occupations and careers than is common in the United States.[66] Although one might expect this to spur demand for occupational change among young adult Turkish elite business professionals, changing one's occupation is still considered a wild move. Occupational identities become quite sticky (students choose and start investing in their majors at age eighteen, and they choose their general area of study even earlier than that) and, as a result, one's occupation constitutes a relatively more influential part of one's self. Unlike the strong welfare states of Northern Europe, Turkey lacks safety nets that would allow Turkish young adults to imagine and try out different career paths more freely. Therefore, calling it quits is always preceded by a long period of evaluation, repeated attempts to make work better within one's current job as well as other corporate settings, scouting for noncorporate alternatives, and sometimes even testing alternatives while still working at one's corporate job. Reaching a decision about whether to quit usually takes months and sometimes even years.

Based on the opt-out narratives I collected in my interviews and many others that I came across during my fieldwork, I constructed a stylized, ideal-typical process of white-collar opt-out. The process often begins with workers' increasing awareness of the negative aspects of their job, such as consistently lacking fulfillment from work and feeling exhausted because of overwork. As a variety of push factors become more salient, the workers usually try to address them in their workplaces. If the problems continue to bother them, the workers consider some form of job change, for example, changing their employer/workplace or their position on the career ladder. If they find a job that seems better, typically a better-paying one, which also usually consists of a trade-off rather than a strictly better outcome—for example, finding a job that is more fulfilling but more demanding or less fulfilling yet more relaxed, they switch to it. As similar problems recur or new ones emerge, workers come to realize—sometimes in the form of epiphanies—that these problems are not related to their specific job or employer, but they are endemic to corporate careers. As the push factors become more acute, they start also to become aware of pull factors—those things outside their careers that may help improve their overall contentment. What follows is a reevaluation of their priorities in life and a consideration of whether they can bear the problems that they identify with corporate careers. In the meantime, they start to prepare themselves mentally, socially, and financially: reaching out to family and friends, paying off their debts and saving money, calculating how long they can survive without any income, and the like. Before they call it quits, they usually rehearse mentally some noncorporate career alternatives and sometimes take some proof-of-concept baby steps. If these white-collar workers believe that they have a promising alternative, at least for a while, some can take a leap of faith and quit. Then, they slow down, stop and think, and enjoy life for a while, depending on their financial resources. Afterward, some find a way to earn a living in a noncorporate setting while others go back to their corporate lives—opting back in from necessity or desire, albeit usually with a mindset that prioritizes well-being over work and career outcomes.

This ideal typical process provides us with a baseline for understanding the largest components of the opt-out experience, allowing us to see that the disparate experiences of white-collar opt-out generally follow a similar story. But, of course, it can only go so far in describing the particularities of individual experience. None of the stages in the above ideal typical process have a predetermined end date or outcome; opting out is an open-ended process with multiple points where white-collar workers may recommit to corporate careers. And if the drive to opt out cannot find a proper venue, if the facilitating conditions are missing or the preventing conditions are strong, the decision to quit may not be realized. Looking more closely at the individual factors gets us a clearer understanding of how white-collar opt-out actually takes place.

Push-Pull Factors in Exiting Corporate Careers

In chapter 3, we explored the wide range of factors that can serve to alienate elite workers from their work: lack of fulfillment, lack of recognition, value mismatches, work-life imbalance. These push factors are complemented by pull factors that together motivate white-collar workers to opt out of the corporate world of work. Many factors I detail in this chapter are interrelated and occur in combination. However, I divide them into push and pull factors for analytical clarity.

PUSH FACTORS
A deep lack of fulfillment from work was often the first factor that pushed these individuals away from their jobs and corporate careers. The desire to quit slowly builds up insofar as workers lack

intrinsic satisfaction from their jobs for which they felt overquali-fied. Erman, the sales manager we met in chapter 3, described his experience of boredom at work with phrases such as "learning nothing new" and "becoming a dull person." And such boredom is not restricted to management roles or sales. Many of my interview-ees reported that, even though management consulting involves problem solving, deploying their existing skills, and developing new ones, the work still came to feel repetitive and boring after a while. Recall Berk, the ex-management consultant who went on to run a startup that seeks social impact, said that in his consulting experience, "I began to feel like Sisyphus"—a comparison that cap-tures many elite workers' prevalent sense of feeling overqualified for and unfulfilled by their so-called good jobs.

When they feel their work is meaningless—like rolling a rock up a hill only to have it tumble back down—workers become disen-gaged. Masking this discontent requires emotional labor, which can add to overwork and burnout.[67] Sarp, who once was a manager in a professional service firm but quit in order to travel around Latin America, complained about how both his clients and colleagues constantly made him feel inauthentic:

> I was fed up with wearing a mask. In consulting, it is all about wearing a mask, maybe in all industries but . . . I realized that I frequently find myself feeling that I'm with people that I don't want to be with, going to places that I don't want to go, speaking about topics that I have no interest in, and that my working life covers a huge portion of my whole life. And this is exhausting. After you notice this and start thinking about it, it stings even deeper, becoming more difficult [to stand].

Even worse, elite workers may begin to feel that their efforts at work actually hurt society, which engenders a significant mismatch between their desire to contribute to some kind of social good and what they are actually doing at work. Ömer, the data scientist working for a Wall Street firm, was dismayed that he was using his skills not to cure cancer but instead to "charge higher interest for indebted families." Gülce, who had left her job as a lawyer at a prestigious law firm, reported that she had been especially unhappy with the projects that she was working on: "They were all megaconstruction projects that ruined the environment and reinforced the authoritarian government in Turkey."

Toxic work environments appear to be another push factor moving people to leave their jobs. My interviewees' narratives about this toxicity reveal how it is undergirded by the pervasive up or out culture of modern corporations.[68] The examples they shared usually revolved around the instrumental use of social networking for individual gains at the expense of colleagues. This could take on a Machiavellian tone: respondents described colleagues stealing the recognition of others' work or gossiping to manipulate supervisors, as well as mobbing or bullying, which disproportionately targeted women. Nisa, who quit her marketing manager job at a consumer goods giant, cited her problematic relationship with her supervisor among her reasons for leaving. She reported how he abused his authority over her, presenting her work to upper management while giving her no credit and sometimes insulting and shouting at her when things went wrong. Songül, who had been a marketing manager at a bank, said that her decision to quit was partly a reaction to how she was treated during a period of corporate restructuring, when she was exposed to an intricate series of misinformation and manipulation. Quitting, she said, was partly a step she took "to save my dignity."

But the strongest push factor expressed by my respondents was work-life imbalance. As many opt-out studies have also noted, difficulties balancing work and family life constitute a strong driver for parents, especially mothers, to quit their demanding corporate jobs. Songül's decision to leave her position as a marketing manager, described above, was also driven by her desire to spend more time with her baby daughter and her feeling that she had been supplanted in her child's eyes by the babysitter. She disclosed how much it hurt her to realize that "my own daughter was treating me as if I am a distant aunt or her babysitter and not her mother."

But work-life imbalance was not experienced by parents only. Many nonparenting interviewees reported that burnout from overwork created problems for their mental and physical health, especially as technology like smartphones had obliterated the spatial and temporal separation between work and nonwork. Necla, an investment banker I interviewed one week after she quit her job, told me that she felt so completely drained after long workdays that she usually found herself sitting on her bed, blankly staring at the wall for an hour or so before going to sleep. She recalled vividly how the red blinking light on her phone, indicating unread emails in her inbox, used to bring tears to her eyes at bedtime, and that she knew she would only wake up to the same grind the following morning. Arda, who had been employed at an elite professional service firm, was also used to feeling the grind. When I asked him to free-associate and develop images about corporate life, he said:

> Some cuts on my face . . . because I had to shave in a hurry, forgot to clip my nails, got out of the house without brushing my teeth. . . . I mean, I could not fit thirty minutes of running in my day; they called me to come back in the middle of my exercise. . . . I started to have red rashes on my skin, here and there on my hands and arms. . . . My body was signaling to me.

In the middle of his thinking, Arda went back to a story he had told earlier in the interview. In a period of overwork in which he and his team were staying in a hotel away from home to finish a project for a client, he felt suffocated and wanted to exercise in the hotel gym. However, five minutes after he started to run on the treadmill, he got a call asking him to come back.

Erman also complained about the heavy workload: "I have not had a single day in five years without my work laptop. Five years! And not a single day! Even vacations." He was contemplating leaving his job for another: "I could still *catapult* myself out of the system." When I probed what he meant by "the system," he answered: "I mean, leaving [the consumer goods giant where he's working], and say, moving to an X firm with a salary that is 70 percent of my current one but I could be a bit happier. I mean [the consumer goods giant where he's working] by the system." Here Erman emphasizes that prioritizing contentment over pay and choosing a "no-name company" over a brand-name global firm feels akin to choosing a life off the beaten track, which he cannot easily do so unless he "catapults" himself out of his current life.

Work-life imbalance can also be exacerbated by the hustle and bustle of metropolitan life in crowded cities like Istanbul and New York, especially for people who value peace and quiet. Thanks to skyrocketing housing costs in global cities, living close to one's workplace is an expensive luxury, even for elite workers; my respondents reported commutes that sometimes consumed two to three hours per day. Hakan, a senior manager at a Big Four company, told me that if he finished his workday during rush hour, he simply waited in his office instead of torturing himself in Istanbul traffic. While this was a rational choice on his end, he also lamented that it reduced the amount of time he spent at home with his family; it also created tensions at the workplace because he passed the time by watching TV, which was frowned upon by some of his colleagues. Didem, who used to be a finance manager at a consumer goods giant, complained that Istanbul was wasting her "time, money, and livelihood," even though she had a large paycheck and worked hard to curate her nonworking life. By contrast, she felt "money has value" in her hometown (a quiet, small city) where she moved upon resigning, and she now enjoyed the invaluable perks of being closer to her aging parents, raising her daughter with her extended family, and kicking off her entrepreneurial venture.

While these push factors loomed large in my interviews with the elite workers who opted out, they were also prevalent among those who were still in the workforce. As Didem's case suggests, push factors alone are often insufficient to lead white-collar workers to quit their jobs unless they work in tandem with pull factors. The interaction between push and pull factors also contributes to workers' alienation, pulling them away from their labor.

PULL FACTORS

While pull factors could potentially be thought of as push factors— because the lack of these things pushes respondents away from work—I treat them as pull factors when my interviewees expressed their motive for opt-out as a desire rather than a complaint, that is, expressions of "positive freedom" or "freedom to" rather than "negative freedom" or "freedom from."[69]

Some respondents stated that family is a source of joy and meaning in and of itself and should not be sacrificed. Family was a high priority for Songül, who said that she had thought a lot after her resignation about whether and in what circumstances she might opt back in: "I lost track of the dilemmas I dealt with. I want to have [another] baby, but if I go back to work, I cannot; I need to postpone. If I postpone having a baby, my age is . . . I mean, being a woman is very difficult in that sense." She later disclosed that she was pregnant with her second baby, and she was considering being a stay-at-home mother for the long term. Some respondents also highlighted family in a broader sense, including parents and extended family. As

I mentioned, Didem disclosed that she resigned to stay close to her aging parents, who were not living in Istanbul. After giving birth to her daughter, she and her partner realized that they want to raise their daughter with the love and support of their extended families.

Some interviewees also expressed a yearning for freedom and autonomy as a reason that led to them to resign. When I asked Sertaç, who had worked as a software engineer at a bank, how he felt after his resignation, he replied with a big smile on his face: "Freedom, dude. Freedom. . . . When I was working, I always wondered how it would feel to walk aimlessly in the streets on a Thursday afternoon. You know, passing time, going to the restaurants at odd hours." One of the first things he did after his opt-out was just to walk around the city during the day. He also mentioned that he wanted to be fully in charge of his periods of work and nonwork, and being attached to a corporation, no matter how flexible the working conditions, could not satisfy his priority of having control over his life. For example, he found it infantilizing to have ask for a day off: "It deeply bothers me to ask for *permission*, as if I am a kid. I find it ridiculous to go to work the day after working hard, building something beautiful, and finishing a project. Just because I have to show up to work . . . I should celebrate instead."

Halis, who used to be a manager at a consumer goods giant but opted out to run his own business in the countryside, expressed his desire to have autonomy over his work, especially over when and how much to work in both the short and long term:

> If you say, "Perhaps I want to be somewhere [other than work] on a Tuesday," it is not easy [to do so] in [a] corporate [career]. If you are thinking, "I have my dreams, I want to see the world, I want to work six months and travel six months," you cannot do it in [a] corporate [career]. . . . Say, I want to learn rock climbing all summer long, no way I can get the whole summer off and keep my job.

Even though he wasn't able to realize these fantasies of extensive travel or summers away from the job (he admitted that he sometimes ended up working longer hours as a business owner than he had in his corporate job), he kept emphasizing the importance of autonomy. After leaving his job, he said, "I began to live more happily as I was managing my own agenda, working for myself."

Another pull factor that drives the decision to quit can be thought of as self-realization. For a few of the respondents, the push factors were not especially salient; nevertheless, they wanted to "do more" with their lives. This "more" was usually expressed with the aphorism, "You only live once," or its equivalent. Cüneyt, who had previously worked as a software engineer at a technology giant in the United States, wanted to work as an entrepreneur, so much so that he had felt that he would regret it if he did not try it. He told me how satisfied he had been with his job in terms of its various rewards (including pay, fulfillment through skill use, and the scale of his work's impact on the world). Nevertheless, once he felt secure of his economic well-being and social status, he quit that job and founded a tech startup. Berk, a former Big Three management consultant whom we met in chapter 3, mentioned that he initially liked having an impact on the world with his consulting work. But he found that the work was often more about bolstering his own ego. As he put it, "There is something in consulting, like, proving yourself, like, you can do anything. Like, I am above these [people to whom he gives business advice]. . . . I got free from proving myself to myself." Rather than devoting himself to self-aggrandizement, Berk wanted to work on projects with social impact and quit his corporate career to build a startup that aimed to bring about greater social equality via education.

These pull factors not only threw various push factors into starker relief but also allowed elite workers to minimize the uncertainty in their post-opt-out lives by substantiating what they were actually going to do with their reclaimed time. These concrete plans enhanced their motivation to quit their jobs, regardless of whether they were able to carry them out.

Escaping Alienation: Golden Handcuffs Versus Safety Nets

Analyzing how push and pull factors undermine worker consent sheds light on the motivational side of these individuals' decisions to walk away from career ladders. Certain conditions must be met, however, for these decisions to be actualized. I categorize these conditions into debilitating and facilitating factors: golden handcuffs and safety nets, respectively.

GOLDEN HANDCUFFS

The popular term "golden handcuffs" refers to financial incentives that aim to keep high-skilled employees tethered to their corporations: employee stock options, deferred payments, bonuses, and more. Cüneyt described one such practice that companies use to "game you to stay and keep working":

> You are getting golden handcuffs after [working] for a while. Because as you keep working, suppose your title changed [with a promotion]. You are offered a bonus of forty thousand dollars' worth of company stocks; first year, ten thousand dollars, second year, another ten thousand, third year. . . . Now, if you leave in year two, you cannot get that [last] twenty thousand.

Here I expand upon this curious concept, golden handcuffs, by including other socioeconomic factors that can also chain business professionals to their high-prestige corporate careers, including maintaining a coherent identity, their social status, or their responsibilities toward their children and families. The golden handcuffs imagery provides us with a crucial parallel to Karl Marx and Friedrich Engels's famous punch line in *The Communist Manifesto*, "The proletarians have nothing to lose but their chains." Elite workers' "golden chains" convey luxury far beyond subsistence; they may not appear as "chains" or "handcuffs" at all from the perspective of the working poor or even many middle-class individuals. Nevertheless, my respondents' narratives of whether to quit their jobs revealed an underlying sense of entrapment and lack of freedom that might be described as a "fear of falling."[70] This fear kept their consent fresh.

Consumer credit—in particular, mortgages and home loans—was the primary and most prevalent financial instrument that kept elite workers dependent on their corporate careers. In addition to being popular saving instruments, mortgages also signal that one is an ideal worker who is fully committed to their job. One interlocutor mentioned that upper-level managers tend to interpret lacking a mortgage loan as a sign that an individual may quit their job one day—the idea being that they are not fully committed to living permanently in the area. This interpretation can exclude a worker from consideration for promotion to upper management roles, where turnover is much costlier to the employer.

Another form of golden handcuffs is the social status represented by an upper-middle-class lifestyle of upscale consumption that signals distinction and superiority.[71] Berk, the ex-management consultant at a Big Three firm, outlined the luxuries he would sacrifice if he quit: "You know, you get used to your lifestyle, you dine in luxury places, you travel as you wish, you go and see beautiful places in the world. . . . And as a [Big Three company name] employee, you have the chance to fly business class and dine in the best restaurants of the world simply thanks to your work. . . . But I could break the cycle." As Juliet Schor's concept of the "work-and-spend cycle" illustrates, for many elite workers, work becomes only a means to consume more and better.[72] This cycle of overspending, in which luxurious consumption culminates in considerable consumer debt, was a recurring theme for my respondents. When I asked Fulya, a manager at a giant consumer goods company, to free-associate about being a white-collar employee, she responded this way:

> A white collar [worker] works, earns money, and spends, works, earns money, spends. . . . What they earn and spend is equal. Five years later [after graduating from college], they get married, have a big fat wedding, then pay for it the next three years. Then, they decide to have a baby, buy a house. They think, "my kid must go to the best school in Istanbul, I must pay fifty thousand liras annually." . . . The white collar [employee] overspends. So much so that they make themself more exhausted.

As Fulya mentioned, responsibilities for childcare and education further discourage elite workers when it comes to quitting their corporate careers. Structured by the upper-middle-class parenting culture of "concerted cultivation," these responsibilities are often felt with a sense of urgency (note Fulya's emphasis that "my kid must go to the best school").[73] The exorbitant costs of upper-middle-class reproduction can lead to considerable debt.[74] And debt can disallow white-collar opt-out. Hakan, a senior manager at a Big Four company, shared that he had contemplated opting out but could not because it would come at the cost of private school for his child: "One and a half years ago, I got very close to resigning with several colleagues to initiate our own [professional service] firm. However, when I learned the price of the private school that our little one [his six-year-old daughter] is going to attend, I said, 'Gentlemen. Let's stop and reconsider.' . . . If I were financially secure, I would absolutely and immediately quit my job."

More broadly, my interviews revealed an overarching status anxiety, of which upscale consumption is but one aspect, that handcuffed these individuals to their corporate careers. This anxiety manifests itself through a success imperative that weaves through elite workers' lives, which has been shaped by the outcomes of school and work tournaments. I find that many elite workers' sense of self-worth was built highly contingent on how well they measured up to conventional success metrics from their prework lives—including classes, exams, and extracurriculars. Some recognized this as a double-edged sword. For instance, when I asked Kaan, the management consultant we met in chapter 2 who described his colleagues as the "elite of the elite," why being successful was so important for him, he quoted Bane, the villain of *The Dark Knight Rises*: "I was born in it, molded by it."

I characterize elite workers' lifelong orientation toward success as success-driven habitus mainly because they have a significant *disposition* to seek high rankings in whatever field they are in, and they prioritize conventional success measures over their well-being and social relationships.[75] The success-driven habitus serves as golden handcuffs because deviance from success is intensely threatening to elite workers' sense of self.[76] Having a high-salary job at a prestigious transnational corporation was among the most important signs of success in respondents' postcollege lives, whereas resigning or even jumping off to a "worse" job at a no-name company was usually interpreted as a sign of failure. Thus, quitting prestigious careers is a daunting prospect for many business professionals, whom Laura Empson has aptly described as "insecure overachievers."[77] Because most world-renowned transnational corporations tend to favor overachievers in their hiring processes, such gatekeeping helps make status anxiety a prevalent factor that drives elite workers to take a more conservative stance when it comes to their careers.

Opting out of prestigious corporate careers can feel like undergoing an identity change that could involve losing a critical pillar of their self-worth. Ayşe, an auditor at a Big Four firm, suffered from burnout such that she "woke up sad every single day." Nevertheless, she carried on instead of opting out because: "I want people to say, 'Yeah, Ayşe can manage this. She is successful.'" Such a strong emphasis on success keeps elite workers' anxiety intact. Many of my respondents shared that what they liked most about their jobs was being part of a select group of people. They often signaled this by associating themselves with elite colleges (for example, by stating, "All my colleagues are Harvard alumni"). Much like Karen Ho's description of investment banking culture in Wall Street as "the culture of smartness,"[78] respondents reported that they constantly judged their "success" at work as an indicator of their intelligence and self-worth. Ayşe mentioned, "One of the most frightening things for me is that people at work would think of me as a dumb person." Selin, a marketing manager at multinational tobacco giant, faced similar anxieties around the notion of success. Negative feedback from her manager led her to question herself: "Am I not successful? Am I not able to manage this situation? A mood of anxiety about it lingers. I am someone who constantly experiences fear of failure."

Regular promotion is another benchmark of success, and delays in getting promoted to higher managerial positions can lead some elite workers to feel that they are not successful. Melih, a software engineer at a world-renowned tech company, told me how he "got used to being an overachiever" and felt uneasy with his "not fast enough rise": "My only discontent is that I could have worked harder and got a promotion earlier. It makes me wonder because *I have always been the most successful person in wherever I was and whatever I was doing*. I am now thinking whether I am losing this ability, something *that defines me* [emphasis added]." While we were discussing what a perfect job would look like for Melih, he mentioned that he loved playing basketball, so he might have wanted to become a basketball player. But even as he described the dream, he changed his mind, saying that he would not be good at it because he was not tall enough, and he would not want to be an "unsuccessful" player.

Emre, a manager at a telecommunications giant, described how these internalized narrow measures of success inevitably come up against the hierarchically structured organization of work: "We were brought up like racing horses and we got used to being number one, but there is only one CEO in the company and so you cannot keep being the most successful all the time. And of course, it makes you question, 'What if I am not enough?'"

Shedding that status anxiety is not easy, even after quitting corporate careers. Ebru, an auditor who had been working at a Big Four firm but decided to abandon her exhausting career and embark upon an elaborate solo travel itinerary throughout South Asia, shared how she came to reevaluate the importance of status in her life. She learned through adventurous experiences that she could get by just fine without her "shiny" career, thanks to the gig economy:

> I understood that I don't need to carry a label like a [brand-name company] employee. If the aim is to earn a living, I can earn it in numerous ways. Before I quit my job, I thought about whether I would starve, but I saw that I can even survive hunger. . . . And I learned that I can trust myself. It is that confidence which carried me over to today.

As she recalibrated her expectations and found that the noncorporate jobs she held, including babysitting (her favorite), event management, and various other gig work, were not that "horrible," she felt secure and in control of her life and hence emancipated. Of course, Ebru's account downplays the precarity of the gig economy.[79] Most people removing golden handcuffs prefer to rely on safety nets.

SAFETY NETS

The decision to quit one's job is highly contingent upon having and activating various safety nets that can ease the deeply entrenched, middle-class anxieties of "falling from grace."[80] In the absence of strong welfare state practices, such as efficacious unemployment benefits, the family functions most often as a safety net to help the opt-out decisions materialize. Sarp put it this way:

> There is a bit of this cushion that I can count on my family. . . .
> If things really go bad, I can always go back to my family home, and if I am hungry, I can call my father and say, "Hi, dad!" I think it is helping in the decision-making process. It works like a safety net. People either save [and rely on that] or if they dared to quit, they rely on that [familial support]. It is much more difficult for the ones who come from point zero.

As Sarp emphasized, having rent-free accommodation at one's parents' house can ease the financial burden of opting out. Nisa, who used to be a marketing manager at a consumer goods giant, described the flip side of that truth: some of her close friends who wanted to quit their jobs could not do so because of Istanbul's exorbitant rents. She said that what helped her the most, even more than her personal savings, was living with her parents. While returning to the nest is usually not an ideal scenario, some interviewees, like Sarp, mentioned that they felt emboldened by knowing that they could count on their parents if things went seriously wrong.

Spouses or romantic partners can also help with the financial burden of opting out. As most opt-out studies highlight, this usually takes a gendered form; it is the woman of a heterosexual couple who can opt out and rely more easily on her breadwinning male partner. Songül, who had been a marketing manager at a bank before opting out, shared that she was able to resign mainly because her husband's income could support their family financially. Gül, who quit the corporate life to become a yoga instructor, mentioned counting on the steady income of her husband and her father, though it was not easy for her: "While I had some savings, I primarily had to rely on my dad and [spouse's name], to be honest, even though doing so hurt my self-esteem." Didem noted that her husband was able to take over an ongoing family business, allowing her to pursue her own entrepreneurship that, as is the case with many startups, was not expected to return a profit immediately.

For many people, however, particularly singles and the upwardly mobile, families cannot provide them with an efficacious safety net. These individuals have to construct their own safety nets by means of personal savings. It takes time to build up such a cushion, and many respondents described also making a deliberate decision to avoid upscale consumption, a unifying theme in my interviewees' description of the yuppie lifestyle. Gülce, who used to work as a lawyer at a prestigious law firm, remarked on "the petulant complaints" of her former colleagues, who wanted to opt out but were caught up in a vicious cycle of upscale consumption that required a high salary to sustain:

> You need to be saving some money for at least six or seven years. If you have no kids and [still] cannot [save], there is no excuse, I think it is ridiculous. I have a close friend who works at [an elite corporate law firm] and keeps whining about leaving her exhausting job. Now she rented an apartment in Kuruçeşme [an upscale neighborhood in Istanbul] with a gorgeous view. If you are paying that much rent, then you are in a cycle. If you are often going out, paying for those cocktails, always eating outside, when you are in that cycle, you begin to feel you need a lot of money. So, yes, money is important but it is this luxury and comfortable lifestyle that she got used to that disallows her to quit.

In contrast, Gülce had saved some money "that could sustain me for a while without depending on my parents. I was nervous [about resigning] but that saving eased my concern." Sertaç, a freelancing software engineer who used to work at a bank, disclosed that in addition to owning his apartment, he had also saved enough money to sustain him for at least six months in case he could not find any source of income once he left his job.

While obtaining a sense of economic security is paramount for white-collar opt-out, dealing with status anxiety or the identity dislocation of leaving prestigious corporate positions also requires social and emotional support from friends, parents, and romantic partners. Helen Rose Fuchs Ebaugh's general theory of role exit posits that voluntary exits from roles that are central to self-identity, such as hard-earned professional-managerial job titles, are contingent upon positive social reinforcement; negative social support can interrupt the exit process.[81] Parents are among the most important sources of such support, especially for young adults.[82] Their support can come in the form of affirmation, even encouragement, for opting out. Fevzi, who used to work as an engineer at a major automobile manufacturer, and Nisa both said it was their mothers who told them that they looked consistently unhappy and exhausted and that they should look for alternatives. Gülce's mother, however, had the opposite reaction: "She looked me in the eye and shouted, 'Have you lost your mind?'" Her mother was shocked that Gülce could even conceive of such an erratic move "that could ruin my life" after she built up such a great career.

For time-deprived business professionals, working constitutes a massive chunk of their waking life and this can render unstructured free time desirable but also unsettling, and it thus requires social support. Gülce mentioned that not only her mother but also her friends kept anxiously asking her about what she was going to do with all her free time after she quit, whether she would "stay idle" or "get bored." Some respondents who opted out mentioned that their significant others helped them to deal with that void by not only providing emotional support but also simply being present in their lives. In addition to being the witnesses who provide a necessary validation to such biographical changes,[83] friends and romantic partners provide professionals who are opting out with a social context they can participate in outside work. Gülce stated that she had been thinking about leaving her job for a while but could not take the leap alone: "Everybody thinks about [quitting] but it is difficult to take action. One of the things that made this possible for me was my partner, who suggested, 'Quit your job and let's travel around the world together!'" Sarp also cited his partner's support in resigning from his job and travel as the incentive: the pair traveling through Latin America together. Mobilizing one's friendship network can also provide crucial social support for the quitting decision and its aftermath. Ebru contemplated her opt-out decision with her close friends and relied on them afterward for support—both emotional support and even economic support via seeking contract-based gigs from them.

Pushed from the workplace and pulled to nonwork spheres of life, some business professionals are left pondering whether they can survive abandoning their years-long investment in their careers and changing the direction of their life trajectories. The metaphorical concepts of safety nets and golden handcuffs, as my respondents used them, paint a picture of people who have made it to the top (of the workplace and, by extension, of the socioeconomic pyramid) through grit and yet have been pushed to an edge beyond which forces are pulling them. What eases the fear of falling here is a safety net (made of family and friends and personal savings), the presence of which or its intentional cultivation help them to gather the courage to remove their golden handcuffs and to make the leap of faith.

POSTCORPORATE TRAJECTORIES

After quitting their corporate jobs, my interlocutors pursued various paths. I identify four major pathways they took with the hope of returning to a balanced life: taking time off, engaging with family, escaping from the city, and changing the mode of earning a living.

Back to One's Self

After working for years and acting on the decision to opt out, every opting-out worker's first step was to take a break for introspection, evaluation, and rest. For some, this break involved going far afield. Sarp had been dreaming of traveling the world for a long time, and when he left his job, he and his partner decided to tour Latin America. They traveled around with little planning, posting pictures from their visits to their Instagram account. After a year, when they ran out of money and their appetite for being on the road had waned, they came back to Istanbul. When I interviewed Sarp, he was looking for a new corporate job but very selectively so. He reported that after much thought the ideal job for him now would allow him to reside away from the metropolis, balance his work and life, and engage with analytical problem solving instead of acting as a manager.

Gülce also made a months-long trip to Latin America with her partner, but their trip was more structured because they had an end date and a plan for afterward. When the trip was done, the pair moved to the United States together, and Gülce was doing volunteer work with some nongovernmental organizations (NGOs) while applying to LLM programs for the year following. In her quest to find a meaningful job, she was considering positions at international nongovernmental organizations (INGOs), for which an LLM degree from a world-renowned university could help very much.

In a few cases, travel turned into a relatively permanent option. Ebru visited a South Asian country following her resignation, intending to stay two weeks, but she had been living there for a couple of years at the time of our interview. On her occasional visits back to Istanbul to see family and friends and sometimes earn some money via contract-based gigs, she pursued a more open-ended self-exploration.

But the exploration of travel did not have to go far. Recall Sertaç, who walked around the city during the day after he first opted out. After spending most of his weekday waking hours at work, even the quotidian aspects of life seemed like an exotic venue for exploration.

Back to Family

Turning one's attention to family, particularly to parenting, is among the most prevalent reasons for opting out as well as a common focus of workers' postemployment energy. As the research on work-family conflict and opting out have pointed out, work and family are both greedy institutions, and especially so for upper-middle-class business professionals. Thus, some professionals, predominantly women, opt-out to devote more time to their family. Recall Songül who wanted to reconnect with her baby after feeling that the child was more attached to her babysitter than to her. She also added that she was pregnant with her second child, and while she had not completely ruled out opting back in, she thought she might remain a stay-at-home mother for the future.

Although parenting is the primary family-related reason for opting out, some workers choose the opt-out path for the sake of a romantic partnership. Fulya decided to quit her job and move to Paris when her partner got a nice expatriate offer there. She mentioned that one of her motivations was to avoid the pitfalls of a long-distance relationship and to keep their bond healthy. Following a months-long trip traveling with her partner, Gülce followed him to the United States instead of coming back to Istanbul.

Back to a Simpler Life

Burnout from the metropolitan life, one of the push factors that drive people to opt out, engenders its own pathway among the possible postquit trajectories: that of abandoning the cosmopolitan city in favor of small town or rural life. *Plaza Köylüleri* (Skyscraper Villagers), a documentary that came out in 2022, exclusively focuses on the increasingly popular trend of such urban flight. *Şehirden Kaçanlar* (Those Who Escaped the City), a growing YouTube channel, features stories of emigration from the cities to rural areas, some of which have millions of views. Another YouTube channel, *Yeni Bir Hayata Adım Atanlar* (Those Who Stepped into a New Life), features stories of drastic turning points in life, most of which involve white-collar opt-out and urban flight.

As noted earlier, Didem returned to her hometown, where she and her young family could reconnect with family social and economic networks. Sarp, who had recently returned from Latin America and was in the job market when I interviewed him, mentioned that he too was on the lookout for opportunities to move to a nonurban context because he viewed metropolitan life as part of the reason for his discontent with his corporate career. He was pessimistic, however, believing that good jobs in his specialty—industrial engineering with an expertise in supply chain management—were likely only available in an urban context; in fact, perhaps only in global cities like Istanbul and New York.

During my fieldwork, I heard many more examples of urban flight, some of which involved even more radical examples, like moving to rural areas to take up subsistence farming. This theme suggests a desire for an even more comprehensive withdrawal of consent—a desire to step away not only from alienating labor but also from the capitalist mode of production writ large.

Back to Fulfilling Work

Switching to a new occupation altogether for paid work is perhaps the thorniest postquit trajectory because it involves a fundamental shift in the mode of earning a living as well as changes in personal identity. Respondents often described it in terms of becoming a new person, a desired but still difficult process. Most respondents' respective postresignation trajectories fell onto one of three pathways: entrepreneurship, freelancing, and occupational change. Note that these paths span distinct positions in the Marxian class structures because they entail becoming an employer, being self-employed, and maintaining an employee status, respectively.

ENTREPRENEURSHIP

Driven by a yearning for freedom and autonomy over their labor, many respondents were attracted to the idea of being their own boss. Such a humanistic impetus, curiously operating hand in hand with the neoliberal zeitgeist, led some professionals toward various forms of entrepreneurship as a way to earn a living after resigning from their corporate posts. Didem and Halis opened small shops producing and selling textiles and olive oil, respectively; Berk ran a nonprofit startup focusing on education; Ümit launched a for-profit, digital marketing startup; Gül opened a wellness café.

FREELANCING

While owning a business or becoming a full-fledged entrepreneur is one way of regaining control over one's labor and carving meaning out of work, another is to seek self-employment via freelancing and contract-based temporary work arrangements, which is becoming more prevalent in the twenty-first century.[84] In this case, the white-collar workers tap into their expertise to earn money, usually by providing customers with various consulting services. Nisa worked as a freelance consultant, giving advice on marketing and accounting; Gülce took on small though well-paying gigs such as legal translation of important documents; and Sertaç worked as a software developer, mostly for international clients.

OCCUPATIONAL CHANGE

While freelancing or becoming an entrepreneur usually involves using one's existing expertise, some of the respondents who left corporate life underwent more profound occupational change. This pathway usually consisted of cultivating new skill sets and expertise, sometimes including a significant departure from previous occupations.

One stereotypical trajectory for an opting-out white-collar worker is to become a yoga instructor, whether as a freelancer or as an employee at a sports club or wellness center. Two of my respondents who opted out, Gül and Deniz, were currently earning a living teaching yoga. And they were not alone: both reported that it was becoming more difficult to get by because the increase in the supply of yoga instructors in the labor market, a non-negligible fraction of them coming from the corporate world, was pushing down hourly rates. That there is a corporate elite–to–yoga teacher pipeline of sorts is a very telling example of the alienating work experience that elite business professionals suffer from. White-collar employees usually start doing yoga as a way of coping with the stress of their urban, modern lives that revolve around their exhausting work; it lets them tap into their bodies and emotional sides that are neglected at work. Deniz said she enjoyed teaching yoga because she could see a tangible result after a hard day at work; in addition to being paid, she found the fruits of her labor were more obvious and positive. She was doing meaningful work; helping people feel better both mentally and physically.

Many of the new professions my respondents embraced, including yoga instruction, required certification and a good deal of training. Fevzi, a former engineer, was in training to become a pilot for a commercial airline; Arda, a former Big Three consultant, had been certified as a sailing instructor; and Suna, another former consultant, was studying to become a psychoanalyst. The common point in all these transitions is that such a career change involves a period of training without earnings, significant effort, and the cultivation of a new self. And their efforts were not always successful: Evren, who was hoping to leave his financial controller position and become a pilot, had failed the tests to be admitted to flight school, partly because he was too tall. He shared that he would be on the lookout to see if the regulations that penalize height for airline pilots change.

Occupational change did not always involve wholesale self-reinvention. Some of my respondents returned to their original occupations by pursuing graduate education and then applying it to new areas. Ece had been an economics major and worked as a marketing manager at a consumer goods giant. But she decided to quit her job to pursue a PhD in economics with a focus on marketing, hoping that she would be happier as an academic. Gülce enjoyed being a lawyer but was unhappy with the environmental and political ramifications of the cases she was handling as well as with overwork. She was motivated to pursue an LLM degree to switch her expertise from corporate law to something else that would be "less evil."

THE AFTERMATH OF WHITE-COLLAR OPT-OUT

A curious question with opt-outs is whether such risky career moves are justified or not. Answering this question conclusively, however, requires longitudinal data, including follow-up interviews with my subjects after some years to see how their postcorporate lives unfolded. There are also the additional complexities of self-reporting and retrospective thinking that we should be careful about in approaching my respondents' aftermath accounts; wishing to justify their risky opt-outs, they could be sharing biased accounts, magnifying the extent of their previous dissatisfaction or current satisfaction. Note that this is not chiefly about the social desirability bias that is typical of interview methodology but rather the specific attitude of my population, that is, their strong desire to seek success in their life course, which eventually meant landing high-prestige corporate positions. With these caveats in mind, attending the before-and-after narratives of my respondents who opted out still helps us further explore what makes a good job good or bad by providing us with the kind of changes—improvements and degradations—business professionals experience in their post-opt-out working arrangements.

When I asked Ebru about common features shared by those who quit—a question I expected her to answer with remarks about gender, class background, occupation, personality, and the like—she instead answered with a big smile, "None of them regret their decisions." This all-embracing answer could be interpreted as a reflection of the success imperative: that they do not regret and they are still "successful." My respondents who opted out also typically reported being more contented with their current jobs and postcorporate lives, despite earning significantly less compared to their previous corporate jobs. What made the difference?

Examining my respondents' narratives, I was able to identify two important shifts in the quality of their working life across the dimensions of work-life balance and fulfillment from work. First, the working hours of respondents who had opted out but were now once again employed were significantly fewer than in their previous jobs, with the exception of those who pursued entrepreneurial endeavors. Based on these respondents' self-reports, their working hours went down from an average of 59 hours per week before they quit their corporate jobs to 37.5 hours per week—almost the typical/legal workweek. Such a major shift in the amount of working time implies a huge improvement in the experience of work-life balance and therefore in the overall quality of (working) life.

The exception of entrepreneurs is also very informative for our understanding of alienation with respect to the importance of feeling connected to one's labor. That those who quit their corporate jobs for entrepreneurial ventures still work long hours (in some cases, even longer hours) and yet report more contentment suggests that when overwork is justified with a sense of ownership (as Halis put it, "I'm building something of my own") or purpose (as Didem put it, "It is a women-only enterprise. . . . I produce for my country"), the individuals can tolerate its negative impacts—at least for a while longer than otherwise. We can even argue that any sort of justification and meaning attributed to one's overwork can ameliorate, if not do away with, its negative effects.

In addition to having less or longer but justified work hours, some respondents mentioned enjoying a clearer temporal delineation of work. Fevzi, the former engineer who was training to become a pilot, shared with me how much he loved the work-life balance in his new job: "When you landed and parked the plane, you're done and you come home with peace of mind. It was not like that when I was working in [the famous car manufacturer that he worked for]. I was always feeling uneasy about work even on the weekends or when I am not working."

Second, subjects who had opted out but were now employed also expressed greater fulfillment from work. This is often described as getting more intrinsic satisfaction from their work and also finding their labor activities more meaningful. Fevzi's account suggests that, while he is at work, flying, which he loves, he is fully immersed in his job. Arda, the former management consultant who was teaching sailing, shared a very similar account. Sertaç also shared with me that he enjoyed freelancing because he could decline the projects he found boring, whereas in his corporate job, he could not get away from them. Ebru's particular love of babysitting highlights how getting intrinsic satisfaction from work intertwines with finding it meaningful. She described how much she loved spending time with children, but it was also a matter of how their parents thanked her, looking her in the eye with gratitude at the end of the day. "I don't earn much," she said, "but I feel my labor has value."

In terms of their work orientation, the respondents typically display a shift from having a stronger job orientation to a stronger calling orientation. In the vignette described in chapter 3, these respondents reported that they became less like Person A and more like Person C (see the vignette in the appendix). I interpret their pre-opt-out work orientations as being caught in a cycle: they typically started working their jobs with a career orientation, like Person B, full of ambition to rise up the corporate ladder. As they experience exhaustion, boredom, and meaninglessness, however, it began to feel more like a "job," something boring but necessary. They typically address it through job change and recalibrate to a career orientation until it begins to feel like a job again. Opting out seems like an attempt to break this cycle, especially through making labor meaningful.

The dynamics of postcorporate life are unpredictable, of course; some corporate opt-outs are actually forced to opt back in, mainly because of financial reasons. Gül's wellness café went bankrupt, and while she continued teaching yoga, she told me that she also began to consider opting back in because she cannot earn much from yoga instruction. Sarp, who had been traveling around Latin America but ran out of money, was looking for a corporate job again. Sarp and Gül thought of corporate jobs as the only viable way of earning a middle-class living; while working in the service sector or manual labor may also be an alternative way of earning a living (like Ebru, who had chosen to keep earning her living rather precariously instead of opting back in), it is usually not considered an option because it cannot sustain a middle-class lifestyle.[85]

————————

This chapter extends the empirical scope of opt-out scholarship beyond American women executives dealing with the double bind of work and family toward nonparenting young adult professional-managerial employees. By examining a broad range of Turkish professional-managerial employees' quality of working life and opt-out narratives, it also extends the opt-out research to contexts outside the United States, casting it as a global phenomenon that highlights the long-standing issues in the nexus of work and well-being. These extensions enabled me to emphasize additional push factors at corporate workplaces besides work-family conflict, such as the lack of fulfillment at work and work-life balance writ large, and additional pull factors that originate from nonwork spheres besides parenting, such as positive freedom and self-realization. With all these factors, I developed a parsimonious model of white-collar opt-out with push and pull factors from work and nonwork spheres of life that refract through a combination of safety nets and golden handcuffs. This account provides us with a baseline understanding of how opt-out decisions are made and actualized within structural constraints and can shed light on a wider array of career transitions, including opting out of academia, artistic labor markets, and humanitarian aid work.[86]

The empirical analysis in this chapter and in chapter 3 shows that high-salary, high-prestige corporate jobs are not sufficient conditions for a happy career and life, and it explains partly the white-collar blues of the transnational Turkish middle class. Respondents who opted out typically earn significantly less compared to their previous corporate jobs, but they feel more satisfied with their current jobs and postcorporate lives. They usually work significantly fewer hours, and even those who do not (primarily entrepreneurs) suggest that the extra work is justified by their sense of ownership and autonomy over their labor, purpose, and/or altruism. They also report that their jobs are more meaningful and that they enjoy their everyday working activities more than before.

With the increasing prevalence of opt-out narratives in popular culture, maybe there is a mimetic aspect to elite workers' withdrawal of consent—that people imitate each other's actions. I have heard from many people—including my subjects—that white-collar people display a greater tendency to fit in and follow the trends; as insecure overachievers they may indeed be conformist. It is possible that these elite workers, many of whom are from the millennial generation, are motivated by a fear of missing out (FOMO). The question that constantly hovers over opt-out narratives is: Will I be happier in a different occupation? Of course, then the question is, How could such a risky decision to forgo so much potential for prestige and wealth became a trend, an event to be imitated? There has to be some sort of a material base and a sufficient number of cases for such a phenomenon to emerge as a culturally desirable and viable action. We may benefit from separate, survey-based research to determine if there is in fact a white-collar exodus in Turkey. Regardless, the opt-out phenomenon is certainly becoming a recurring theme in Turkey's popular culture. Perhaps the most telling sign of this is the exploding popularity of Kaan Sekban.

"Congratulations! You Are Fired!"

Kaan Sekban quit his job to pursue his dreams of becoming an actor after working ten years as a banker, and he tells his story in his biographical satire *Tebrikler Kovuldunuz!*—the first book we saw in the introduction. He had toyed with the idea for some time, taking acting classes on the weekends. Then one day, after an emotional acting exercise, he realized that he had become a banker in order not to disappoint his family again—as he had when he took the selective middle school exams at age eleven. He stayed in his banking job for a little while, until he could loosen the golden handcuffs of his mortgage payments and the credit card debts from his aspirational consumption. But he did eventually make the leap, and today, Sekban is one of the most popular stand-up comedians in Turkey. His stand-up show became a hit and made him famous; he has performed it in New York and London, to a mostly white-collar Turkish audience. His show, a three-hour long stand-up act—an aberration in the genre—revolves around his story of opting out and his incisive satire of the corporate world of work. I was able to see him live, and I can easily say that his story resonated with the audience members, who were mostly white-collar workers. During the intermission and after the show, I overheard people praising the accuracy of his satirical account of white-collar labor and the lifestyle centered around it. After the show, there was a long line of people waiting for a signature on their copies of his book. In addition to his stand-up show, his comedy sketches, which he shares with the hashtag *#YakamBeyazBeynimAyaz* (roughly translated as "My collar is white, my brain is frozen"), usually go viral on social media.

Sekban's story is more than an anecdote considering his American counterpart, Anish Shah, a former McKinsey consultant, also opted out and moved from Chicago to New York to become a full-time standup comedian, carving a niche of "corporate comedy." Moreover, many other stories and themes of opting out have begun to populate social media in the past several years. In addition to the popular YouTube channels I mentioned above, the tales of white-collar opt-out in Turkey have appeared in television shows such as the Netflix show *Uysallar* (*Wild Abandon*, released in 2022), movies such as *Küçük Şeyler* (*La Belle Indifference*, released in 2019), and documentaries such as *Beyaz Yaka* (*White Collar*, released in 2021). Regardless of whether there is an opt-out revolution in Turkey—no statistical evidence for such a phenomenon was found in the United States as well[87]—these opt-out narratives and their popularization help us shed more light on the discouraging quality of working life experiences of the transnational Turkish middle class.

CONCLUSION

Rethinking Alienation and Middle-Class Formation in the Age of Globalization

When I'm retired, my life is my own,
I've made all my payments, it's time to go home,
Wonder what happened betwixt and between,
When I went to work in tall buildings.

—JOHN HARTFORD, "IN TALL BUILDINGS"

This book has explored various aspects of the formation of the transnational Turkish middle class by examining three interrelated questions that unfold over the life course of employment: Who can (and can't) obtain high-prestige, high-salary white-collar jobs at transnational corporations (TNCs)? Once they have landed these jobs, how do Turkish elite business professionals think about the quality of their working lives? Why and how do some of them opt out of their enviable corporate careers? The answers shed light on a surprising feature of my respondents' experience of quality of (working) life, what I call white-collar blues.

I began my inquiry by contextualizing the problem within the theories of the middle classes in chapter 1. Highlighting the transnational aspects of class formation in semiperiphery countries, I outlined the historical processes that contributed to the emergence of Turkey's transnational middle class. This investigation specifically emphasized crisis-ridden Turkey forgoing its developmentalist ideology and adhering to the Washington Consensus instead. The Turkish economy's global integration and embrace of neoliberalism since the 1980s—an Anglo-American-centered transnationality with an overall welfare retrenchment accompanied by privatizations in education and health care—constitute the key macro-level processes that undergirded the country's transnational middle class. In particular, the increasing prevalence of TNCs in Turkey and their emergence as the primary employers of its most educated and qualified labor force marked the rise of Turkish yuppiedom vis-à-vis its old middle class, whose primary employer was the state. The most distinctive features of the culture of this ascendant new middle class consist of consumerism and careerism with a global orientation.

After covering the macro-level processes that structured the rise of the transnational middle class in Turkey, I turned to its meso-level (i.e., institutional and organizational) makings in chapter 2. Conceptualizing hiring as a potential moment of gatekeeping and social closure, I examined the processes through which senior undergraduates are recruited to entry-level white-collar jobs at TNCs. I found that the hiring practices at these companies disproportionately prefer students from a select group of colleges. This limited focus, together with the increasing privatization of education in Turkey since the 1980s, tilts the playing field in favor of wealthier families from the very earliest phases of the hiring process. The elimination practices in the later steps demonstrate the importance of transnational forms of cultural capital—English-language skills, high-quality international experience, and a cosmopolitan outlook and taste—all of which heavily depend on class background. And the job interviews at these firms—particularly the final ones conducted by revenue-generating managers—tend to suffer from class homophily, often subtly yet systematically preferring candidates from richer backgrounds. These findings suggest that the elimination practices of TNCs during hiring shape the transnational middle class as an exclusive group with a homogeneous class culture and contribute to the reproduction of social inequalities writ large.

In chapter 3, I turned to a micro-level analysis of class formation, examining the quality of working life narratives of the transnational Turkish middle class. I identified two major dimensions of satisfaction and discontent: (1) experiencing work as fulfilling versus experiencing it as lacking intrinsic satisfaction and meaning, and (2) having a good work-life balance versus being overworked. Analyzing the narratives of my respondents across these dimensions, I found that, while a small fraction of white-collar workers feels contented with their jobs, a non-negligible proportion feels disappointed, exhausted, or both. Contrary to their high hopes for and expectations from their careers, and despite having the best corporate jobs in the labor market, disappointment and exhaustion loom large in the lived experiences of Turkey's transnational middle class. Their experiences have many of the hallmarks of alienated labor, inviting us to revisit the question of what makes a good job good or bad.

I subsequently examined the subset of Turkish elite business professionals who opt out and thus forgo their privileged positions and corporate careers. I interpreted opting out as a withdrawal of worker consent in the face of alienating labor and found that it is, first, contingent on how much the push factors of the workplace resonate with the pull factors of nonwork spheres of life. However, this push-pull interaction is a necessary but insufficient condition for opting out, which, second, depends on the interplay between safety nets (such as economic resources and social support from family and friends) and the golden handcuffs (such as upscale consumption, credit card and mortgage debt, and status anxiety) that tend to keep elite workers tethered to corporate careers. If and when they opt out, elite workers' immediate postcorporate trajectories consist of four distinct paths "back" to a more balanced life: back to one's self, back to family, back to a simpler life, and back to fulfilling work. They typically earn less but also work fewer hours and get more fulfillment from their new jobs, and they become markedly more contented with their lives.

In this conclusion, I put my examination of the Turkish case into a broader context within Turkey and beyond by exploring transnational middle-class formation elsewhere. Then I extend the alienation theory to encompass professional-managerial labor. I conclude with a discussion of this extension's implications for our understanding of the quality of working life and higher education.

FISSURES IN THE REMADE
TURKISH MIDDLE CLASS

The fragmentation of the Turkish middle class in general and the emergence of the transnational Turkish middle class in particular have important political implications for our understanding of contemporary Turkish politics. Even as the relaxation of capital controls encouraged the emergence of the transnational middle class, the shift from import- to export-oriented growth models led to the expansion of another middle-class fraction: those employed by Turkey's export-heavy domestic firms.[1] These firms, which came to be known as "the Anatolian Tigers" or "the Islamic Capital" (small to medium-size enterprises often located in Turkey's periphery instead of Istanbul) boomed after the 1980s as well.[2] And the conservative middle-class fraction they engendered has risen in numbers and become more powerful under the aegis of the AKP (Adalet ve Kalkınma Partisi, the Justice and Development Party) since the 2000s.[3] In addition to the transnational Turkish middle class's valorization of international cosmopolitanism over the public sector and service-oriented professions, the AKP has also cultivated patronage relationships that extend into the selective distribution of public employment,[4] constituting a good deal of this emerging conservative middle class.

This expanding, more domestically embedded middle class competes with the transnational middle class in accumulating cultural capital, and the AKP's increasingly totalitarian stance on education lays this intra-middle-class competition bare.[5] Islamization of public schools in the last decade, while creating a favorable environment for conservative middle-class families, has engendered a "reproduction crisis" for nonconservative middle-class families, who feel forced to choose private schools to distance their children from Islamization while also ensuring their upward mobility.[6]

Coupled with the recent economic instability (especially the recent devaluation of the Turkish lira against the U.S. dollar and the euro and skyrocketing inflation), the AKP's increasing hostility toward secular lifestyles has left the highly educated utterly frustrated with their overall quality of life and future prospects, further reinforcing the transnational Turkish middle class's aspirations to transcend Turkey and move to the Global North. Emigration of high-skilled Turkish labor to the Global North (the Turkish brain drain) has taken off in the past decade, leading to a significantly larger and more disgruntled and oppositional Turkish diaspora in the Northern European and North American countries.

Many of these dynamics had already come to the fore in the largest and longest protest event in Turkish history, the Gezi Park Resistance in 2013. Like the American professional-managerial class's involvement in the formation of the New Left of the 1960s to the 1970s in the United States,[7] the increasingly dissatisfied Turkish professionals emerged as a significant political protagonist with the Gezi Resistance,[8] just like their counterparts around the world,[9] demonstrating a loud opposition to the AKP's authoritarianism.[10] For its part, the AKP has skillfully stoked the sociopolitical polarization between these transnational/secular and domestic/conservative middle-class fractions to consolidate its social base by means of "us versus them" politics and culture wars. It remains an open question how the frustrations and struggles (or lack thereof) of the transnational middle class will affect the ongoing democratic backsliding in Turkey and the nation's future.

TRANSNATIONAL MIDDLE-CLASS FORMATION BEYOND TURKEY AND THE GLOBAL SOUTH

As I stressed in chapter 1, focusing on the creation of Turkey's transnational middle class revealed how TNCs have functioned as key carriers of globalization by not only diffusing goods and commodities (cultural and material alike) but also spreading a common work culture, encouraging and facilitating global labor mobility, and entrenching the unequal global division of labor between core and periphery countries. This process of transnational middle-class formation is hardly unique to Turkey.

What follows is a discussion of how transnational middle-class formations have unfolded in the rest of the world. I outline this comparative exploration through the conceptual construct of the North–South divide, situating Turkey within the Global South. The North–South divide (or its equivalents) facilitates clearer analytical explanations by assuming both fundamental differences between the North and South and similarities within the North and within the South. To resist unhelpful reifications of these inherently relational concepts, it's important to consider the construct's limits. The term "Global South," for example—which captures very diverse political-economic units of analysis, including periphery and semiperiphery economies or postsocialist and so-called third world economies—is beneficial *only* when compared to the Global North. And even though the term "transnational" does not entail any inherent focus, in the context of the Global South, I use it to characterize an Anglo-American-centered transnationalism under the aegis of U.S. hegemony since the 1980s.[11] It is important at this point to consider that, even though the Global South is highly heterogeneous, there are ways in which all Global South experiences bear certain commonalities vis-à-vis the Global North. This can be seen most easily through a consideration of the transnational European middle classes.

The European Union encouraged the rise of a "European transnational middle class" built around a supranational, European identity.[12] Meanwhile, as in the Global South, TNCs, particularly North European ones, helped transnationally mobile professional-managerial groups ascend by structuring the economic integration of Europe via foreign direct investment.[13] The European transnational middle classes, akin to their Global South counterparts, are comprised mostly of well-educated business professionals. These professional-managerial groups—sometimes called "Eurostars"—were the main beneficiaries of Europe's economic integration.[14] And just like the rift between the conservative Turkish middle class and the transnational Turkish middle class, the cosmopolitanism of these European professionals is often seen as a cleavage dividing the locally embedded from transnationally mobile fractions of the middle class, reflecting a general classed experience of globalization and transnationalism.[15]

Nevertheless, unlike the high-skill immigrants from the Global South, members of the Western European transnational middle classes enjoy an almost frictionless cross-border mobility within the Global North. Their ease of mobility, undergirded by the EU's politico-legal infrastructure, stretches the range of jobs that they can hold in other EU countries beyond professional-managerial jobs at TNCs.[16] Thus, a broader range of professionals can move between countries, and physical border crossing figures more prominently in the experience of the transnational European middle class[17] than it does for most Global South transnational middle classes, whose transnational experience depends primarily on working at the local branches of TNCs of the Global North.

Unlike most members of the Global South transnational middle classes, "Eurostars" often feel sufficiently rooted in their countries of origin and thus employ "partial exit strategies," which refers to a more selective transnational engagement; instead of immigrating outright, they opt for frequent international travel for various reasons, such as seeking health care or public education for children abroad.[18] Their motivations for immigrating, compared to those of their Global South counterparts, thus appear to be more cultural and personal than economic or political, although migrants from Central and Eastern Europe are notable exceptions.[19] Global North business professionals too are certainly motivated by career interests insofar as transnational work experience enables promotions and upward mobility.[20] However, the upward mobility to be gained from South-to-North transnational work experience is considerably steeper than can be achieved by intra-North mobility. As a result, South-to-North migrants may be able to achieve a greater improvement in quality of life than their intra-North counterparts—both regaining civil liberties increasingly lost in the Global South and securing higher material returns.[21] Of course, the alarming rise of right-wing populism worldwide, with its strong anti-immigrant stance, complicates the immigration processes and globalization as we have known it. It is a curious process to see how nationalist leadership across the board will continue engaging with unrolling globalization, and we will see to what extent they succeed.

While the experiences of the transnational middle classes of the Global North and South diverge quite dramatically, experiences of transnational middle-class formation within the Global South also show variations that reveal the effects of globalization across different conditions. The emergence of the transnational Turkish middle class can be taken as representative of other transnational middle-class formations in the Global South—including Egypt, Morocco, and India[22]—insofar as they were all undergirded by the shift from developmentalism to neoliberalism and the global integration of hitherto protected national economies.[23] Nonetheless, the extent and penetration of these transitions differed, as did the precise formations that emerged.

For example, Iran, with its curtailed global integration, affords a sharp contrast with Turkey and highlights the importance of foreign direct investment and TNCs in engendering transnational middle classes. During the neoliberalization and global integration of the Global South economies in the 1980s and 1990s, postrevolution Iran continued with the developmentalism of the Pahlavi era.[24] Coupled with the Iran-Iraq War and ongoing U.S.-led embargoes and sanctions, foreign direct investment and the presence of TNCs in Iran remained relatively negligible until the 2002 passage of the famous Law on Encouragement and Protection of Foreign Investment.[25] Although the Iranian economy has opened since then and "hegemonic professionals" have increased in number—mainly because of the expansion of higher education by the state in the 1990s and 2000s[26]—the size and prominence of a transnational middle class in Iran have still been limited compared to many Global South countries. The emigration of highly skilled Iranians has played a greater role than domestic outposts of TNCs in the formation of a transnational Iranian middle class.[27]

On the other hand, the transition to a capitalist economy seen in postsocialist countries such as Poland, Hungary, and the Czech Republic runs counter to Iran's closure: Since the fall of the Berlin Wall, foreign direct investment to Central and Eastern Europe has soared,[28] and TNCs have spurred new class formation processes

in postcommunist economic systems,[29] particularly through privatization of state-owned enterprises.[30] Young adults with cultural
capital were the winners of these transitions,[31] and for these "communist yuppies" (as with my respondents) "working for a large
multinational corporation" loomed large in their ambitions.[32]

Overall, this book proposes putting TNCs forward as influential
agents of transnational middle-class formation and social change.
Considering all these cases together, we can even claim that TNCs
are engendering a truly global middle class—the combined total of
the transnational middle classes of each country. This proposition
becomes more plausible from a micro-level perspective as well. For
example, it is quite reasonable to think that there is a great deal of
overlap in the life experiences of a McKinsey consultant in Kenya,
Brazil, and Turkey, and even the United States. Passing through
similar filters of recruitment, working at not just isomorphic but
almost *identical* workplaces, experiencing global mobility through
the same paths, and socially coming together at annual company
events, the professional-managerial employees of TNCs tend to
form a more homogenous stratum in the global social stratification.
Further research, such as ethnographic accounts of such annual
company events, could help examine how TNCs facilitate such a
formation and the broader implications of it, such as whether it
would engender a more cosmopolitan middle-class attitude and
culture around the world.

AN IMMANENT CRITIQUE OF
GLOBAL CAPITALISM

Here I frame the totality of my empirical excursions into the lives of
Turkish upper-middle-class business professionals as an immanent
critique of capitalism in its most recent neoliberal and globalized

form. In particular, this is a critique of its ideological core, the American dream,[33] as it unfolds and beckons transnationally in the Global South, including Turkey. By the very design of this research, I spotlighted the so-called winners of capitalism: professional-managerial employees of prestigious TNCs. In other words, I explored the employment conditions under which there is seemingly sufficient room for living the good life under the capitalist world order. I chose to "study up"—if not the top—and asked what happens if everything mostly goes right, especially for people coming from a nonwealthy background, be it working or middle-class. This book is partly motivated by the prospect of making an a fortiori argument for a stronger critique of capitalism's ills. Suppose we are the poster child of meritocracy: we behaved ourselves and were good sons and daughters, studied hard and succeeded through one high-stakes test after another, survived demanding schooling and extracurriculars simultaneously, successfully graduated from the top colleges, immediately secured the best corporate positions in "tall buildings" of global cities, and strove for more—sought higher positions at more prestigious firms with higher pay that would allow us to consume more and better. In short, suppose we are the admired success stories with respect to the scripts laid out by the American dream. What then?

Toward an Extended Theory of Alienation

As summarized above, the book's main findings prompt us to extend and generalize the Marxian theory of alienation to better account for the quality of (working) life of the middle classes, including its privileged upper and transnational fractions, as well as the working class. This extension proposes a more relational, subjective, and pluralistic understanding of alienation than that of the original

Marxist one that focuses primarily on degrading manual labor anchored to subsistence.

Recall in chapter 3 that, by rethinking the alienation theory of young Karl Marx pragmatically with an emphasis on the effects of alienation, I identified four different deficits that accompany and structure alienation of labor. First, there is the loss of workers' recognition of their productive/creative powers in the end product (i.e., loss of authorship). Second, there is the loss of human freedom and autonomy implicated in when, how long, how to, and on what to work. Third, there is the loss of living up to one's (human) potential through engaging with creative and intrinsically satisfying activity while at work, and fourth, the limitation of human potential at nonworking times as well because of overwork and a lack of energy, time, and sometimes capacity to engage with active leisure and self-actualization.

From the Marxian perspective, crafts labor of the precapitalist era is the implicit benchmark against which Marx compares alienated labor under the early phases of capitalism in England. Craftspeople, whose labor incorporates both design and execution, enjoy the ideal working conditions: they can derive intrinsic satisfaction and meaning from their labor through authorship; they are the owners of their business and hence their products; and, thanks to their ownership and authorship, they have maximum freedom and autonomy over their labor and can express their authenticity via exercising their judgment over creative labor.[34]

As such, crafts labor seems to provide craftspeople with a fulfilling working life.[35] Experiencing one's labor as fulfilling could be thought of as a postmaterial value.[36] Borrowing from the language of humanistic psychology, we can think of fulfilling work as a genuine human need. Work is one of the fundamental conduits of human flourishing;[37] as such, it is a path to the self-realization that stands at the top of Abraham Maslow's famous hierarchy of needs.[38]

Maslow's hierarchy lists a range of needs as building blocks of human motivation: physiological needs like food, water, and shelter are at the base, followed by safety, belonging and love, esteem (for example, prestige), and self-actualization.

The majority of high-status white-collar jobs seem to fulfill many of these needs. Corporate careers often promise a kind of existential security, a silver bullet that satisfies most of these needs simultaneously: in addition to the financial means to meet physiological needs well beyond, TNCs usually provide their professional-managerial employees with status as well as a ready-made social environment of potential friends in the workplace.[39] As many of my respondents discovered, however, the lives enabled by corporate careers often fall short of the pinnacle of self-realization because of a fundamental trade-off and tension between security and freedom. The decreasing prospects of homeownership, a hitherto marker of middle class-ness, illustrates this trade-off. As I touched upon in chapter 4, skyrocketing real estate prices, particularly in the global cities of New York, London, and Istanbul, put homeownership increasingly out of reach, even for the privileged upper and trans-national middle classes. Homeownership in these cities came to be possible only at the cost of "debt bondage," that is, decades-long installments of massive mortgage payments keep these professionals at their high-paying corporate careers despite their discontent. This is a classic double bind because having a mortgage loan is an unspoken prerequisite for promotion to higher managerial positions.

We have seen how white-collar labor characterized by overwork and unfulfilling work can undermine physical and mental health and well-being as well as social relations and leisure,[40] thereby leaving the occupants of enviable white-collar jobs frustrated and dissatisfied, much less flourishing. In other words, such pursuit of security via corporate careers can cost them dearly as they pursue its promised benefits.

I argue that alienation, in its most general form, is the depressing experience of separation from laboring activity—be it manual, emotional, aesthetic, or intellectual labor—which is typically accompanied by an impoverished life experience. Work is colossally important in our lives—whether highlighted by a transcendental understanding that work undergirds our humanity or the inconvenient fact that most of our waking lives are devoted to it. And such vital importance suggests that paid work that does not directly contribute to human flourishing beyond pecuniary compensation is prone to alienation, which often manifests itself as an aversion toward work. Such disengagement from labor stems from a range of work and nonwork conditions that manifested and experienced in multiple ways with varying intensities, as I have demonstrated throughout chapters 3 and 4. Therefore, instead of posing alienation as a binary variable, I conceive of alienation and human flourishing as facilitated by labor as processes, pulling us toward the opposite poles on a spectrum of contentment with work.

While there are common drivers of alienating labor, such as overwork and routine, the tone, intensity, and taste of alienation are idiosyncratic. This is mainly because deriving, finding, and constructing meaning (from work)—a substantial aspect of our experience of working—is, by definition, a subjective and open-ended process. After all, the same working conditions—though conducive to providing a certain set of meanings or lack thereof—can be experienced quite variously by different people. Nevertheless, one of the most profound experiences of working-class as well as middle-class alienation is of domination and powerlessness: we feel that we are forced to sell our labor on a market instead of developing and experiencing it freely.

The philosophical accounts of alienation that Marx built on revolve around an external entity's domination of the actual builder of that very external entity. Georg Wilhelm Friedrich Hegel famously argued that history is nothing but the cumulative process of self-realization of the Spirit, which surpasses its self-alienation as human beings raise their consciousnesses. Ludwig Feuerbach, on the other hand, contended that instead of seeing human beings as self-alienated God, we must see God as self-alienated human beings; by projecting their own images and calling it God, human beings become alienated from themselves.[41] Religion, therefore, is the self-alienation of humans: this humanmade God dominates its own makers, human beings, through religion. Following the shift from Hegelian idealism to Feuerbachian humanism, young Marx first applied this framework of alienation as domination to Hegel's *Philosophy of Right*, arguing that the state is a humanmade product that nonetheless dominates human beings as an external and alien/ inhuman being in the realm of politics.[42] Afterward, Marx applied the same framework to capitalism and argued that alienation in the realm of economics looks like human domination by capital, which is the externalized productive powers of human beings. Following the most distinctive common denominator of all these accounts of alienation in the spheres of religion, politics, and economics, I argue that a generalized theory of alienation can be understood as a process of human beings' dominating themselves via an external entity that they themselves produce.

When we examine the elite business professionals' discontents through this lens of *alienation as self-domination*, we can see rather clearly that they feel trapped in their careers by their *human capital*, which they have meticulously and industriously built themselves (unlike most of their working-class counterparts, who didn't have the chance to do so). Their grit, hard work, and delayed gratification throughout their childhood, adolescence, and young adulthood brought them to where they are, enabling them to succeed through high-stakes tests, arduous schooling and extracurriculars, and selective hiring in the labor market. Several of my interviewees even referred to themselves and other white-collar workers as "corporate slaves" who cling to corporate careers despite their persistent discontent. While it is rather absurd to think of their experience as indentured labor or slavery—and they are surely aware of that—it still captures part of their lived experience of lacking freedom (even though they hold admired positions that seem to give a lot of freedom to them thanks to their high income and human capital). The term "golden handcuffs" captures a similar paradoxical experience of having good jobs but feeling miserable and trapped. Another sign of this shared experience of domination shows itself in the narratives of white-collar workers as a yearning for ownership or "being one's own boss."

Would the elite workers' experience as "corporate slaves," chained to their corporate careers with golden handcuffs, mean the proletarianization of white-collar workers and middle classes? While this question begs for further research examining the contemporary white-collar labor processes in detail, I argue that white-collar professional labor conforms to the proletarianization thesis, although it requires some drastic alterations: that white-collar employees indeed end up feeling they have nothing but their *intellectual* labor to sell to earn a *middle-class* living. These two italicized additions to the Marxian aphorism constitute the key difference between precarious manual laborers and service-sector workers and their relatively well-off white-collar counterparts. While "the middle-class way of living" is quite an amorphous term, we can simply assume it refers to a rather comfortable and secure lifestyle, one that goes beyond subsistence if not to abundance. Nevertheless, the neoliberal erosion of welfare states and the resulting decline in the quality of public education and health care has increasingly encouraged self-reliance. Coupled with the powerful script of the American dream of upward mobility and occupational prestige, which consecrates a materialistic and competitive lifestyle as *the* middle-class way of living, working at a high-salary, high-prestige corporate job turns out to feel like a *necessity* of a happy and content life.

Prioritizing the lived experience of powerlessness and paid work as forced labor also reveals the relativistic nature of alienation, or simply, *alienation as relative deprivation*. Drawing from work narratives and paying close attention to the subjective experiences of my elite worker respondents (as opposed to deriving their job quality from objective conditions of their employment), we can see the importance of highly educated, white-collar workers' expectations to their experience of quality of working life. "Relative deprivation" is a key concept for theories of collective violence.[43] It is also closely related to the concept of anomie, which highlights a lack of means to achieve culturally recognized goals.[44] Here I simply use "relative deprivation" to capture the white-collar experience of "a discrepancy between the 'ought' and the 'is,'" between what they expect and what they get.[45] The core premise of relative deprivation is that "people may be subjectively deprived with reference to *their expectations* even though an objective observer might not judge them to be in want [emphasis added]."[46] Considering my case of inquiry—elite workers who earn high salaries and have comfortable lives and yet feel disappointed—the discontents of my respondents can indeed be articulated as expressions of their relative deprivation. Objectively speaking, they are financially better off and not as precarious as the working class; as I showed, however, this does not automatically translate into experiencing even the best corporate jobs as "good jobs."

As we saw in chapters 2 and 3, the majority of respondents' experience of alienation as relative deprivation stems from their high hopes and expectations that they formed prior to their corporate careers. Just like Paul Willis found that working-class students "learn to labor" in schools and end up being funneled to working-class jobs,[47] Amy Binder and colleagues found that middle-class students in elite colleges "learn to define and desire 'prestigious' jobs,"[48] a very narrow range of white-collar labor of the sort I covered in this book, and end up being funneled to higher echelons of the labor market. Nevertheless, my respondents' frequent refrain that "a college degree is unnecessary for my job" highlights a significant shortcoming: although their demanding college education has armed them with high-level skills and correspondingly high expectations, the actual content of their white-collar jobs turns out to require minimal use of those skills. They desire to have world-scale impacts via their work; however, the reality often does not match these expectations. Such falling short of expectations contrasts with being dubbed as the winners of capitalism (as professional-managerial employees) or of neoliberal globalization (as transnational elite business professionals). The persistence of social inequalities keeps the stakes of having a stable, prestigious, and well-paying white-collar job high and reinforces the normative power of the American dream, which tacitly labels people who cannot make it to such positions as failures.[49] Coupled with a status anxiety fueled by such inequality, the highly educated people's inertia of overachieving, or what I call success-driven habitus, keeps them at their corporate careers and their consent to alienating labor fresh.

Thinking of alienation as relative deprivation highlights the importance of human agency. Echoing Michael Burawoy's discussion of blue-collar workers' making their boring, shop-floor jobs bearable (turning their experience of bad jobs into better jobs),[50] I showed how white-collar workers can experience good jobs as bad jobs, as alienating labor. Of course, unlike the precarious blue-collar or service-sector workers, elite white-collar workers have an opportunity to break the cycle if they realize that they can indeed survive without working for a while and that they can flourish without their corporate jobs—as we have seen in the tales of opt-out in chapter 4. However, the withdrawal of worker consent in the face of unfulfilling work and overwork, that is, alienating labor, does not necessarily mean opting out of corporate careers altogether—indeed, "job crafting" is such an alternative.[51] Rather, I suggest considering the withdrawal of consent as a heightened sense of agency insofar as white-collar workers feel and act freer in prioritizing nonwork aspects of life; and in their careers and jobs, they feel and act freer by prioritizing intrinsic satisfaction and meaning over prestige and salary. Alienation can undermine elite workers' consent and motivate them to loosen golden handcuffs and cultivate safety nets, which encourages purposeful redirection of one's agency away from self-domination toward human flourishing.

In addition to rethinking alienation as self-domination and relative deprivation, we can keep extending the alienation theory by examining two distinct quality of working life experiences I covered in-depth in earlier chapters: underemployment and overwork. The contrast between the issues emphasized by the white-collar workers who love their jobs and those who do not puts these two experiences forward as key drivers of middle-class alienation.

First, underemployment is a determinant of whether my respondents can derive fulfillment from their work, much as it is for their blue-collar counterparts. In chapter 3, I highlighted the way skill mismatch and the design versus execution binary contributes to alienation. The Marxian account of alienation, which mainly deals with blue-collar workers on shop floors, can also be seen as a case of skill mismatch or, to be more precise, underemployment: Marx believed that proletarian jobs composed of repetitive tasks constitute underemployment for every human being given humans' productive and creative potential. If we think of a skill spectrum from low- to high-skilled labor, with manual labor typically considered at one end and knowledge work at the other, even highly educated, white-collar workers can experience underemployment.

In addition, when the mismatch occurs at the higher echelons of the skill spectrum, it imparts a distinctively resentful taste because of the high expectations of middle-class workers.

Although Émile Durkheim considered skill mismatch to be an anomaly in the capitalist division of labor,[52] we see it again and again as more of a rule than an exception. In addition to the labor processes as conceived within a factory or even a country, there is a transnational aspect of alienation as underemployment. As I argued in chapter 3, TNCs tend to amplify the design versus execution gap in the labor process on a global scale, deepening the divide between core versus periphery countries. This shows itself most explicitly in the contrast between the headquarters and branches of TNCs: headquarters are workplaces where the global design of business processes takes place, whereas in the branches, work mostly consists of local or regional execution of those global designs. At best, branch employees could edit the design, not author it. A comparison of the array of jobs available at the higher echelons of labor markets in core versus periphery countries reveals a skills gap between them. Such an unequal global division of labor creates some structural conditions for underemployment and alienation of not only blue-collar labor but also white-collar labor. It also partly explains the immigration of high-skilled workers from the Global South to the Global North and the increasing prevalence of work visas, such as the famous H-1B visa that grants work authorization in the United States, in the competition among the world's advanced economies.

Some Turkish elite business professionals working in New York City were more sanguine regarding how much fulfillment they get from their jobs than were their counterparts in Istanbul. Once the New York workers recognized that their skills were in proper use and that their education and training had not been in vain, their work could be fulfilling. Working on cutting-edge problems with a select group of people as their colleagues, they felt that their lives were advancing, that they not only earned a lot but were also learning and contributing to something; their efforts seemed meaningful to them. Working at the headquarters of major TNCs whose operations cover the whole globe, they knew that their efforts at work would have large-scale impacts. Sometimes they even felt proud of their jobs.

Second, overwork looms large in the experience of white-collar workers. Thinking of alienation as overwork indeed provides us with perspective on the quality of working life: we can consider the importance of the nonwork portion of our lives for our well-being and how (over)work influences that portion and, by extension, our experience of human flourishing or lack thereof. When a worker perceives their work and nonworking aspects of life as a zero-sum phenomenon, work-life balance becomes of paramount importance—because overwork usurps not only time but also emotional and physical energy, motivation, and eventually the capacity to engage with creative and intrinsically satisfying activities when away from the job.

Consent to overwork is prevalent today, however, and can be seen as a key triumph of capitalism. This was not always the case, as Max Weber's incisive account of the precapitalist norm suggests:

> With remarkable frequency, the raising of the piecework rate did not result in *more*, but in *less*, work being done in the same period of time, because the workers responded to the raising of the piecework rate not by *increasing* but by *reducing* the amount they worked in a day. . . . The extra money appealed to him less than the reduction in work. . . . Wherever capitalism has begun its work of increasing the "productivity" of human labor by increasing its intensity, it has run up against . . . this leitmotiv of the precapitalist economic labor.[53]

But today's workers, unlike Weber's pieceworkers, are firmly in the toils of the desire to earn more money—indeed, earning more is now an entrenched imperative thanks to the vicious "work-and-spend cycle" induced by advanced capitalism.[54] In addition to the desire to earn more, the prioritization of career success and status over intrinsic satisfaction is another key reason why a highly educated workforce can put up with overwork even at the expense of health, well-being, and social relationships. Alienation of white-collar labor points toward a different instrumentalization of work than blue-collar alienation because the main motivation differs: if blue-collar workers' main goal of working is primarily need-based (i.e., subsistence), elite workers' main goal can be thought as greed/ambition-based (i.e., status through success and consumption). At the same time, I would push back against one of the core premises of Marxian alienation theory that instrumentalization of labor is, by definition, alienating. Thinking of work as a means rather than as an end in itself can be liberating *if* a sound justification is provided. Here, justification does not mean finding an excuse but an active and agentic acceptance of one's conditions and being genuinely contented with one's answer to the question, Why am I working in my current job?

Overwork and its discontents can be thought of separately from underemployment because overwork can still hurt workers even if work is fulfilling. As I discussed in chapter 3, unlike my white-collar respondents who reported a good work-life balance, those who were overworked often reported work-family conflict, decay of physical and mental health, diminished and unfulfilling leisure time, social deprivation, and self-blaming—even when they found their jobs fulfilling. Thinking of alienation as overwork independent of the content of work enables us to see the limits of the production-centered Marxian perspective: while work is one of the fundamental venues of self-actualization and contentment, there is absolutely more to life than work. Human flourishing can emanate from other sources and experiences, including family and friends, parenthood, charity and social responsibility, participation in social movements, and production and active consumption of art. An abused understanding and practice of a work ethic, a peculiarly American one with roots in Protestantism, often accompanies overwork and puts work in utter competition with these alternative sources of fulfillment. The result can be an impoverished life experience despite high levels of income and luxurious consumption habits.

Approaching the primacy of work thesis—a key premise of both sociology of work and class—from a perspective that takes nonwork aspects of life seriously reveals some additional caveats: What about doing boring work for the greater good of humanity, such as a clerk working at a nongovernmental organization (NGO) that fights for social justice? Or how about having an instrumental relation with one's work but reducing the workday to four hours, as Bertrand Russell recommended in his essay *In Praise of Idleness*, or to three hours, as John Maynard Keynes famously estimated almost a century ago in his essay *Economic Possibilities for Our Grandchildren*?[55]

To express his discontent, one of my white-collar respondents likened himself to Sisyphus of Greek mythology—an extremely crafty human being condemned by the gods to the eternal punishment of a dull, strenuous, meaningless, and repetitive task of rolling a giant boulder up a hill only for it to roll down. Although it may just sound like a witty remark, I wonder what would have happened in the Sisyphus story if he was condemned to roll that boulder for only three or four hours per day but was free afterward to live a decent life with his family, friends, and community? Conversely, what about the quality of working life experience of a heart surgeon whose job makes the world a better place and is inherently meaningful and challenging—both intellectually and dexterously—but who is consistently working seventy hours per week? These are thorny questions that challenge the primacy of work thesis, and they may point toward an alternative way of relating to work without valorizing it. Marx was clear that higher pay cannot remove alienation.[56] A reduced amount of alienating labor, on the other hand, could indeed go a long way. Alongside the emerging debates of universal basic income schemes and economic degrowth,[57] maybe it is time to revisit Paul Lafargue's polemical and electrifying essay, *The Right to Be Lazy*.[58]

RETHINKING QUALITY OF WORKING LIFE

Extending alienation theory to cover professional-managerial labor has two serious implications for our understanding of quality of working life. First, my discussion of alienation as underemployment asserts that overqualification is not restricted to manual labor and the precarious service sector alone. Elite workers also suffer from repetitive aspects of their jobs, high-stress workplaces, value mismatches, and an overall failure to attach meaning to their labor. It suggests that we bring issues of meaningful and intrinsically satisfying work more emphatically to the center of the debates on job quality,[59] the future of work,[60] and work redesign.[61] Note that this does not mean we should forgo the importance of the material aspects of good jobs, especially good pay and job security, which are obviously indispensable to satisfy our most basic human needs. However, there is more to what makes a good job good—the fact that these elite jobs are better than many others is not enough to make them good. The benchmark for understanding whether a job is good needs to go beyond the "is" and embrace the "ought."

Second, it is a clear-cut social injustice to have structural unemployment in an environment of persistent overwork. Elite workers' seventy-hour workweeks, known as 9-9-6 (from 9 A.M. to 9 P.M., six days a week), could even be considered an indirect form of social closure; after all, cutting these strenuous work schedules down to the typical forty-hour workweek could almost double the amount of so-called good jobs in the labor market, while certainly making them better jobs than they are. Reducing working time, such as through four-day workweek initiatives, which have become increasingly common after the COVID-19 pandemic (thanks to its all-encompassing nature, inconveniently easing the coordination aspect of collective action problems), would immediately boost the quality of working life of the overworked while helping decrease unemployment. Of course, as Weber's quote illustrated, working time sits at the heart of capital-labor conflict (recall that in the Marxist parlance, working time is a direct multiplier of the amount of exploited surplus value), which has been dangerously tilting in favor of capital in the past decades. Let's not forget that it was largely labor unions that brought about the landmark achievement of the eight-hour workday and a reduction in working time (without compromising salaries) and that this is still a key labor demand for our individual and collective well-being. Today, it is perhaps as crucial as higher minimum wages and job security, especially given that longer work hours put greater pressure on the environment and add to the looming climate crisis.[62]

Future research that would further qualify the extended alienation theory I outlined here and test some of my arguments empirically in other work contexts should include additional abductive analyses of other deviant case studies, such as the professionals who earn not only sufficient material, psychological, and social benefits (i.e., the lower steps in Maslow's hierarchy of needs) but also have a calling orientation to their occupation. Research on the lived experience of the quality of working life of such scientists, medical doctors, social workers, NGO workers, academics, and artists could be the next step of a research program that investigates what makes a good job good or bad.

RETHINKING MERITOCRACY AND
HIGHER EDUCATION

My examination of white-collar blues as experienced by the transnational Turkish middle class also has implications for meritocracy and higher education. The occupational regret stories among the highly educated spotlight some structural determinants of alienation, as I discussed in chapters 1 and 2. The distribution of students to universities and majors via high-stakes testing—arguably, the backbone of the myth of meritocracy in Turkey—and the difficulty of changing majors in college are among the root causes of occupational regret among Turkish young adults. An encompassing transformation of higher education is necessary to combat such narrowing down of potential career paths at an early age. Such transformation should be motivated not only to prevent occupational regret but also to cast higher education as a platform for building both individual flourishing and a stronger civil society. This upgrade should shift the emphasis on higher education from treating universities as training grounds for the business world and stepping stones to higher-paying careers toward a liberal arts model that treats college campuses as relatively autonomous spaces in which students find their own voices and wants. Given that the post-Fordist economy actually demands a more flexible workforce, there is arguably even an economic incentive for such an upgrade; it is wasteful to teach skills that are of no use. My respondents' shared sentiment of "not needing a college degree" for their jobs should be taken seriously and, as we have seen in chapter 2, the prevalence of cultural matching in hiring at many TNCs could be easily interpreted as a sign of the saturation of the highly skilled labor supply.

Higher education institutions are indeed vital not only for individual but also for collective well-being. Yet a pernicious prioritization of corporate careers at the expense of many other meaningful and satisfactory career paths has plagued higher education. Amy Binder and colleagues found that almost 50 percent of Harvard's 2014 graduates *learned* to pursue careers only in consulting, finance, and tech industries.[63] Much like their American counterparts, the most successful Turkish students also tend to favor a narrow range of career paths, mostly preferring to work for TNCs upon graduation. This suggests that "career funneling" is, in fact, a global problem of higher education. Surely, employer branding activities of TNCs on elite college campuses and more perniciously, "corporate partnership programs" constitute a significant part of the reason for such an erosion.[64] And universities—and particularly their career centers—would do well to challenge (not accommodate) this trend and encourage their students to consider pursuing a broader range of careers and occupations.

This peculiar narrowing down of potential careers symbolically reproduces the normative power of the American dream script, which prescribes that high-income and high-status occupations are the only viable way forward for a happy life. Nevertheless, my examination of white-collar blues and tales of opt-out help us demystify fast-track corporate careers and make the case for a different way forward. Can we revalorize careers in the public sector and restructure welfare states, thereby helping promote "a plurality of criteria of worth"?[65] Considering the precarious times we live in—persistent social inequalities, rising xenophobia and authoritarianism around the globe, a horrible pandemic and the threat of future pandemics, and accelerating climate change—perhaps it is time to ask ourselves why and how the best and brightest of us ended up desiring only a narrow range of careers with the accompanying "one-dimensional" taste of life that Herbert Marcuse aptly described more than half a century ago[66] and whether or not adherence to such a limited vision helps us to ameliorate these pressing problems.

METHODOLOGICAL APPENDIX

Studying Elite Workers

I drew my empirical material from two waves of fieldwork in Istanbul and New York City during the spring and summer of 2017 and 2018. This fieldwork enabled me to collect over one hundred semistructured in-depth interviews with various constituencies of the transnational middle class of Turkey, including business professionals, graduating seniors at elite universities, and human resources (HR) professionals involved in the hiring process at transnational corporations (TNCs). I engaged in "theoretical sampling" and mainly followed external and chain referrals for recruitment.[1] In this appendix, I share the details for each of these groups of interviews such as sampling and recruitment, durations of interviews, and the like.

To protect the privacy of my interviewees, I use pseudonyms, and occasionally I generalize some details. For example, instead of saying that Person X is an investment banker, I may write that she or he is working in a professional service firm, a category that includes management consulting, accounting, auditing, and corporate law. I used such forms of distortion more often for my New Yorker subjects because they are more identifiable than the subjects from Istanbul.

The interviews were held in Turkish. All the quotes in this book, including the ones I took from sources in Turkish, are my own translation. All the interviews were recorded, with a few exceptions—some did not feel comfortable with being recorded. At the end of all the interviews, except those for therapists and HR professionals, I handed my interviewees a tablet on which they filled out an online survey that asked for demographic and socioeconomic information about them. I also took detailed notes after each interview.

In addition to these notes, the interviews were also transcribed and coded using the qualitative data analysis software, NVivo 12, following "flexible coding."[2] I first passed through my interview notes and developed index codes that anchored the transcripts to my interview schedules; later, I developed analytical codes for each empirical chapter. In developing my analytical codes, I first sampled both extreme cases (such as the most contented and discontented business professionals) as well as typical ones, and afterward, I expanded to the others iteratively, updating my analytical codes.

ELITE WORKERS

My sampling strategy for elite business professionals and managers, the heart of this study, followed two steps. First, I limited my population to the graduates of the top six universities in Turkey as well as graduates of the nation's elite private high schools (some of whose alumni pursue college education at prestigious American and European universities instead of Turkish ones). I next narrowed this group down to a sampling frame by choosing fifty companies (see table A.1). Most of these companies are listed in Fortune Global 500; they are among the top-tier TNCs in their sectors. They are also the most prestigious companies that Turkish elite college graduates desire to work for (which I validated via my interviews with senior

Table A.1 The list of transnational corporations that comprises the sampling frame

Category	Company	Category	Company
Technology	Amazon		Procter & Gamble
	Apple		Unilever
	Google		L'oréal
	Microsoft		Philip Morris
	Facebook	**Consumer goods**	British American Tobacco
Management consulting	McKinsey & Co.		Pepsi Co.
	Boston Consulting Group		Coca-Cola
	Bain & Co.		Danone
	Oliver Wyman		Nestlé
	Accenture		Peugeot
Law	White & Case	**Manufacturing**	Ford
	Baker McKenzie		Daimler-Mercedes
Auditing	PricewaterhouseCoopers		Citigroup
	Deloitte		HSBC
	Ernst & Young		Merrill Lynch
	KPMG		Deutsche Bank
Information Technology (IT)	IBM	**Finance and insurance**	Credit Suisse
	SAP		J. P. Morgan
	Oracle		Goldman Sachs
Telecom	Vodafone		Marsh
	Turkcell		Allianz
Pharmaceutical	Pfizer		Macquire Capital
	GsK	**Oil and energy**	BP
	Novartis		Shell

undergraduates of an elite public university). While I was mostly loyal to this sampling frame of companies, I occasionally made some exceptions; for example, if the company of a potential subject was not on this list but was equal in prestige with a company that was, I interviewed that person.

To recruit interviewees from this sampling frame, I used a premium LinkedIn account for scouting purposes and leveraged my own personal social network. These are usually time-deprived individuals, and it is relatively difficult to arrange interviews with them. I followed the social scientists' advice on eliciting qualitative data from elite professionals, and I relied on referrals from close ties for both initial access and building rapport.[3] I then also used snowball recruitment to capture the maximum variation and to cover both typical and deviant cases with respect to quality of working life.

I interviewed seventeen business professionals in New York and thirty-one in Istanbul. Detailed demographic and socioeconomic information about these respondents can be found in tables A.2 and A.3. The interviews lasted ninety-five minutes on average, ranging from forty-eight minutes to 157 minutes. My questions revolved around (1) their career histories and experiences of quality of working life, (2) transnational employment, and (3) their experiences of job searching and recruitment processes.

Halfway through each interview, I also used a vignette instrument, which can be found at the end of this appendix. I used it mainly to explore and understand people's work orientations and to differentiate between a job, career, and calling orientation.[4] I adapted the vignette from Amy Wrzesniewski et al.'s work to better accommodate the elite labor experience, particularly the descriptions for Person B and Person C. In the middle of each interview, I handed the respondent a sheet of paper with the vignette text on the front side and asked them read it, then turn the page over and think aloud while answering a series of questions written on the back. In tables A.2 and A.3, I report my respondents' work orientation scores based on their answers to these questions, ranging from 0 to 3, that is, from "not at all like me" to "very much like me."

My main motivation for using this instrument was to encourage respondents to talk more deeply and intimately about their work experiences. Comparing their own experiences with such artificial yet realistic experiences turned out to be very fruitful and illuminated how these individuals related to the phenomenon of working in general. I also included an additional question and asked my interviewees to comment on a famous saying, "Choose a job you love, and you will never have to work a day in your life."

Afterward, I asked respondents to rank their current job satisfaction from 1 to 10, where 1 means "I cannot be more dissatisfied" and 10 is "I cannot be more satisfied," followed by a question about why they gave this rating. I also often asked them to give me examples of people that they know or the kinds of jobs that would lead people to answer with a score of 10 out of 10. Tables A.2 and A.3 display the job satisfaction scores of my elite worker samples in Istanbul and New York, respectively.

CORPORATE OPT-OUTS

To reach out to corporate opt-outs who were once employees of the prestigious transnational corporations but left, I followed the same sampling and recruitment strategy that I used for the elite business professionals. However, as they constitute a population that is more difficult to find and locate, I occasionally deviated from the sampling frame above.

I interviewed seventeen ex-business professionals in Istanbul. The interviews lasted ninety-eight minutes on average, ranging from sixty to 160 minutes. My questions revolved around

Table A.2 Socioeconomic and demographic details of the interviewees in Istanbul

Subject	Gender	Age	Class Location, Income	Class Location, Lifestyle	Parents' Class, Income	Parents' Class, Lifestyle
Evren	Male	Late-twenties	Upper-middle	Upper-middle	Middle	Middle
Başak	Female	Mid-thirties	Upper-middle	Middle	Working	Working
Selin	Female	Mid-twenties	Upper-middle	Upper-middle	Middle	Middle
Erman	Male	Late twenties	Upper-middle	Middle	Middle	Middle
Lila	Female	Late twenties	Upper-middle	Upper-middle	Upper-middle	Upper-middle
Yasemin	Female	Mid-twenties	Middle	Middle	Upper-middle	Middle
Tuğba	Female	Mid-twenties	Middle	Middle	Middle	Middle
Serkan	Male	Late-twenties	Middle	Upper	Middle	Lower-middle
Cengiz	Male	Late twenties	Middle	Middle	Middle	Middle
Gökhan	Male	Mid-thirties	Middle	Middle	Middle	Middle
Aylin	Female	Late twenties	Middle	Upper-middle	Middle	Middle
Yeşim	Female	Mid-twenties	Upper-middle	Upper-middle	Middle	Middle
Kıvanç	Male	Late-twenties	Middle	Middle	Upper-middle	Upper-middle
Onur	Male	Late-twenties	Upper-middle	Upper-middle	Upper-middle	Upper-middle
Metin	Male	Early thirties	Middle	Middle	Upper-middle	Upper-middle
Soner	Male	Mid-twenties	Upper-middle	Upper-middle	Upper-middle	Upper-middle
Ebru	Female	Early thirties	Middle	Middle	Upper-middle	Upper-middle
Arif	Male	Late twenties	Upper middle	Middle	Lower-middle	Lower-middle
Emre	Male	Early thirties	Middle	Upper-middle	Middle	Lower-middle
Ecem	Female	Late twenties	Middle	Upper-middle	Middle	Middle
Hakan	Male	Mid-thirties	Upper-middle	Upper-middle	Upper class	Upper-middle
Leyla	Female	Mid-thirties	Upper	Upper-middle	Middle	Upper-middle
Fulya	Female	Mid-thirties	Upper-middle	Middle	Upper-middle	Upper-middle
Kaan	Male	Late twenties	Upper-middle	Upper-middle	Upper-middle	Middle
Olcay	Male	Late twenties	Upper-middle	Upper-middle	Lower-middle	Middle
Pelin	Female	Mid-twenties	Upper-middle	Upper-middle	Upper-middle	Upper-middle
Nazım	Male	Late twenties	Middle	Upper-middle	Lower-middle	Lower-middle
Necla	Female	Early thirties	Upper-middle	Middle	Middle	Middle
Uğur	Male	Early thirties	Upper	Upper	Upper-middle	Upper-middle
Irmak	Female	Early thirties	Middle	Middle	Upper-middle	Upper-middle
Yılmaz	Male	Early thirties	Upper-middle	Middle	Middle	Lower-middle

Graduate Degree	Industry	Workplace Authority	Annual Gross Income	Job Satisfaction [1 to 10]	Job Orientation [0 to 3]	Career Orientation [0 to 3]	Calling Orientation [0 to 3]
MS	Food and beverages	Expert	Ł75–90k	6	2	2	0
—	Pharmaceuticals	Senior expert	Ł105–125k	2.5	3	0	0
—	Tobacco	Manager	Ł60–75k	7	2	3	1
—	Consumer goods	Manager	Ł200–250k	5	2	2	0
MBA	Consumer goods	Expert	Ł75–90k	7	0	3	1
—	Retail	Expert	Ł75–90k	8	3	2	0
—	Engineering consultancy	Expert	Ł60–75k	7	1	3	0
—	Food and beverages	Expert	Ł125–150k	7.5	0	3	0
MS	Automative	Manager	Ł150–200k	7	0	2	2
—	Insurance	Manager	Ł125–150k	5	3	1	0
—	Technology	Expert	Ł125–150k	8	1	1	0
—	Technology	Manager	Ł300–400k	7	2	1	2
MA	Telecommunications	Expert	Ł150–200k	8	0	1	3
—	Consumer goods	Manager	Ł150–200k	7	1	2	0
MS	Automative	Expert	Ł60–75k	8	1	2	0
—	Management consultancy	Expert	Ł400–500k	8	0	1	3
MS	Management consultancy	Manager	Ł125–150k	7	1	3	0
—	Finance	Expert	Ł125–150k	7	2	1	0
—	Telecommunications	Manager	Ł105–125k	7	1	3	2
—	Management consultancy	Expert	Ł75–90k	6.5	1	2	0
MBA	Auditing and accounting	Senior manager	Ł150–200k	6	3	0	0
MBA	Management consultancy	Manager	Ł300–400k	7	0	0	2
—	Manufacturing	Expert	Ł200–250k	7	1	2	3
—	Management consultancy	Expert	Ł200–250k	7	2	1	2
LLM	Corporate law	Manager	Ł300–400k	8	0	2	2
—	Management consultancy	Expert	Ł150–200k	8	1	3	2
—	Finance	Expert	Ł150–200k	8	2	1	1
—	Finance	Manager	Ł300–400k	4	3	0	0
MBA	Management consultancy	Manager	Ł600–750k	7	0	0	2
—	Manufacturing	Expert	Ł125–150k	7	2	1	0
MS	Technology	Expert	Ł150–200k	7	0	2	1

Table A.3 Socioeconomic and demographic details of the interviewees in New York City

Subject	Gender	Age	Class Location, Income	Class Location, Lifestyle	Parents' Class, Income	Parents' Class, Lifestyle
Ayşe	Female	Late twenties	Middle	Upper-middle	Upper-middle	Upper-middle
Ömer	Male	Early thirties	Middle	Middle	Middle	Middle
Alper	Male	Late twenties	Upper-middle	Upper-middle	Upper-middle	Upper-middle
Melih	Male	Mid-twenties	Upper-middle	Upper-middle	Upper-middle	Upper-middle
Furkan	Male	Early thirties	Upper	Middle	Middle	Lower-middle
Canan	Female	Early thirties	Upper-middle	Upper	Upper-middle	Upper-middle
Muhsin	Male	Mid-thirties	Upper-middle	Upper-middle	Upper-middle	Middle
Çağla	Female	Early thirties	Upper-middle	Upper-middle	Upper-middle	Middle
Ozan	Male	Early thirties	Upper-middle	Upper-middle	Upper-middle	Upper-middle
Nisan	Female	Early thirties	Upper-middle	Upper-middle	Upper-middle	Middle
Dilay	Female	Early thirties	Middle	Upper-middle	Upper-middle	Upper-middle
Ramazan	Male	Mid-thirties	Upper	Upper	Lower-middle	Lower-middle
Umut	Male	Early forties	Upper	Upper	Lower-middle	Lower-middle
Reyhan	Female	Early forties	Upper-middle	Middle	Middle	Lower-middle
Filiz	Female	Late twenties	Upper-middle	Upper-middle	Upper-middle	Upper-middle
Ahmet	Male	Late twenties	Upper-middle	Upper-middle	Upper-middle	Upper-middle
Tolga	Male	Mid-twenties	Middle	Middle	Upper-middle	Middle

Graduate Degree	Industry	Workplace Authority	Annual Gross Income	Job Satisfaction [1 to 10]	Job Orientation [0 to 3]	Career Orientation [0 to 3]	Calling Orientation [0 to 3]
—	Auditing and accounting	Expert	$75–100k	6.5	1	3	1
PhD dropout	Finance	Expert	$100–125k	6	3	1	0
MS	Management consultancy	Expert	$75–100k	6	1	2	1
MS	Technology	Expert	$200–250k	8	0	2	2
—	Technology	Manager	$450–500k	10	0	0	2
LLM	Corporate law	Expert	$175–200k	6	3	1	1
PhD	Management consultancy	Expert	$150–175k	8	0	2	2
—	Technology	Expert	$100–125k	4	1	3	0
MBA	Finance	Manager	$250–300k	2	3	2	0
PhD	Management consultancy	Expert	$125–150k	7	2	2	0
PhD	Management consultancy	Expert	$175–200k	7	0	3	1
MBA	Consumer goods	Manager	$300–350k	7	0	3	1
PhD	Management consultancy	Partner	+$1M	7	2	1	0
PhD	Management consultancy	Manager	$125–150k	7	0	3	1
MS and MBA	Finance	Manager	$175–200k	5	0	2	3
MBA	Management consultancy	Manager	$150–175k	8	1	2	2
—	Management consultancy	Manager	$125–150k	8	0	3	2

(1) their career histories and stories of opt-out; (2) their experiences of the aftermath of their opt-out; and (3) their work orientation, job satisfaction, and ideal work narratives. In this third group of interviews, I used the same vignette instrument, although I asked them to think of their most recent corporate job in answering these questions. I also asked them to use the same instrument to evaluate their current jobs if they were currently working. In some cases, I asked them to speculate in their answer as if they had the job that they envisioned for themselves in the future. I asked them to rank their satisfaction with both their current situation and their most recent job.

PSYCHOTHERAPISTS

From my interviews with elite business professionals, I learned that some see psychotherapists to cope with their problems. Thinking of therapists whom elite business professional patients visit to talk about their work-related discontents as an alternative depository of crucial information, I interviewed five psychotherapists in Istanbul. These interviews lasted forty-nine minutes on average, ranging from thirty-three to seventy-five minutes. My questions to them revolved around what kind of patterns of complaints they heard from their white-collar patients and how their white-collar patients made sense of their work-related problems. I used these interviews for triangulation.

UNDERGRADUATES IN THEIR SENIOR YEAR

To interview undergraduates in their senior year, I decided to pick only one university for convenience. The one selected is a public school that is one of Turkey's top six universities. I relied on my own personal social network to find the initial batch of interviews and, from then on, I snowballed. The majors that I targeted were mostly engineering, management, and economics because these are the main majors of elite business professionals. The interviews were held either on campus or at one of the coffee shops around the campus.

I interviewed fifteen senior undergraduates who had been in the labor market. These interviews lasted sixty-one minutes on average, ranging from thirty-four to eighty-three minutes. My questions revolved around how and why they chose the majors they did, their internship and recruitment experiences, how they navigated the elite labor market, their expectations about their job prospects, and how they talked about postcollege careers with their friends.

HR PROFESSIONALS

To interview HR professionals who are responsible for the recruitment of recent graduates for entry-level jobs at TNCs, I followed, with some exceptions, the same company list that I constructed for my interviews with elite business professionals. In my sampling of HR professionals, I tried to cover as many different companies and industries as possible, and I complemented this with my interviews with managers, who told me a great deal about their recruitment processes. I also tried to cover both junior and senior HR professionals to gauge their different perspectives as well as to inquire about historical trends in hiring.

I interviewed thirteen HR professionals who are responsible for the recruitment of recent graduates for entry-level jobs at transnational corporations.[5] My interviews lasted fifty-eight minutes on average, ranging from thirty-one to eighty-four minutes. My questions revolved around their practices and experiences of hiring, such as how the overall hiring process unfolds, how they target potential employees, what a desirable and undesirable white-collar candidate looked like, why and how they identified whether a job applicant fits a vacancy, and how they think job applicants navigate recruitment processes.

My questions to revenue-generating managers who engaged in hiring at TNCs revolved around their own experiences of hiring, and included a hypothetical question: What advice would you give to your nephew or niece, a high schooler now, who told you that they want to end up like you, working in such a prestigious company as a manager?

SUPPLEMENTAL INTERVIEWS

I also conducted some supplemental interviews during my fieldwork. These included an interview with one of the authors of the famous white-collar novels that I mention in the introduction to this book. I also interviewed two Turkish elite business professionals in London and one in Frankfurt. My main motivation in doing these interviews was to assess the differences of quality of working life experience between New Yorkers, and Londoners and residents of Frankfurt. In other words, I wanted to see whether my choice of New York would engender serious problems in generalization regarding the part of the transnational Turkish middle class that is located abroad. While the number of these interviews is too few to be conclusive, they suggest a good deal of overlap in terms of quality of working life experiences, which is the main concern of the book. I also interviewed three professors at an elite public university. These helped me to get to know my senior undergraduates better as well as learn more about the historical trends of highly skilled employment in Turkey, which is mostly comprised of their students.

VIGNETTE TO ASSESS WORK ORIENTATIONS

Adapted from Wrzesniewski et al., "Jobs, Careers, and Callings."

PERSON A

Person A works primarily to earn enough money to support their life outside their job. If Person A was financially secure, they would no longer continue with their current line of work, but would really rather do something else instead. Person A's job is basically a necessity of life, a lot like breathing or sleeping. Person A often wishes the time would pass more quickly at work. Person A greatly anticipates weekends and vacations. If Person A lived their life over again, Person A probably would not go into the same line of work. Person A would not encourage their friends and children to enter the same line of work.

PERSON B

Person B is basically okay with their work. But Person B plans to move on to a better, higher-level job; hence, they are willing to invest their time, energy, and even money to this end. For Person B, the prestige of their job and of the corporation that they work for is important, and Person B has several goals for the future pertaining to the positions they would eventually like to hold. For Person B, being successful is very important. Although sometimes Person B's work seems a waste of time, Person B knows that they must do sufficiently well in this current position to move on. Person B is also eager to get a promotion, which they view as a recognition of their good performance and a sign of their success in competition with their coworkers.

PERSON C

Person C is very pleased that they are in this line of work. Person C feels good about their work because they think it makes the world a better place, and because they enjoy what they do at work. Person C is fine with taking their work home with them and on vacations, too. Because what Person C does for a living is a vital part of who they are, it is one of the first things Person C tells people about themself. Person C's work is one of the most important parts of their life and Person C would be pretty upset if they were forced to stop working. Person C would encourage their friends and children to enter this line of work.

- How much do you think you are like Person A on a scale ranging from "very much like me," "somewhat like me," "a little like me," or "not at all like me"?

  very much like me ☐ somewhat like me ☐ a little like me ☐
  not at all like me ☐

- How much do you think you are like Person B on a scale ranging from "very much like me," "somewhat like me," "a little like me," or "not at all like me"?

  very much like me ☐ somewhat like me ☐ a little like me ☐
  not at all like me ☐

- How much do you think you are like Person C on a scale ranging from "very much like me," "somewhat like me," "a little like me," or "not at all like me"?

  very much like me ☐ somewhat like me ☐ a little like me ☐
  not at all like me ☐

- What do you think of the following quote? "Choose a job you love, and you will never have to work a day in your life."

NOTES

INTRODUCTION

1. In this book, I use the terms transnational corporations (TNCs), multinational companies (MNCs), and multinational enterprises (MNEs) interchangeably. For the nuances between them, see Tim Bartley, "Transnational Corporations and Global Governance," *Annual Review of Sociology* 44, no. 1 (2018): 147–48, https://doi.org/10.1146/annurev-soc-060116-053540.

2. Throughout the book, I use the term "Turkish" to refer to Turkish citizenship, regardless of ethnicity. Although the terms "Turk" and "Turkish" could potentially refer to the nuance between Turkish ethnicity and citizenship, there is no established convention in the English language to signal the difference. In Turkey, this is an important matter of debate in the struggle to launch a more inclusive definition of civic citizenship. For more on this issue, see Ioannis N. Grigoriadis, "Türk or Türkiyeli? The Reform of Turkey's Minority Legislation and the Rediscovery of Ottomanism," *Middle Eastern Studies* 43, no. 3 (2007): 423–38, https://doi.org/10.1080/00263200701246116.

3. Annette Lareau, *Unequal Childhoods: Class, Race, and Family Life*, 2nd ed. (University of California Press, 2011).

4. Indeed, many interviewees were paying rent and were not homeowners. This can be explained by a combination of skyrocketing housing prices in Istanbul and New York City (like other global cities), seeking expensive lifestyles, and their age. See the appendix for detailed

socioeconomic and demographic information of my subjects, including their subjective assessments of their and their parents' class locations by income and by consumption and lifestyle.

5. Kaan Sekban, *Tebrikler Kovuldunuz!* (Okuyan Us Yayınları, 2017).
6. Yüce Zerey, *The Profesyonel* (Doğan Yayıncılık, 2014).
7. Erdem Aksakal, *Mezeleri Güzel: Bir Beyaz Yakalının İtirafları* (Ot Kitap, 2016).
8. Yüce Zerey, *Fabrika Ayarlarına Dön* (Doğan Yayıncılık, 2016).
9. Sarp Mogan, *Beyaz Yalaka: Kariyer İçin Hayat Feda Etme Sanatı* (Okuyan Us Yayınları, 2017).
10. For example, the back flap of *Tebrikler Kovuldunuz!* ends with the following: "*This is the story* of the ones who have to go to work every morning, instead of running towards their dreams . . ." [emphasis added]. The back flap of *The Profesyonel* begins: "The Professional . . . The king of PowerPoint presentations. The queen of Outlook . . . The hazelnut syrup of lattes . . . *This is your story* . . ." [emphasis added].
11. Cihan Tuğal, " 'Resistance Everywhere': The Gezi Revolt in Global Perspective," *New Perspectives on Turkey* 49 (2013): 156–59, https://doi.org/10.1017/S0896634600002077; Cihan Tuğal, "Elusive Revolt: The Contradictory Rise of Middle-Class Politics," *Thesis Eleven* 130, no. 1 (2015): 87–88, https://doi.org/10.1177/0725513615602183.
12. Some observers even consider them part of a transnational capitalist class whose interests overlap with those of the capitalist classes more than the traditional middle class. See Meltem Yilmaz Şener, "Turkish Managers as a Part of the Transnational Capitalist Class," *Journal of World-Systems Research* 13, no. 2 (2008): 119–41; Leslie Sklair, *The Transnational Capitalist Class* (Blackwell, 2001).
13. See Michèle Lamont, "From 'Having' to 'Being': Self-Worth and the Current Crisis of American Society," *British Journal of Sociology* 70, no. 3 (2019): 660–707, https://doi.org/10.1111/1468-4446.12667; Hartmut Rosa, *Resonance: A Sociology of Our Relationship to the World* (Polity, 2019), 24–25.
14. See Alejandro Portes, *Economic Sociology: A Systematic Inquiry* (Princeton University Press, 2010), 83–99.
15. By class formation, I do not refer to the process of the emergence of class as a collective actor seeking its own (material) interests. As will

become clear in the following chapters, I refer to the emergence of a *shared life experience* and a respective *class identity* revolving around it. In this book, I explore primarily the work-related aspects of class formation and its entanglements with globalization.

16. Throughout the book, I use the North-South divide as a theoretically informed shorthand of global inequality, particularly concerning economic development and division of labor. In world-systems parlance, for instance, the North refers to core economies, whereas the South refers to semiperiphery and periphery economies. See Christopher Chase-Dunn and Marilyn Grell-Brisk, "World-System Theory," in *International Relations* (Oxford University Press, 2019), https://doi.org /10.1093/obo/9780199743292-0272. I reflect upon the limitations of using this concept in the conclusion.

17. Stefan Timmermans and Iddo Tavory, "Theory Construction in Qualitative Research: From Grounded Theory to Abductive Analysis," *Sociological Theory* 30, no. 3 (2012): 179, https://doi.org/10.1177/0735275112457914.

18. I used these five interviews mainly for triangulation.

19. Portes, *Economic Sociology*, 83–99.

20. Laura Empson, "Elite Interviewing in Professional Organizations," *Journal of Professions and Organization* 5, no. 1 (2018): 58–69, https://doi.org /10.1093/jpo/jox010; Brooke Harrington, "Studying Elite Professionals in Transnational Settings," in *Professional Networks in Transnational Governance*, ed. Leonard Seabrooke and Lasse Folke Henriksen (Cambridge University Press, 2017), 39–49, https://doi.org/10.1017/9781316855508 .003.

21. Mario Luis Small and Jessica McCrory Calarco, *Qualitative Literacy* (University of California Press, 2022), 18–20, https://doi.org/10.1525 /9780520390676.

22. David Conradson and Alan Latham, "Transnational Urbanism: Attending to Everyday Practices and Mobilities," *Journal of Ethnic and Migration Studies* 31, no. 2 (2005): 227–33, https://doi.org/10.1080/13691830 42000339891.

23. See Rhacel Salazar Parreñas, *Servants of Globalisation: Migration, Women and Domestic Work* (Stanford University Press, 2015); Saskia Sassen, *Globalization and Its Discontents* (New Press, 1998); Sklair, *The Transnational Capitalist Class*.

24. See Donald Tomaskovic-Devey and Dustin Avent-Holt, *Relational Inequalities* (Oxford University Press, 2019), https://doi.org/10.1093/oso/9780190624422.001.0001.

25. Pierre Bourdieu, *Distinction: A Social Critique of the Judgement of Taste* (Harvard University Press, 1984), 479–81.

26. For Mexico, see Sarah Babb, *Managing Mexico: Economists from Nationalism to Neoliberalism* (Princeton University Press, 2001), https://doi.org/10.2307/j.ctv36zrv2; for Poland, see Elizabeth Cullen Dunn, *Privatizing Poland: Baby Food, Big Business, and the Remaking of Labor* (Cornell University Press, 2015), https://doi.org/10.7591/9781501702204; for others, see Rachel Heiman, Carla Freeman, and Mark Liechty, eds., *The Global Middle Classes: Theorizing Through Ethnography* (School for Advanced Research, 2012), https://doi.org/10.1177/0094306114531284u.

27. Laura Empson, *Leading Professionals: Power, Politics, and Prima Donnas* (Oxford University Press, 2017); Lauren A. Rivera, *Pedigree: How Elite Students Get Elite Jobs* (Princeton University Press, 2015); Karen Ho, *Liquidated* (Duke University Press, 2009), https://doi.org/10.1215/9780822391371.

28. Jeffrey J. Sallaz, *Labor, Economy, and Society* (Polity, 2013).

29. See Arne L. Kalleberg, *Good Jobs, Bad Jobs: The Rise of Polarized and Precarious Employment Systems in the United States, 1970s–2000s* (Russell Sage Foundation, 2011).

30. See Jeffrey Guhin and Joseph Klett, "School Beyond Stratification: Internal Goods, Alienation, and an Expanded Sociology of Education," *Theory and Society* 51, no. 3 (2022): 371–98, https://doi.org/10.1007/S11186-022-09472-6; Hartmut Rosa, *Social Acceleration: A New Theory of Modernity* (Columbia University Press, 2013); Rosa, *Resonance*; Hartmut Rosa, *The Uncontrollability of the World* (Polity, 2020); Tad Skotnicki and Kelly Nielsen, "Toward a Theory of Alienation: Futurelessness in Financial Capitalism," *Theory and Society* 50, no. 6 (2021): 837–65, https://doi.org/10.1007/s11186-021-09440-6.

31. For a notable exception, see Michael L. Siciliano, *Creative Control: The Ambivalence of Work in the Culture Industries* (Columbia University Press, 2021).

32. See Karl Marx and Friedrich Engles, "Manifesto of the Communist Party," in *The Marx-Engels Reader*, 2nd ed., ed. Robert C. Tucker (Norton, 1978 [1888]), 500.

1. TRANSNATIONAL CORPORATIONS AND REMAKING
THE TURKISH MIDDLE CLASS

1. The Big Three refers to McKinsey & Company, Boston Consultancy Group, and Bain & Company; they are the world's three largest management consultancy firms by revenue, and they are among the most prestigious white-collar employers.
2. Jennifer Bair, "Global Commodity Chains: Genealogy and Review," in *Frontiers of Commodity Chain Research*, ed. Jennifer Bair (Stanford University Press, 2009), 1–34, https://doi.org/10.1515/9780804779760-003; Saskia Sassen, *The Mobility of Labor and Capital: A Study in International Investment and Labor Flow* (Cambridge University Press, 1988), https://doi.org/10.1017/CBO9780511598296; Nina Bandelj, *From Communists to Foreign Capitalists* (Princeton University Press, 2008), https://doi.org/10.1515/9781400841257.
3. Tim Bartley, "Transnational Corporations and Global Governance," *Annual Review of Sociology* 44, no. 1 (2018): 147–48, https://doi.org/10.1146/annurev-soc-060116-053540.
4. Arthur S. Alderson and Jason Beckfield, "Power and Position in the World City System," *American Journal of Sociology* 109, no. 4 (2004): 811–51, https://doi.org/10.1086/378930.
5. Şahan Savaş Karataşlı, "The Origins of Turkey's 'Heterodox' Transition to Neoliberalism: The Özal Decade and Beyond," *Journal of World-Systems Research* 21, no. 2 (2015): 387–416, https://doi.org/10.5195/jwsr.2015.8.
6. Ho-fung Hung, "Recent Trends in Global Economic Inequality," *Annual Review of Sociology* 47, no. 1 (2021): 356–58, https://doi.org/10.1146/annurev-soc-090320-105810.
7. Rachel Heiman, Carla Freeman, and Mark Liechty, eds., *The Global Middle Classes: Theorizing Through Ethnography* (School for Advanced Research, 2012), https://doi.org/10.1177/0094306114531284u.
8. Lars Meier and Hellmuth Lange, eds., *The New Middle Classes: Globalizing Lifestyles, Consumerism and Environmental Concern* (Springer, 2009).
9. William I. Robinson, *A Theory of Global Capitalism: Production, Class, and State in a Transnational World* (Johns Hopkins University Press, 2004), 31.

10. Diane E. Davis, "The Sociospatial Reconfiguration of Middle Classes and Their Impact on Politics and Development in the Global South: Preliminary Ideas for Future Research," *Political Power and Social Theory* 21 (2010): 243, https://doi.org/10.1108/S0198-8719(2010)0000021014.

11. Louise Walker, *Waking from the Dream: Mexico's Middle Classes After 1968* (Stanford University Press, 2013), 166.

12. Lawrence P. King and Iván Szelényi, *Theories of the New Class: Intellectuals and Power* (University of Minnesota Press, 2004), xxxi.

13. Caglar Keyder, ed., *Istanbul: Between the Global and the Local* (Rowman & Littlefield, 1999), 14–15; Hayri Kozanoğlu, *Yuppieler, Prensler ve Bizim Kuşak* (İletişim, 1993), 57.

14. Davis, "The Sociospatial Reconfiguration of Middle Classes," 246.

15. "Transnational upper middle class" sounds wordy because, in non-Western contexts like Turkey, the term "transnational" typically implies some privilege. Besides, I contend that an upper middle class should always be considered part of the middle class. As will be evident in the following pages, thinking of elite workers as middle class and not upper class is imperative for a better understanding of white-collar blues (although it may be the opposite for C-level executives).

16. For an excellent account of the middle class-democracy nexus, see Celso M. Villegas, "The Middle Class as a Culture Structure: Rethinking Middle-Class Formation and Democracy Through the Civil Sphere," *American Journal of Cultural Sociology* 7, no. 2 (2019): 135–73, https://doi .org/10.1057/s41290-018-0061-2. For an account of the limits of using middle-class language in African contexts, see Dieter Neubert and Florian Stoll, "The Narrative of 'the African Middle Class' and Its Conceptual Limitations," in *Middle Classes in Africa: Changing Lives and Conceptual Challenges*, ed. Lena Kroeker, David O'Kane, and Tabea Scharrer (Palgrave Macmillan, 2018), 57–79, https://doi.org/10.1007/978-3-319-62148-7_3.

17. Immanuel Wallerstein, "Class-Formation in the Capitalist World-Economy," *Politics & Society* 5, no. 3 (1975): 368–69, https://doi.org /10.1177/003232927500500304.

18. See Georg Simmel, "The Triad," in *The Sociology of Georg Simmel*, ed. Kurt H. Wolff (Free Press, 1950), 145–77.

19. Karl Marx and Friedrich Engles, "Manifesto of the Communist Party," in *The Marx-Engels Reader*, 2nd ed., ed. Robert C. Tucker (Norton, 1978 [1888]), 500.

20. Erik Olin Wright, "The Comparative Project on Class Structure and Class Consciousness: An Overview," *Acta Sociologica* 32, no. 1 (1989): 5.

21. See Harry Braverman, *Labor and Monopoly Capital: The Degradation of Work in the Twentieth Century* (Monthly Review Press, 1974), 281.

22. Wright C. Mills, *White Collar: The American Middle Classes* (Oxford University Press, 1956), 63–65.

23. While these three dominate the research on middle classes, there are also other approaches. Most notable is the neo-Durkheimian approach of micro classes, which argues that occupations are more meaningful categories than "big classes." For more details on the micro-class approach, see Kim A. Weeden and David B. Grusky, "The Case for a New Class Map," *American Journal of Sociology* 111, no. 1 (2005): 141–212, https://doi.org/10.1086/428815. For the Durkheimian roots of this approach, see David Grusky, "Foundations of a Neo-Durkheimian Class Analysis," in *Approaches to Class Analysis*, ed. Erik Olin Wright (Cambridge University Press, 2005), 51–81, https://doi.org/10.1017/CBO9780511488900.004. While having solid merits of better mapping micro classes to political attitudes and lifestyle practices, I think this approach moves us too far away from the middle class and its central problem of ambiguity, which is key to my analysis of white-collar blues and alienation from good jobs.

24. See John Ehrenreich and Barbara Ehrenreich, "The Professional-Managerial Class," in *Between Labor and Capital*, ed. Pat Walker (South End Press, 1979), 5–45; Nicos Poulantzas, *Classes in Contemporary Capitalism* (New Left Books, 1975), https://doi.org/10.2307/2063170; King and Szelényi, *Theories of the New Class*.

25. Erik Olin Wright, *Class Structure and Income Determination* (Academic Press, 1979).

26. Ehrenreich and Ehrenreich, "The Professional-Managerial Class."

27. Loïc J. D. Wacquant, "Making Class: The Middle Class(es) in Social Theory and Social Structure," in *Bringing Class Back In: Contemporary and Historical Perspectives*, ed. Scott G. McNall, Rhonda F. Levine, and Rick Fantasia (Westview, 1991), 46.

28. See Anthony Giddens, "Class Structuration and Class Consciousness," in *Classes, Power, and Conflict: Classical and Contemporary Debates*, ed. Anthony Giddens and David Held (Macmillan Education UK, 1982), 157–74; John H. Goldthorpe, "On the Service Class, Its Formation and

Future," in *Social Class and Division of Labor*, ed. Anthony Giddens and Gavin Mackenzie (Cambridge University Press, 1982), 162–85.

29. See Goldthorpe, "On the Service Class, Its Formation and Future"; Robert Erikson and John H. Goldthorpe, *The Constant Flux: A Study of Class Mobility in Industrial Societies* (Oxford University Press, 1992).

30. See Wacquant, "Making Class," 50; Erik Olin Wright, "Class Analysis," in *Class Counts* (Cambridge University Press, 2000), 27–34, https://doi.org/10.1017/cbo9780511488917.

31. See Wacquant, "Making Class," 51.

32. See E. P. Thompson, *The Making of the English Working Class* (Pantheon, 1963).

33. Wacquant, "Making Class," 52.

34. See Pierre Bourdieu, "Forms of Capital," in *Handbook of Theory and Research for the Sociology of Education*, ed. J. G. Richardson (Greenwood, 1986), 241–58.

35. See Pierre Bourdieu, *Distinction: A Social Critique of the Judgement of Taste* (Harvard University Press, 1984), 114.

36. See Bourdieu, *Distinction*, 128–29, 140.

37. See Bourdieu, *Distinction*, 479–81.

38. See Michèle Lamont, *Money, Morals, and Manners: The Culture of the French and American Upper-Middle Class* (University of Chicago Press, 1992).

39. See Lauren A. Rivera, *Pedigree: How Elite Students Get Elite Jobs* (Princeton University Press, 2015).

40. Annette Lareau, *Unequal Childhoods: Class, Race, and Family Life*, 2nd ed. (University of California Press, 2011).

41. In their defense, though, the theories of new middle class mostly flourished before globalization took off in the 1980s and 1990s.

42. See Robinson, *A Theory of Global Capitalism*, 2, 12–13.

43. See Bandelj, *From Communists to Foreign Capitalists*; Sassen, *The Mobility of Labor and Capital*.

44. William K. Carroll, *The Making of a Transnational Capitalist Class: Corporate Power in the Twenty-First Century* (Zed, 2010); Leslie Sklair, *The Transnational Capitalist Class* (Blackwell, 2001).

45. William I. Robinson, "Social Theory and Globalisation: The Rise of a Transnational State," *Theory and Society* 30, no. 2 (2001): 157–200.

46. See Kevan Harris, "Unraveling the Middle Classes in Postrevolutionary Iran," *Political Power and Social Theory* 37 (2020): 105, https://doi.org/10.1108/S0198-871920200000037006.
47. See Walker, *Waking from the Dream*, 6.
48. See William I. Robinson, "Global Capitalism Theory and the Emergence of Transnational Elites," *Critical Sociology* 38, no. 3 (2012): 354, https://doi.org/10.1177/0896920511411592.
49. See Davis, "The Sociospatial Reconfiguration of Middle Classes," 253–54.
50. See Shana Cohen, *Searching for a Different Future: The Rise of a Global Middle Class in Morocco* (Duke University Press, 2004).
51. For the Egyptian example, see Anouk de Koning, "Introduction," in *Global Dreams: Space, Class, and Gender in Middle-Class Cairo* (American University in Cairo Press, 2009), xv–xxxvi. For the Indian example, see Irani Lilly, *Chasing Innovation: Making Entrepreneurial Citizens in Modern India* (Princeton University Press, 2019); Smitha Radhakrishnan, *Appropriately Indian: Gender and Culture in a New Transnational Class* (Duke University Press, 2011).
52. See Stephan Haggard and Robert R. Kaufman, *Development, Democracy, and Welfare States* (Princeton University Press, 2009), https://doi.org/10.1515/9780691214153.
53. See Sarah Babb and Alexander Kentikelenis, "Markets Everywhere: The Washington Consensus and the Sociology of Global Institutional Change," *Annual Review of Sociology* 47, no. 1 (2021): 522, https://doi.org/10.1146/annurev-soc-090220-025543.
54. See Robinson, "Social Theory and Globalisation," 179.
55. Robinson, "Global Capitalism Theory and the Emergence of Transnational Elites," 355; Heiman, Freeman, and Liechty, *The Global Middle Classes*, 14.
56. See Saskia Sassen, *A Sociology of Globalization* (Norton, 2006), 173–78.
57. See Sassen, *The Mobility of Labor and Capital*.
58. See Saskia Sassen, *The Global City: New York, London, Tokyo* (Princeton University Press, 1991).
59. See Keyder, *Istanbul*.
60. Robinson, *A Theory of Global Capitalism*, 31.
61. See Radhakrishnan, *Appropriately Indian*.
62. See Lilly, *Chasing Innovation*.

63. See de Koning, "Introduction."
64. A. Ricardo López and Barbara Weinstein, eds., *The Making of the Middle Class: Toward a Transnational History* (Duke University Press, 2012), 18–19, https://doi.org/10.1080/03071022.2013.807637.
65. See Meier and Lange, *The New Middle Classes.*
66. Fiona Devine and Mike Savage, "The Cultural Turn, Sociology and Class Analysis," in *Rethinking Class: Culture, Identities and Lifestyle* (Bloomsbury, 2005), 1–23.
67. Davis, "The Sociospatial Reconfiguration of Middle Classes," 246.
68. Steve Derne, "Globalization and the Making of a Transnational Middle Class: Implications for Class Analysis," in *Critical Globalization Studies*, ed. Richard P. Appelbaum and William I. Robinson (Routledge, 2005), 177–79.
69. See Steve Derne, "Making the Transnational Middle Class in India," in *Globalization on the Ground: Media and the Transformation of Culture, Class, and Gender in India* (Sage, 2008), 90–126, https://doi.org/10.4135/9788132100386.n3.
70. See Derne, "Globalization and the Making of a Transnational Middle Class," 180.
71. Irmak Karademir Hazır, "Boundaries of Middle-Class Identities in Turkey," *Sociological Review* 62, no. 4 (November 1, 2014): 675–97, https://doi.org/10.1111/1467-954X.12114; Meltem Yilmaz Şener, "Turkish Managers as a Part of the Transnational Capitalist Class," *Journal of World-Systems Research* 13, no. 2 (2008): 119–41.
72. Sencer Ayata, "The New Middle Class and the Joys of Suburbia," in *Fragments of Culture: The Everyday of Modern Turkey*, ed. Deniz Kandiyoti and Ayşe Saktanber (I. B. Tauris, 2002), 25–42; Çağlar Keyder, "Globalization and Social Exclusion in Istanbul," *International Journal of Urban and Regional Research* 29, no. 1 (2005), https://doi.org/10.1111/j.1468-2427.2005.00574.x.
73. T. Deniz Erkmen, "Houses on Wheels: National Attachment, Belonging, and Cosmopolitanism in Narratives of Transnational Professionals," *Studies in Ethnicity and Nationalism* 15, no. 1 (2015): 26–47, https://doi.org/10.1111/sena.12122.
74. Sklair, *The Transnational Capitalist Class.*
75. For example, the exorbitant costs of living in the global cities, especially for housing, means that even the high income levels of business professionals and managers do not necessarily translate into wealthy,

upper-class lives. Many of them, particularly single young adults, cannot afford homeownership in the cities where they live, a hitherto solid marker of being middle-class. See also Robinson, *A Theory of Global Capitalism*, 36. Similarly, thinking of these business professionals as part of the capitalist class prematurely resolves the inherent ambiguity of middle classes toward one side of the capital-labor conflict, whereas the participation of new middle classes in the recent global protest wave nudges us, at the very least, to keep considering and investigating the political ambiguity of the middle classes. See Göran Therborn, "Class in the 21st Century," *New Left Review*, no. 78 (November–December 2012): 5–29. Note that, a vulgar Marxist approach that overextends the boundaries of the working class to include every nonpropertied and working individual would also fail us here. See Cihan Tuğal, "Elusive Revolt: The Contradictory Rise of Middle-Class Politics," *Thesis Eleven* 130, no. 1 (2015): 82, https://doi .org/10.1177/0725513615602183.

76. See Carroll, *The Making of a Transnational Capitalist Class*; Joshua Murray, "Interlock Globally, Act Domestically: Corporate Political Unity in the 21st Century," *American Journal of Sociology* 122, no. 6 (2017): 1617–63, https://doi.org/10.1086/691603.

77. See David Conradson and Alan Latham, "Transnational Urbanism: Attending to Everyday Practices and Mobilities," *Journal of Ethnic and Migration Studies* 31, no. 2 (2005): 227–33, https://doi.org/10.108 0/1369183042000339891; Adrian Favell, *Eurostars and Eurocities: Free Movement and Mobility in an Integrating Europe* (Blackwell, 2008), 259, https://doi.org/10.1002/9780470712818.

78. See Sassen, *A Sociology of Globalization*, 178.

79. For example, see Hung, "Recent Trends in Global Economic Inequality"; cf. Hagen Koo, "The Global Middle Class: How Is It Made, What Does It Represent?," *Globalizations* 13, no. 4 (2016): 440–53, https://doi .org/10.1080/14747731.2016.1143617.

80. See Radhakrishnan, *Appropriately Indian*, 16–19.

81. See Derne, "Making the Transnational Middle Class in India"; Derne, "Globalization and the Making of a Transnational Middle Class."

82. Ehrenreich and Ehrenreich, "The Professional-Managerial Class."

83. Poulantzas, *Classes in Contemporary Capitalism*.

84. See Radhakrishnan, *Appropriately Indian*; cf. Sassen, *A Sociology of Globalization*, 164–65.

85. See Rakesh Khurana, *From Higher Aims to Hired Hands: The Social Transformation of American Business Schools and the Unfulfilled Promise of Management as a Profession* (Princeton University Press, 2007).

86. See Steven Peter Vallas, "Work and Employment," in *The Wiley-Blackwell Companion to Sociology*, ed. George Ritzer and William Yagatich (Wiley, 2012), 418–43, https://doi.org/10.1002/9781444347388.ch23.

87. For another aspect of the transnationalization of white-collar labor via "virtual migration," see Aneesh Aneesh, *Virtual Migration: The Programming of Globalization* (Duke University Press, 2006).

88. See Donald Tomaskovic-Devey and Dustin Avent-Holt, *Relational Inequalities* (Oxford University Press, 2019), https://doi.org/10.1093/oso/9780190624422.001.0001.

89. See Donald Tomaskovic-Devey et al., "Rising Between-Workplace Inequalities in High-Income Countries," *Proceedings of the National Academy of Sciences of the United States of America* 117, no. 17 (2020): 9277–83, https://doi.org/10.1073/PNAS.1918249117/SUPPL_FILE/PNAS.1918249117.SAPP.PDF.

90. See Jonathan V. Beaverstock, "Transnational Elites in the City: British Highly-Skilled Inter-Company Transferees in New York City's Financial District," *Journal of Ethnic and Migration Studies* 31, no. 2 (2005): 245–68, https://doi.org/10.1080/1369183042000339918; Ödül Bozkurt and Alexander T. Mohr, "Forms of Cross-Border Mobility and Social Capital in Multinational Enterprises," *Human Resource Management Journal* 21, no. 2 (2011): 138–55, https://doi.org/10.1111/J.1748-8583.2010.00147.X.

91. See Swethaa S. Ballakrishnen, *Accidental Feminism: Gender Parity and Selective Mobility Among India's Professional Elite* (Princeton University Press, 2021).

92. See Paul Osterman, "In Search of the High Road: Meaning and Evidence," *ILR Review* 71, no. 1 (2018): 3–34, https://doi.org/10.1177/0019793917738757.

93. See May Al-Dabbagh, "Serial Migrant Mothers and Permanent Temporariness in Dubai," *Migration Studies*, 2022, https://doi.org/10.1093/MIGRATION/MNAC020; Sam Scott, "The Social Morphology of Skilled Migration: The Case of the British Middle Class in Paris," *Journal of*

Ethnic and Migration Studies 32, no. 7 (2006): 1105–29, https://doi.org /10.1080/13691830600821802.

94. See Karataşlı, "The Origins of Turkey's 'Heterodox' Transition to Neoliberalism," 390.

95. Karl Polanyi, The Great Transformation: The Political and Economic Origins of Our Time (Beacon, 2001 [1944]).

96. See Davis, "The Sociospatial Reconfiguration of Middle Classes"; Harris, "Unraveling the Middle Classes in Postrevolutionary Iran."

97. See Faruk Birtek, "The Rise and Fall of Etatism in Turkey, 1932–1950: The Uncertain Road in the Restructuring of a Semiperipheral Economy," Review (Fernand Braudel Center) 8, no. 3 (1985): 407–38.

98. See Yunus Kaya, "Proletarianization with Polarization: Industrialization, Globalization, and Social Class in Turkey, 1980–2005," Research in Social Stratification and Mobility 26, no. 2 (2008): 165, https://doi.org /10.1016/j.rssm.2007.11.003.

99. See Caglar Keyder, State and Class in Turkey: A Study in Capitalist Development (Verso, 1987).

100. See Miguel A. Centeno and Joseph N. Cohen, "The Arc of Neoliberalism," Annual Review of Sociology 38, no. 1 (2012): 326, https://doi.org /10.1146/annurev-soc-081309-150235.

101. See Karataşlı, "The Origins of Turkey's 'Heterodox' Transition to Neoliberalism."

102. See Yeşim Arat and Şevket Pamuk, "Uneven Economic Development and Domestic Politics," in Turkey Between Democracy and Authoritarianism (Cambridge University Press, 2019), 136–37, https://doi.org/10.1017 /9781139022385.006.

103. See Fikret Şenses, "Structural Adjustment Policies and Employment in Turkey," New Perspectives on Turkey 15 (July 21, 1996): 65–93, https:// doi.org/10.1017/S0896634600002491.

104. See Keyder, Istanbul, 20; Ziya Öniş, "The Dynamics of Export-Oriented Growth in a Second Generation NIC: Perspectives on the Turkish Case, 1980–1990," New Perspectives on Turkey 9 (1993): 76, https://doi .org/10.1017/s0896634600002223.

105. See Şevket Pamuk, Uneven Centuries: Economic Development of Turkey Since 1820 (Princeton University Press, 2018), 287, https://doi.org/10.23943 /princeton/9780691166377.001.0001.

106. See Ziya Öniş, "Liberalization, Transnational Corporations and Foreign Direct Investment in Turkey: The Experience of the 1980s," in *Recent Industrialization Experience of Turkey in a Global Context*, ed. Fikret Şenses (Greenwood, 1994), 108.

107. See Nezih Neyzi, "The Middle Classes in Turkey," in *Social Change and Politics in Turkey: A Structural-Historical Analysis*, ed. Kemal Karpat (Brill, 1973), 123–28.

108. See Harris, "Unraveling the Middle Classes in Postrevolutionary Iran," 119–20.

109. Neyzi, "The Middle Classes in Turkey," 131.

110. See Kemal H. Karpat, ed., *Social Change and Politics in Turkey: A Structural-Historical Analysis* (Brill, 1973), 57–59.

111. Nilüfer Göle, *Mühendisler ve İdeoloji Öncü Devrimcilerden Yenilikçi Seçkinlere* (Metis Yayınları, 1986), 114–15.

112. Neyzi, "The Middle Classes in Turkey," 131.

113. See Ziya Öniş, "International Context, Income Distribution and State Power in Late Industrialization: Turkey and South Korea in Comparative Perspective," *New Perspectives on Turkey* 13 (1995): 45, https://doi.org/10.1017/s089663460000234x.

114. The most prominent examples include Morocco, India, and Mexico. See Walker, *Waking from the Dream*; Cohen, *Searching for a Different Future*; Lilly, *Chasing Innovation*; Radhakrishnan, *Appropriately Indian*.

115. See Kaya, "Proletarianization with Polarization," 172.

116. See Keyder, *Istanbul*, 19.

117. Despite the discouraging strict capital controls, a few foreign-owned firms did partner with the Turkish companies and state-owned enterprises, mostly to import the technological know-how, essential to import substitution industrialization (ISI). See Geoffrey Jones, "Learning to Live with Governments: Unilever in India and Turkey, 1950–80," in *Entrepreneurship and Multinationals: Global Business and the Making of the Modern World* (Edward Elgar, 2013), 165–89; Şevket Pamuk, "Uneven Centuries: Turkey's Experience with Economic Development Since 1820," *Economic History Review* 72, no. 4 (2019): 1145, https://doi.org/10.1111/ehr.12938; Asli M. Colpan and Geoffrey Jones, "Business Groups, Entrepreneurship and the Growth of the Koç Group in Turkey," *Business History* 58, no. 1 (2016): 69–88, https://doi.org/10.1080/00076791.2015.1044521.

118. See Jones, "Learning to Live with Governments," 187; Şener, "Turkish Managers as a Part of the Transnational Capitalist Class," 125.

119. See United Nations Conference on Trade and Development, "World Investment Report 1999: Foreign Direct Investment and the Challenge of Development," United Nations Conference on Trade and Development (UNCTAD) World Investment Report (WIR) (United Nations, 1999), 409, https://doi.org/10.18356/8e79f24c-en.

120. See OECD, "Employment in Foreign Affiliates," in *OECD Factbook 2010: Economic, Environmental and Social Statistics* (OECD Publishing, 2010), 83–99, https://doi.org/10.1787/factbook-2010-29-en.

121. See Asu Aksoy, *Küreselleşme ve İstanbul'da Istihdam* (Friedrich-Ebert Stiftung, 1996), 33, as cited in Keyder, *Istanbul*, 19.

122. See Ayşe Öncü and Deniz Gökçe, "Macro-Politics of De-Regulation and Micro-Politics of Banks," in *Strong State and Economic Interest Groups*, ed. Metin Heper (De Gruyter, 1991), 112, https://doi.org/10.1515/9783110859966.99.

123. See The Banks Association of Türkiye, "24.12.2022 Tarihi İtibarıyla Gruplar Bazında, Banka ve Bankaların Şube Sayıları," December 12, 2024, https://www.tbb.org.tr/modules/banka-bilgileri/banka_sube_bilgileri.asp.

124. The Banks Association of Türkiye, "Banking Sector in Turkey 1960–2020," June 2021, https://www.tbb.org.tr/en/Content/Upload/Dokuman/1188/Banking_Sector_In_Turkey_1960-2020.pdf.

125. The Big Four refers to the four largest accounting and professional services networks in the world: Deloitte, Ernst & Young, KPMG, and PricewaterhouseCoopers.

126. In addition to transnational corporations (TNCs), market liberalization in general and increasing foreign direct investment (FDI) in particular also engendered some ascending Turkish professional service firms, such as elite Turkish corporate law firms that serve international clientele, which, while rarer, share the reputation of prestigious TNCs. For the Indian case, see Ballakrishnen, *Accidental Feminism*.

127. See United Nations Conference on Trade and Development, "World Investment Report 1994: Transnational Corporations, Employment and the Workplace" (United Nations, 1994), 197–98.

128. See Henry J. Rutz and Erol M. Balkan, "Globalization, Middle-Class Formation, and 'Quality' Education: Hyper-Competition in Istanbul,

Turkey," *International Journal of Diversity in Organisations, Communities and Nations* 3, no. 1 (2003): 1–6, https://doi.org/10.18848/1447-9532/CGP/v03i01.

129. See Ahmet Öncü and Erol Balkan, "Nouveaux Riches of the City of Minarets and Skyscrapers: Neoliberalism and the Reproduction of the Islamic Middle Class in İstanbul," *Research and Policy on Turkey* 1, no. 1 (2016): 34, https://doi.org/10.1080/23760818.2015.1099780.

130. See Deniz Kandiyoti and Ayşe Saktanber, eds., *Fragments of Culture: The Everyday of Modern Turkey* (I. B. Tauris, 2002), 5.

131. See Hazır, "Boundaries of Middle-Class Identities in Turkey."

132. Cem Emrence, "After Neo-Liberal Globalization: The Great Transformation of Turkey," *Comparative Sociology* 7, no. 1 (2008): 54–55, https://doi.org/10.1163/156913308X260466.

133. See Keyder, "Globalization and Social Exclusion in Istanbul," 124.

134. Emrence, "After Neo-Liberal Globalization," 54.

135. See Şener, "Turkish Managers as a Part of the Transnational Capitalist Class"; Z. Umut Türem, "Engineering Competition and Competitive Subjectivities: 'Self' and Political Economy in Neoliberal Turkey," in *The Making of Neoliberal Turkey*, ed. Cenk Özbay et al. (Routledge, 2016), 33–52, https://doi.org/10.4324/9781315562766-10.

136. Kozanoğlu, *Yuppieler, Prensler ve Bizim Kuşak*, 76. Emphasis added.

137. Tuğal, "Elusive Revolt," 83.

138. See Göle, *Mühendisler ve İdeoloji Öncü Devrimcilerden Yenilikçi Seçkinlere*.

139. Ahmet Haşim Köse and Ahmet Öncü, "A Class Analysis of the Professional and Political Ideologies of Engineers in Turkey," in *The Ravages of Neo-Liberalism: Economy, Society, and Gender in Turkey*, ed. Nesecan Balkan and Sungur Savran (Nova Science, 2002), 146.

140. See Kozanoğlu, *Yuppieler, Prensler ve Bizim Kuşak*, 41.

141. See Henry J. Rutz and Erol M. Balkan, *Reproducing Class: Education, Neoliberalism, and the Rise of the New Middle Class in Istanbul* (Berghahn, 2009), 43.

142. See Kandiyoti and Saktanber, *Fragments of Culture*, 9.

143. See Wendy Nelson Espeland and Michael Sauder, *Engines of Anxiety: Academic Rankings, Reputation, and Accountability* (Russell Sage Foundation, 2016).

144. See Lauren A. Rivera, "Hiring as Cultural Matching: The Case of Elite Professional Service Firms," *American Sociological Review* 77, no. 6 (2012): 999–1022, https://doi.org/10.1177/0003122412463213.

145. See Julian Go and Monika Krause, "Fielding Transnationalism: An Introduction," *Sociological Review Monographs* 30 (2016): 9, https://doi .org/10.1111/2059-7932.12000. For an example of how the globalization of the field of art gave way to "the new types of 'global capital,'" see Larissa Buchholz, "What Is a Global Field? Theorizing Fields Beyond the Nation-State," *Sociological Review Monographs* 60, no. 2016 (2016): 47, https://doi.org/10.1111/2059-7932.12001.

146. Hiroki Igarashi and Hiro Saito, "Cosmopolitanism as Cultural Capital: Exploring the Intersection of Globalization, Education and Stratification," *Cultural Sociology* 8, no. 3 (2014): 224, https://doi.org /10.1177/1749975514523935.

147. See Annick Prieur and Mike Savage, "Emerging Forms of Cultural Capital," *European Societies* 15, no. 2 (2013): 246–67, https://doi.org/10.1080 /14616696.2012.748930.

148. See D. Weenink, "Cosmopolitanism as a Form of Capital: Parents Preparing Their Children for a Globalizing World," *Sociology* 42, no. 6 (2008): 1089–1106, https://doi.org/10.1177/0038038508096935.

149. Stephanie Lee Mudge, "What Is Neo-Liberalism?," *Socio-Economic Review* 6, no. 4 (2008): 704, https://doi.org/10.1093/ser/mwn016.

150. For the limits of the cosmopolitan attitudes of Turkish elite business professionals and managers, particularly when it comes to Turkey's inherent ethnic issues, see Deniz İlhan, "Turkish Transnational Business Professionals in Istanbul: Globalization, Cosmopolitanism and the Emerging Elite" (master's thesis, Bogazici University, 2010).

151. T. Deniz Erkmen, "Stepping into the Global: Turkish Professionals, Employment in Transnational Corporations, and Aspiration to Transnational Forms of Cultural Capital," *Current Sociology* 66, no. 3 (2016): 421, https://doi.org/10.1177/0011392116653236.

152. See Zeynep Yanaşmayan, "Does Education 'Trump' Nationality? Boundary-Drawing Practices Among Highly Educated Migrants from Turkey," *Ethnic and Racial Studies* 39, no. 11 (2016): 2041–59, https:// doi.org/10.1080/01419870.2015.1131315.

153. See Elif Öznur Acar, "Türkiye'den OECD Ülkelerine Nitelikli İşgücü Göçü: Bir Panel Veri Analizi," *Uluslararası Ekonomi ve Yenilik Dergisi* 3, no. 1 (2017): 2, https://doi.org/10.20979/ueyd.266025.

154. See OECD, "How Do OECD Countries Compare in Their Attractiveness for Talented Migrants?," *Migration Policy Debates*, 2019, https://www.oecd.org/migration/mig/migration-policy-debates-19.pdf.

155. See Özlem Altan-Olcay and Evren Balta, *The American Passport in Turkey: National Citizenship in the Age of Transnationalism* (University of Pennsylvania Press, 2020), https://doi.org/10.9783/9780812297065.

2. BECOMING ELITE WORKERS

1. See Daniel Bertaux and Paul Richard Thompson, "Introduction," in *Pathways to Social Class: A Qualitative Approach to Social Mobility*, ed. Daniel Bertaux and Paul Richard Thompson (Clarendon, 1997), 1–31.

2. See Samuel Bowles and Herbert Gintis, *Schooling in Capitalist America: Educational Reform and the Contradictions of Economic Life* (Basic Books, 1976).

3. See Erik Olin Wright, "Class Analysis," in *Class Counts* (Cambridge University Press, 2000), 21–23, https://doi.org/10.1017/cbo9780511488917.

4. See Wright, "Class Analysis," 25–26.

5. Paul Willis, *Learning to Labor: How Working Class Kids Get Working Class Jobs* (Cambridge University Press, 2017).

6. Lauren A. Rivera, *Pedigree: How Elite Students Get Elite Jobs* (Princeton University Press, 2015).

7. Lauren A. Rivera, "Hiring as Cultural Matching: The Case of Elite Professional Service Firms," *American Sociological Review* 77, no. 6 (2012): 999, https://doi.org/10.1177/0003122412463213.

8. Lauren A. Rivera, "Go with Your Gut: Emotion and Evaluation in Job Interviews," *American Journal of Sociology* 120, no. 5 (2015): 1339–89, https://doi.org/10.1086/681214.

9. Amy J. Binder, Daniel B. Davis, and Nick Bloom, "Career Funneling: How Elite Students Learn to Define and Desire 'Prestigious' Jobs," *Sociology of Education* 89, no. 1 (2016): 20–39, https://doi.org/10.1177/0038040715610883.

10. See Henry J. Rutz and Erol M. Balkan, *Reproducing Class: Education, Neoliberalism, and the Rise of the New Middle Class in Istanbul* (Berghahn, 2009), 43; Ahmet Öncü and Erol Balkan, "Nouveaux Riches of the City of Minarets and Skyscrapers: Neoliberalism and the Reproduction of

the Islamic Middle Class in İstanbul," *Research and Policy on Turkey* 1, no. 1 (2016): 35, https://doi.org/10.1080/23760818.2015.1099780.

11. See Deniz Kandiyoti and Ayşe Saktanber, eds., *Fragments of Culture: The Everyday of Modern Turkey* (I. B. Tauris, 2002), 2.

12. See Rutz and Balkan, *Reproducing Class*, 47.

13. See Henry J. Rutz and Erol M. Balkan, "Globalization, Middle-Class Formation, and 'Quality' Education: Hyper-Competition in Istanbul, Turkey," *International Journal of Diversity in Organisations, Communities and Nations* 3, no. 1 (2003): 3, https://doi.org/10.18848/1447-9532/CGP/v03i01.

14. See Rutz and Balkan, *Reproducing Class*, 46–50; Fatma Gök, "The Privatization of Education in Turkey," in *The Ravages of Neo-Liberalism: Economy, Society, and Gender in Turkey*, ed. Neşecan Balkan and Sungur Savran (Nova Science, 2002), 93–104.

15. See Kandiyoti and Saktanber, *Fragments of Culture*, 9.

16. Öncü and Balkan, "Nouveaux Riches of the City of Minarets and Sky-scrapers," 34.

17. See Hayri Kozanoğlu, *Yuppieler, Prensler ve Bizim Kuşak* (İletişim, 1993), 76.

18. Unlike the United States, medicine and law degrees in Turkey do not require attendance at professional graduate schools, and they can be attained as college degrees, although with different requirements than other majors.

19. Attending other universities such as Galatasaray, Bilgi, Yıldız Technical, and Özyeğin might still provide a similar trajectory, although the path would be somewhat more difficult to follow.

20. See Kozanoğlu, *Yuppieler, Prensler ve Bizim Kuşak*, 77.

21. Here I use the notion of ideal both in its Weberian sense of an ideal type and in the sense of perfection to highlight the most desirable aspects of white-collar job applicants.

22. See David Farrugia, "Class and the Post-Fordist Work Ethic: Subjects of Passion and Subjects of Achievement in the Work Society," *Sociological Review*, no. 2011 (2019): 1–16, https://doi.org/10.1177/0038026118825234.

23. See David Farrugia, "The Formation of Young Workers: The Cultivation of the Self as a Subject of Value to the Contemporary

Labour Force," *Current Sociology* 67, no. 1 (2019): 47–63, https://doi
.org/10.1177/0011392118793681.

24. See D. Weenink, "Cosmopolitanism as a Form of Capital: Parents Preparing Their Children for a Globalizing World," *Sociology* 42, no. 6 (2008):
1089–1106, https://doi.org/10.1177/0038038508096935; Hiroki Igarashi
and Hiro Saito, "Cosmopolitanism as Cultural Capital: Exploring the
Intersection of Globalization, Education and Stratification," *Cultural Sociology* 8, no. 3 (2014): 222–39, https://doi.org/10.1177/1749975514523935.

25. A striking instance of this is Korean "kirogi families . . . in which the
mothers and children live overseas in English-speaking countries while
the fathers remain in Korea to work." See Hagen Koo, "The Global Middle Class: How Is It Made, What Does It Represent?," *Globalizations* 13,
no. 4 (2016): 448, https://doi.org/10.1080/14747731.2016.1143617.

26. See T. Deniz Erkmen, "Stepping into the Global: Turkish Professionals,
Employment in Transnational Corporations, and Aspiration to Transnational Forms of Cultural Capital," *Current Sociology* 66, no. 3 (2016):
422–24, https://doi.org/10.1177/0011392116653236.

27. It is true that the Erasmus program and the universities' formal criteria provide important opportunities for further equality and upward
mobility. The fact that the universities provide one year of mandatory
English preparation for students who are not proficient in English or
they provide free language courses other than English sets a somewhat
meritocratic ground. As I discussed before with the case of learning
and practicing a foreign language, however, even with these equal-
izing efforts, the students with upper-class and upper-middle-class
upbringing are still in a more advantageous position than those from
the lower classes.

28. See Luc Boltanski and Eve Chiapello, *The New Spirit of Capitalism* (Verso,
2005).

29. See Rivera, *Pedigree*.

30. Amy J. Binder and Andrea R. Abel, "Symbolically Maintained Inequality: How Harvard and Stanford Students Construct Boundaries Among
Elite Universities," *Sociology of Education* 92, no. 1 (2019): 41–58, https://
doi.org/10.1177/0038040718821073.

31. For an elaborate account of this popular label, see Mücahit Bilici,
"Black Turks, White Turks: On the Three Requirements of Turkish

Citizenship," *Insight Turkey* 11, no. 3 (2009): 23–35; Deniz İlhan, "Turkish Transnational Business Professionals in Istanbul: Globalization, Cosmopolitanism and the Emerging Elite" (master's thesis, Bogazici University, 2010), 83–91.

32. Hiring discrimination in Turkey is unfortunately an extremely understudied problem. Examining how various vectors of inequality along the categories of class, gender, ethnicity, and religious orientation intersect with each other is vital to understanding the reproduction of social inequalities in Turkey and requires a much longer discussion. In further iterations of this research, I hope to cover the intersectional dynamics in hiring in more detail.

33. See Rivera, *Pedigree*, 25.

34. Rutz and Balkan, *Reproducing Class*, 46.

3. DISAPPOINTED AND EXHAUSTED

1. Arne L. Kalleberg, *Good Jobs, Bad Jobs: The Rise of Polarized and Precarious Employment Systems in the United States, 1970s–2000s* (Russell Sage Foundation, 2011).

2. Laura Nader, "Up the Anthropologist—Perspectives Gained from Studying Up," in *Reinventing Anthropology*, ed. Dell Hymes (Pantheon, 1972), 284–311.

3. Charles Duhigg, "Wealthy, Successful and Miserable," *New York Times Magazine*, February 21, 2019, https://www.nytimes.com/interactive /2019/02/21/magazine/elite-professionals-jobs-happiness.html.

4. See Stefan Timmermans and Iddo Tavory, "Theory Construction in Qualitative Research: From Grounded Theory to Abductive Analysis," *Sociological Theory* 30, no. 3 (2012): 167–86, https://doi.org/10.1177 /0735275112457914.

5. Michael Burawoy's analyses of worker games, which revealed the importance of agency for manufacturing workers dealing with boredom at work, can be thought of as such an example of exploiting surprising cases. See Michael Burawoy, *The Politics of Production: Factory Regimes Under Capitalism and Socialism* (Verso, 1985); Michael Burawoy, *Manufacturing Consent: Changes in the Labor Process Under Monopoly Capitalism* (University of Chicago Press, 1979). For manual labor made into

chic and meaningful careers, see also Richard E. Ocejo, *Masters of Craft: Old Jobs in the New Urban Economy* (Princeton University Press, 2017).

6. See Paul Osterman, "Introduction to the Special Issue on Job Quality: What Does It Mean and How Might We Think About It?," *ILR Review* 66, no. 4 (2013): 739–52, https://doi.org/10.1177/001979391306600401; Patricia Findlay, Arne L. Kalleberg, and Chris Warhurst, "The Challenge of Job Quality," *Human Relations* 66, no. 4 (2013): 441–51, https://doi.org/10.1177/0018726713481070.

7. See Alan Felstead, Duncan Gallie, and Francis Green, *Unequal Britain at Work* (Oxford University Press, 2015); Francis Green, "Assessing Job Quality in the Affluent Economy," in *Demanding Work: The Paradox of Job Quality in the Affluent Economy* (Princeton University Press, 2007), 1–23; Duncan Gallie, "Production Regimes and the Quality of Employment in Europe," *Annual Review of Sociology* 33, no. 1 (2007): 85–104, https://doi.org/10.1146/annurev.soc.33.040406.131724; Duncan Gallie, ed., *Employment Regimes and the Quality of Work* (Oxford University Press, 2007), https://doi.org/10.1093/acprof:oso/9780199230105.001.0001; Duncan Gallie, ed., *Economic Crisis, Quality of Work, and Social Integration: The European Experience* (Oxford University Press, 2013), https://doi.org/10.1093/acprof:oso/9780199664719.001.0001; Carola Frege and John Godard, "Varieties of Capitalism and Job Quality: The Attainment of Civic Principles at Work in the United States and Germany," *American Sociological Review* 79, no. 5 (2014): 942–65, https://doi.org/10.1177/0003122414548194.

8. See Paul Osterman and Beth Shulman, "Introduction," in *Good Jobs America* (Russell Sage Foundation, 2011), 1–22; David R. Howell and Arne L. Kalleberg, "Declining Job Quality in the United States: Explanations and Evidence," *RSF: The Russell Sage Foundation Journal of the Social Sciences* 5, no. 4 (2019): 1, https://doi.org/10.7758/rsf.2019.5.4.01.

9. See Howell and Kalleberg, "Declining Job Quality in the United States," 5.

10. See Paul Osterman, "In Search of the High Road: Meaning and Evidence," *ILR Review* 71, no. 1 (2018): 5–7, https://doi.org/10.1177/0019793917738757.

11. See Kalleberg, *Good Jobs, Bad Jobs.*

12. See Andrew Brown, Andy Charlwood, and David A. Spencer, "Not All That It Might Seem: Why Job Satisfaction Is Worth Studying Despite It Being

a Poor Summary Measure of Job Quality," *Work, Employment and Society* 26, no. 6 (2012): 1007–18, https://doi.org/10.1177/0950017012461837.

13. See Jeffrey J. Sallaz, "Labor and Capital in the Twenty-First Century: Rereading Braverman Today," *Employee Responsibilities and Rights Journal* 26, no. 4 (2014): 299–311, https://doi.org/10.1007/s10672-014-9251-4.

14. For detailed reviews on alienation, see Peter W. Archibald, "Using Marx's Theory of Alienation Empirically," *Theory and Society* 6, no. 1 (1978): 119–32, https://doi.org/10.1007/BF01566160; Dan S. Chiaburu, Tomas Thundiyil, and Jiexin Wang, "Alienation and Its Correlates: A Meta-Analysis," *European Management Journal* 32, no. 1 (2014): 24–36, https://doi.org/10.1016/j.emj.2013.06.003; Devorah Kalekin-Fishman and Lauren Langman, "Introductory Background," *Current Sociology* 56, no. 4 (2008): 507–16, https://doi.org/10.1177/0011392108090938; Devorah Kalekin-Fishman and Lauren Langman, "Alienation: The Critique That Refuses to Disappear," *Current Sociology* 63, no. 6 (2015): 916–33, https://doi.org/10.1177/0011392115591612.

15. See Melvin Seeman, "On the Meaning of Alienation," *American Sociological Review* 24, no. 6 (1959): 783–91, https://doi.org/10.1126/science.135.3503.554; Melvin Seeman, "Alienation Studies," *Annual Review of Sociology* 1, no. 1 (August 1975): 91–123, https://doi.org/10.1146/annurev.so.01.080175.000515.

16. See Archibald, "Using Marx's Theory of Alienation Empirically."

17. See James E. Twining, "Alienation as a Social Process," *Sociological Quarterly* 21, no. 3 (1980): 417–28, https://doi.org/10.1111/j.1533-8525.1980.tb00622.x.

18. Robert Blauner, *Alienation and Freedom: The Factory Worker and His Industry* (University of Chicago Press, 1964).

19. Harry Braverman, *Labor and Monopoly Capital: The Degradation of Work in the Twentieth Century* (Monthly Review Press, 1974).

20. See Sallaz, "Labor and Capital in the Twenty-First Century"; Steven Peter Vallas, "New Technology, Job Content, and Worker Alienation: A Test of Two Rival Perspectives," *Work and Occupations* 15, no. 2 (May 17, 1988): 148–78, https://doi.org/10.1177/0730888488015002002; Steven Peter Vallas, "White-Collar Proletarians? The Structure of Clerical Work and Levels of Class Consciousness," *Sociological Quarterly* 28, no. 4 (1987): 523–40, https://doi.org/10.1111/j.1533-8525.1987.tb00310.x.

21. Burawoy, *The Politics of Production*; Burawoy, *Manufacturing Consent*.
22. Karl Marx, "Economic and Philosophic Manuscripts of 1844," in *The Marx-Engels Reader*, 2nd ed., ed. Robert C. Tucker (Norton, 1978 [1844]), 74.
23. For an exception, see Jana Costas and Peter Fleming, "Beyond Dis-Identification: A Discursive Approach to Self-Alienation in Contemporary Organizations," *Human Relations* 62, no. 3 (2009): 353–78, https://doi.org/10.1177/0018726708101041. Other noteworthy studies that focus on the white-collar work experience have taken office clerks as their main object of study. See Wright C. Mills, *White Collar: The American Middle Classes* (Oxford University Press, 1956). Mills's audacious work on white-collar workers in the United States illustrates, in what Braverman would later treat in his deskilling thesis, the mechanization of office work and the convergence between office and factory in terms of alienation experience. See Braverman, *Labor and Monopoly Capital*, 203–47.
24. Arlie Russell Hochschild, *The Managed Heart: Commercialization of Human Feeling* (University of California Press, 1979).
25. See Amy S. Wharton, "The Sociology of Emotional Labor," *Annual Review of Sociology* 35, no. 1 (2009): 147–65, https://doi.org/10.1146/annurev-soc-070308-115944.
26. A great contemporary example from cinema is Maren Ade's *Toni Erdmann*, Palme d'Or nominee of 2016, which tells the story of an alienated elite management consultant. Maren Ade, dir., *Toni Erdmann* (Germany-Austria: Komplizen Film, 2016).
27. Michael L. Siciliano, *Creative Control: The Ambivalence of Work in the Culture Industries* (Columbia University Press, 2021).
28. See Siciliano, *Creative Control*, 123–24.
29. For a similar account of alienating labor of ghostwriting, see Michel Anteby and Nicholas Occhiuto, "Stand-In Labor and the Rising Economy of Self," *Social Forces* 98, no. 3 (2019): 1287–1310, https://doi.org/10.1093/sf/soz028.
30. See Mary Blair-Loy and Jerry A. Jacobs, "Globalization, Work Hours, and the Care Deficit Among Stockbrokers," *Gender & Society* 17, no. 2 (2003): 230–49, https://doi.org/10.1177/0891243202250777; Amy S. Wharton and Mary Blair-Loy, "Long Work Hours and Family Life," *Journal of Family Issues* 27, no. 3 (2006): 415–36, https://doi.org/10.1177

/0192513X05282985; Amy S. Wharton and Mary Blair-Loy, "The 'Over-time Culture' in a Global Corporation: A Cross-National Study of Finance Professionals' Interest in Working Part-Time," *Work and Occupations* 29, no. 1 (2002): 32–63, https://doi.org/10.1177/0730888402029001003; Erin L. Kelly and Phyllis Moen, *Overload: How Good Jobs Went Bad and What We Can Do About It* (Princeton University Press, 2020); Phyllis Moen et al., "Time Work by Overworked Professionals," *Work and Occupations* 40, no. 2 (2013): 79–114, https://doi.org/10.1177/0730888413481482; Erin L. Kelly et al., "Changing Work and Work-Family Conflict," *American Sociological Review* 79, no. 3 (2014): 485–516, https://doi.org/10.1177/0003122414531435; Alexandra Michel, "Transcending Socialization," *Administrative Science Quarterly* 56, no. 3 (2011): 325–68, https://doi.org/10.1177/0001839212437519; Alexandra Michel, "Participation and Self-Entrapment: A 12-Year Ethnography of Wall Street Participation Practices' Diffusion and Evolving Consequences," *Sociological Quarterly* 55, no. 3 (2014): 514–36, https://doi.org/10.1111/tsq.12064.

31. Gideon Kunda, *Engineering Culture: Control and Commitment in a High-Tech Corporation*, Rev. ed. (Temple University Press, 2006).
32. Mary Blair-Loy, *Competing Devotions: Career and Family Among Women Executives* (Harvard University Press, 2003).
33. See Scott Schieman, Paul Glavin, and Melissa A. Milkie, "When Work Interferes with Life: Work-Nonwork Interference and the Influence of Work-Related Demands and Resources," *American Sociological Review* 74, no. 6 (2009): 966–88, https://doi.org/10.1177/000312240907400606.
34. See Moen et al., "Time Work by Overworked Professionals."
35. See Wharton and Blair-Loy, "Long Work Hours and Family Life."
36. See Schieman, Glavin, and Milkie, "When Work Interferes with Life."
37. John H. Goldthorpe et al., *The Affluent Worker: Industrial Attitudes and Behaviour* (Cambridge University Press, 1968); John H. Goldthorpe et al., *The Affluent Worker in the Class Structure* (Cambridge University Press, 1969).
38. Daniel Kahneman and Angus Deaton, "High Income Improves Evaluation of Life but Not Emotional Well-Being," *Proceedings of the National Academy of Sciences* 107, no. 38 (2010): 16489–93, https://doi.org/10.1073/pnas.1011492107.

39. Arne L. Kalleberg, "Work Values and Job Rewards: A Theory of Job Satisfaction," *American Sociological Review* 42, no. 1 (1977): 124, https://doi.org/10.2307/2117735.

40. I compiled these statistics based on the surveys my respondents filled out, and I used the surveys to inquire about their subjective class identifications by consumption and lifestyle, among other details. I asked them to consider their and their parents' consumption habits and locate these in a fivefold class map. See the appendix in this book for additional details.

41. See Amy Wrzesniewski et al., "Jobs, Careers, and Callings: People's Relations to Their Work," *Journal of Research in Personality* 31, no. 1 (1997): 24, https://doi.org/10.1006/jrpe.1997.2162.

42. The respondents who were able to recognize Person C's job satisfaction and fulfillment were mostly the people who thought that they were like Person C and that they themselves had a "calling" orientation. These people also had higher job satisfaction compared to others. The minority who did not feel like Person C yet were still able to recognize Person C as a contented worker were also quite certain that they were not like Person C at all.

43. Burawoy, *Manufacturing Consent*.

44. See Braverman, *Labor and Monopoly Capital*, 203–47. For an insightful revisit of the deskilling debate, see Aneesh Aneesh, "Skill Saturation: Rationalization and Post-Industrial Work," *Theory and Society* 30, no. 3 (2001): 363–96.

45. See Arne L. Kalleberg, *The Mismatched Worker* (Norton, 2007).

46. From the Marxian perspective, given humans' productive and creative potential, proletarian jobs that consist of repetitive tasks constitute underemployment for any human being, even those who do not have higher education as we think of it today.

47. Aneesh highlights a distinction even between "[p]rogramming for a definite task" and "programming for an imagined outcome," where the latter provides the computer scientist with more room for play and creativity. Aneesh, "Skill Saturation," 375.

48. For an account of how the "algocratic" governance of global labor processes, especially visible in information technology labor, has a similar effect of robbing workers of autonomy over labor via "skill

saturation," see Aneesh, "Skill Saturation"; Aneesh Aneesh, "Global Labor: Algocratic Modes of Organization," *Sociological Theory* 27, no. 4 (2009): 347–70.

49. After I graduated in 2011 with a degree in industrial engineering, I started working at Procter & Gamble's supply chain department of oral care products in Istanbul, with the title of assistant manager. I had studied the supply chain and its optimization in college, with a specific emphasis on mathematical modeling, so I was excited to learn how complicated the supply chain of oral care products, spanning the whole globe, actually was, a promising intellectual challenge. When I asked my supervisor whether we would be working on mathematical models to optimize the design of these supply chains, he told me that the models were all crafted at the company's headquarters in Geneva, Switzerland, and Cincinnati, Ohio, and that I just needed to click "execute" on a computer, get the results, and make sure that the actual process on the ground was flowing smoothly with respect to that plan. I remember that I was taken aback by this answer because I knew that I had been trained to design and craft these models, not simply execute them.

50. Lauren A. Rivera, *Pedigree: How Elite Students Get Elite Jobs* (Princeton University Press, 2015); Amy J. Binder, Daniel B. Davis, and Nick Bloom, "Career Funneling: How Elite Students Learn to Define and Desire 'Prestigious' Jobs," *Sociology of Education* 89, no. 1 (2016): 20–39, https://doi.org/10.1177/0038040715610883.

51. I personally know at least four such people in my immediate network of friends, and I have heard of others during my fieldwork.

52. Some physics PhD students end up working in Wall Street firms. See Aneesh, "Skill Saturation," 386.

53. Costas and Fleming, "Beyond Dis-Identification."

54. Michel, "Transcending Socialization."

55. Max Horkheimer and Theodor W. Adorno, "The Culture Industry: Enlightenment as Mass Deception," in *Dialectic of Enlightenment: Philosophical Fragments* (Stanford University Press, 2002 [1944]), 94–136.

56. See Jessi Streib, *The Power of the Past: Understanding Cross-Class Marriages* (Oxford University Press, 2015), https://doi.org/10.1093/acprof:oso/9780199364428.001.0001; Christine R. Schwartz, "Trends and

Variation in Assortative Mating: Causes and Consequences," *Annual Review of Sociology* 39, no. 1 (2013): 451–70, https://doi.org/10.1146/annurev-soc-071312-145544.

57. See Ofer Sharone, "Why Do Unemployed Americans Blame Themselves While Israelis Blame the System?," *Social Forces* 91, no. 4 (2013): 1429–50, https://doi.org/10.1093/sf/sot050.

58. The cultural difference between the United States and Turkey, or the way my respondents set Turkish work culture in opposition to "professionalism," can in fact be best understood from a Zelizerian perspective of relational work. Most corporate nonwork activities—such as weekend retreats—can best be understood through this lens: these activities, which are actually a form of economic exchange between the company and its workers, are disguised as a form of kindly caring for the workers by the company, usually through managers' friendly faces.

4. WHITE-COLLAR OPT-OUT

1. In the United States, for instance, the postpandemic Great Resignation has attracted a great deal of attention. Most of that employee turnover consisted of people in low-paid service positions switching to better jobs, often within the same sector. But the shift also laid bare the discontentment with work even among well-to-do, high-income professionals; 11 percent of high-income workers in the United States reported that they quit a job during 2021. See Kim Parker and Juliana Menasce Horowitz, "Majority of Workers Who Quit a Job in 2021 Cite Low Pay, No Opportunities for Advancement, Feeling Disrespected," *Pew Research Center*, March 9, 2022, https://www.pewresearch.org/short-reads/2022/03/09/majority-of-workers-who-quit-a-job-in-2021-cite-low-pay-no-opportunities-for-advancement-feeling-disrespected/.

2. See Juliet Schor, *The Overspent American: Upscaling, Downshifting, and the New Consumer* (Basic Books, 1998); Juliet Schor, *The Overworked American: The Unexpected Decline of Leisure* (Basic Books, 1991).

3. See Mary Blair-Loy, *Competing Devotions: Career and Family Among Women Executives* (Harvard University Press, 2003); Pamela Stone, *Opting Out? Why Women Really Quit Careers and Head Home* (University of California Press, 2007); Pamela Stone and Meg Lovejoy, *Opting Back*

In (University of California Press, 2019), https://doi.org/10.2307/j
.ctvpb3w8p.

4. Erich Fromm, *Escape from Freedom* (Farrar & Rinehart, 1941).
5. For an extensive overview, see Peter W. Hom et al., "One Hundred Years of Employee Turnover Theory and Research," *Journal of Applied Psychology* 102, no. 3 (2017): 530–45, https://doi.org/10.1037/apl0000103.
6. See Karen M. Olsen, Therese E. Sverdrup, and Arne L. Kalleberg, "Turnover and Transferable Skills in a Professional Service Firm," *Journal of Professions and Organization* 6, no. 1 (2019): 2–16, https://doi.org/10.1093/JPO/JOY022.
7. Lisa Belkin, "The Opt-Out Revolution," *New York Times Magazine*, October 26, 2003, https://www.nytimes.com/2003/10/26/magazine/the-opt-out-revolution.html.
8. See Christine Percheski, "Opting Out? Cohort Differences in Professional Women's Employment Rates from 1960 to 2005," *American Sociological Review* 73, no. 3 (2008): 498, https://doi.org/10.1177/000312240807300307.
9. See Percheski, "Opting Out?," 513.
10. See Joni Hersch, "Opting Out Among Women with Elite Education," *Review of Economics of the Household* 11, no. 4 (2013): 469–506, https://doi.org/10.1007/s11150-013-9199-4; Stone, *Opting Out?*
11. See Stone, *Opting Out?*, 66; Hersch, "Opting Out Among Women with Elite Education," 473.
12. Blair-Loy, *Competing Devotions*. See also Katherine Weisshaar, "From Opt Out to Blocked Out: The Challenges for Labor Market Re-Entry After Family-Related Employment Lapses," *American Sociological Review* 83, no. 1 (2018): 34–60, https://doi.org/10.1177/0003122417752355.
13. Stone, *Opting Out?*
14. Stone, *Opting Out?*
15. Stone and Lovejoy, *Opting Back In.*
16. See M. J. Budig and P. England, "The Wage Penalty for Motherhood," *American Sociological Review* 66, no. 2 (2001): 204–25, https://doi.org/10.2307/2657415; Shelley J. Correll, Stephen Benard, and In Paik, "Getting a Job: Is There a Motherhood Penalty?," *American Journal of Sociology* 112, no. 5 (2007): 1297–1338, https://doi.org/10.1086/511799.
17. For an exception, see Elizabeth D. Wilhoit, "Opting Out (Without Kids): Understanding Non-Mothers' Workplace Exit in Popular

Autobiographies," *Gender, Work & Organization* 21, no. 3 (2014): 260–72, https://doi.org/10.1111/gwao.12034.

18. See Erin L. Kelly and Phyllis Moen, *Overload: How Good Jobs Went Bad and What We Can Do about It* (Princeton University Press, 2020), 35–36.

19. See Seymour Spilerman, "Careers, Labor Market Structure, and Socio-economic Achievement," *American Journal of Sociology* 83, no. 3 (1977): 551–93, https://doi.org/10.1086/226595; Harold L. Wilensky, "Orderly Careers and Social Participation: The Impact of Work History on Social Integration in the Middle Mass," *American Sociological Review* 26, no. 4 (1961): 521, https://doi.org/10.2307/2090251.

20. See Valentina Cuzzocrea and Dawn Lyon, "Sociological Conceptualisations of 'Career': A Review and Reorientation," *Sociology Compass* 5, no. 12 (2011): 1031, https://doi.org/10.1111/j.1751-9020.2011.00429.x.

21. See Arne L. Kalleberg and Ted Mouw, "Occupations, Organizations, and Intragenerational Career Mobility," *Annual Review of Sociology* 44, no. 1 (2018): 283–303, https://doi.org/10.1146/annurev-soc-073117-041249; Rachel A. Rosenfeld, "Job Mobility and Career Processes," *Annual Review of Sociology* 18, no. 1 (1992): 39–61, https://doi.org/10.1146/annurev.so.18.080192.000351.

22. See Arne L. Kalleberg, "Precarious Work, Insecure Workers: Employment Relations in Transition," *American Sociological Review* 74, no. 1 (2009): 1–22, https://doi.org/10.1177/000312240907400101; Kalleberg and Mouw, "Occupations, Organizations, and Intragenerational Career Mobility."

23. See David Farrugia, "Class and the Post-Fordist Work Ethic: Subjects of Passion and Subjects of Achievement in the Work Society," *Sociological Review*, no. 2011 (2019): 1–16, https://doi.org/10.1177/0038026118825234; Patricia Findlay, Arne L. Kalleberg, and Chris Warhurst, "The Challenge of Job Quality," *Human Relations* 66, no. 4 (2013): 441–51, https://doi.org/10.1177/0018726713481070; Arne L. Kalleberg, *Good Jobs, Bad Jobs: The Rise of Polarized and Precarious Employment Systems in the United States, 1970s–2000s* (Russell Sage Foundation, 2011); Steven Peter Vallas, "Work and Employment," in *The Wiley-Blackwell Companion to Sociology*, ed. George Ritzer and William Yagatich (Wiley, 2012), 418–43, https://doi.org/10.1002/9781444347388.ch23.

24. See Eileen Appelbaum et al., *Manufacturing Advantage: Why High-Performance Work Systems Pay Off* (Cornell University Press, 2000); Blair-Loy, *Competing Devotions.*

25. See Zygmunt Bauman, *Liquid Modernity* (Polity, 2000); Ulrich Beck, *Risk Society: Towards a New Modernity* (Sage, 1992).

26. Luc Boltanski and Eve Chiapello, *The New Spirit of Capitalism* (Verso, 2005).

27. See Jesse Potter, "The Ghost of the Stable Path: Stories of Work-Life Change at the 'End of Career,' " *Work, Employment and Society* 34, no. 4 (2019): 1–16, https://doi.org/10.1177/0950017019870751.

28. Michael B. Arthur and Denise M. Rousseau, eds., *The Boundaryless Career: A New Employment Principle for a New Organizational Era* (Oxford University Press, 1996); Sherry E. Sullivan and Michael B. Arthur, "The Evolution of the Boundaryless Career Concept: Examining Physical and Psychological Mobility," *Journal of Vocational Behavior* 69, no. 1 (2006): 19–29, https://doi.org/10.1016/j.jvb.2005.09.001; Lisa A. Mainiero and Sherry E. Sullivan, *The Opt-Out Revolt: Why People Are Leaving Companies to Create Kaleidoscope Careers* (Davies-Black, 2006).

29. Cuzzocrea and Lyon, "Sociological Conceptualisations of 'Career.' "

30. Paul Osterman, ed., *Broken Ladders: Managerial Careers in the New Economy* (Oxford University Press, 1996).

31. Arthur and Rousseau, *The Boundaryless Career.*

32. Potter, "The Ghost of the Stable Path."

33. Brian W. Halpin and Vicki Smith, "Employment Management Work: A Case Study and Theoretical Framework," *Work and Occupations* 44, no. 4 (2017): 339–75, https://doi.org/10.1177/0730888417720714; Steven Peter Vallas and Angèle Christin, "Work and Identity in an Era of Precarious Employment: How Workers Respond to 'Personal Branding' Discourse," *Work and Occupations* 45, no. 1 (2018): 3–37, https://doi.org/10.1177/0730888417735662; Steven Peter Vallas and Emily R. Cummins, "Personal Branding and Identity Norms in the Popular Business Press: Enterprise Culture in an Age of Precarity," *Organization Studies* 36, no. 3 (2015): 293–319, https://doi.org/10.1177/0170840614563741; Steven Peter Vallas and Andrea L. Hill, "Reconfiguring Worker Subjectivity: Career Advice Literature and the 'Branding' of the Worker's Self," *Sociological Forum* 33, no. 2 (2018): 287–309, https://doi.org/10.1111/socf.12418.

34. Gianpiero Petriglieri, Jennifer Louise Petriglieri, and Jack Denfeld Wood, "Fast Tracks and Inner Journeys: Crafting Portable Selves for Contemporary Careers," *Administrative Science Quarterly* 63, no. 3 (2018): 479–525, https://doi.org/10.1177/0001839217720930.

35. Douglas T. Hall, Jeffrey Yip, and Kathryn Doiron, "Protean Careers at Work: Self-Direction and Values Orientation in Psychological Success," *Annual Review of Organizational Psychology and Organizational Behavior* 5, no. 1 (2018): 129–56, https://doi.org/10.1146/annurev-orgpsych-032117-104631.

36. Maury Peiperl and Yehuda Baruch, "Back to Square Zero: The Post-Corporate Career," *Organizational Dynamics* 25, no. 4 (1997): 7–22, https://doi.org/10.1016/S0090-2616(97)90033-4.

37. Mainiero and Sullivan, *The Opt-Out Revolt.*

38. See Ingrid Biese, *Opting Out and In: On Women's Careers and New Lifestyles* (Routledge, 2017), 4, https://doi.org/10.4324/9781315637006.

39. See Potter, "The Ghost of the Stable Path."

40. Stephen R. Barley, "Careers, Identities, and Institutions: The Legacy of the Chicago School of Sociology," in *Handbook of Career Theory*, ed. Michael B. Arthur, Douglas T. Hall, and Barbara S. Lawrence (Cambridge University Press, 1989), 53, https://doi.org/10.1017/CBO9780511625459.005.

41. Sherry E. Sullivan and Yehuda Baruch, "Advances in Career Theory and Research: A Critical Review and Agenda for Future Exploration," *Journal of Management* 35, no. 6 (2009): 1543, https://doi.org/10.1177/0149206309350082.

42. See Blair Wheaton and Ian H. Gotlib, "Trajectories and Turning Points over the Life Course: Concepts and Themes," in *Stress and Adversity over the Life Course: Trajectories and Turning Points*, ed. Blair Wheaton and Ian H. Gotlib (Cambridge University Press, 1997), 1–26, https://doi.org/10.1017/CBO9780511527623.001.

43. See Andrew Delano Abbott, "On the Concept of Turning Point," in *Time Matters: On Theory and Method* (University of Chicago Press, 2001), 240–60.

44. See Helen Rose Fuchs Ebaugh, *Becoming an Ex: The Process of Role Exit* (University of Chicago Press, 1988).

45. Blair-Loy, *Competing Devotions*, 142–71.

46. Herminia Ibarra, *Working Identity: Unconventional Strategies for Reinventing Your Career* (Harvard Business School Press, 2003).

47. See Ibarra, *Working Identity*, 17.

48. Ebaugh, *Becoming an Ex.*

49. Ibarra, *Working Identity*, 167.

50. See Cuzzocrea and Lyon, "Sociological Conceptualisations of 'Career,'"
    1032–33.
51. Erik Olin Wright, "The Biography of a Concept: Contradictory Class
    Locations," in *Classes* (Verso, 1985), 19–63.
52. Alejandro Portes, *Economic Sociology: A Systematic Inquiry* (Princeton
    University Press, 2010), 83–99.
53. Nicos Poulantzas, *Classes in Contemporary Capitalism* (New Left Books,
    1975), 278–79, https://doi.org/10.2307/2063170.
54. John H. Goldthorpe, "On the Service Class, Its Formation and Future,"
    in *Social Class and Division of Labor*, ed. Anthony Giddens and Gavin
    Mackenzie (Cambridge University Press, 1982); Robert Erikson and
    John H. Goldthorpe, *The Constant Flux: A Study of Class Mobility in Indus-
    trial Societies* (Oxford University Press, 1992).
55. Cihan Tuğal, "Elusive Revolt: The Contradictory Rise of Middle-Class
    Politics," *Thesis Eleven* 130, no. 1 (2015): 83, https://doi.org/10.1177
    /0725513615602183.
56. Wright C. Mills, *White Collar: The American Middle Classes* (Oxford Uni-
    versity Press, 1956), 70–76.
57. Poulantzas, *Classes in Contemporary Capitalism*, 292.
58. See Pierre Bourdieu, *Distinction: A Social Critique of the Judgement of Taste*
    (Harvard University Press, 1984).
59. Michael Burawoy, *Manufacturing Consent: Changes in the Labor Process
    Under Monopoly Capitalism* (University of Chicago Press, 1979).
60. Ted Robert Gurr, *Why Men Rebel* (Princeton University Press, 1970), 23,
    https://doi.org/10.4324/9781315631073.
61. Gurr, *Why Men Rebel*, 24.
62. See also Jeffrey Guhin and Joseph Klett, "School Beyond Stratification:
    Internal Goods, Alienation, and an Expanded Sociology of Education,"
    Theory and Society 51, no. 3 (2022): 371–98, https://doi.org/10.1007
    /S11186-022-09472-6.
63. Tad Skotnicki and Kelly Nielsen, "Toward a Theory of Alienation:
    Futurelessness in Financial Capitalism," *Theory and Society* 50, no. 6
    (2021): 837–65, https://doi.org/10.1007/s11186-021-09440-6.
64. Schor, *The Overworked American*; Schor, *The Overspent American*.
65. See Burawoy, *Manufacturing Consent*; Ashley Mears, "Working for
    Free in the VIP: Relational Work and the Production of Consent,"

American Sociological Review 80, no. 6 (2015): 1099–1122, https://doi
.org/10.1177/0003122415609730.

66. This comparison is only to put the Turkish case in perspective, and does not necessarily mean that the United States is doing well in this regard. See Amy J. Binder, Daniel B. Davis, and Nick Bloom, "Career Funneling: How Elite Students Learn to Define and Desire 'Prestigious' Jobs," *Sociology of Education* 89, no. 1 (2016): 20–39, https://doi.org /10.1177/0038040715610883.

67. Arlie Russell Hochschild, *The Managed Heart: Commercialization of Human Feeling* (University of California Press, 1979).

68. See Karen Ho, *Liquidated* (Duke University Press, 2009), https://doi.org /10.1215/9780822391371.

69. Fromm, *Escape from Freedom*.

70. Barbara Ehrenreich, *Fear of Falling: The Inner Life of the Middle Class* (Pantheon, 1990).

71. See Bourdieu, *Distinction*.

72. See Schor, *The Overworked American*; Schor, *The Overspent American*.

73. See Annette Lareau, *Unequal Childhoods: Class, Race, and Family Life*, 2nd ed. (University of California Press, 2011).

74. See Caitlin Zaloom, *Indebted: How Families Make College Work at Any Cost* (Princeton University Press, 2019).

75. I emphasize that experiencing status anxiety is conditional upon *assuming* meritocracy; whether the society is meritocratic or not is tangential to my inquiry. Rather, I stress that these people put a lot of work into their achievements so that, regardless of their ascriptions, they feel they made their way with their grit.

76. For the concept of hysteresis effect, see Bourdieu, *Distinction*, 109.

77. Laura Empson, *Leading Professionals: Power, Politics, and Prima Donnas* (Oxford University Press, 2017).

78. Ho, *Liquidated*.

79. See Steven Peter Vallas and Juliet B. Schor, "What Do Platforms Do? Understanding the Gig Economy," *Annual Review of Sociology* 46, no. 1 (2020): 273–94, https://doi.org/10.1146/annurev-soc-121919-054857.

80. Katherine S. Newman, *Falling from Grace: Downward Mobility in the Age of Affluence* (University of California Press, 1999).

81. Ebaugh, *Becoming an Ex*.

82. See Jennifer M. Silva, "Constructing Adulthood in an Age of Uncertainty," *American Sociological Review* 77, no. 4 (2012): 505–22.
83. See Silva, "Constructing Adulthood in an Age of Uncertainty," 508.
84. See Stephen R. Barley and Gideon Kunda, *Gurus, Hired Guns, and Warm Bodies: Itinerant Experts in a Knowledge Economy* (Princeton University Press, 2004).
85. They could also very well be found as *overqualified* and hence not get the job because the employer suspects that they might just leave it after a while.
86. See Christopher L. Caterine, *Leaving Academia* (Princeton University Press, 2020), https://doi.org/10.1515/9780691209869; Pierre-Michel Menger, "Artistic Labor Markets and Careers," *Annual Review of Sociology* 25 (1999): 541–74; Silke Roth, *The Paradoxes of Aid Work: Passionate Professionals* (Routledge, 2015), 148–67.
87. Percheski, "Opting Out?," 513.

CONCLUSION

1. For a similar dynamic that unfolded in Latin America and East Asia, see Diane E. Davis, *Discipline and Development: Middle Classes and Prosperity in East Asia and Latin America* (Cambridge University Press, 2004), https://doi.org/10.1017/CBO9780511499555.
2. See Ömer Demir, Mustafa Acar, and Metin Toprak, "Anatolian Tigers or Islamic Capital: Prospects and Challenges," *Middle Eastern Studies* 40, no. 6 (2004): 166–88, https://doi.org/10.1080/0026320042000282937.
3. See Neşecan Balkan, Erol Balkan, and Ahmet Öncü, eds., *The Neoliberal Landscape and the Rise of Islamist Capital in Turkey* (Berghahn, 2015).
4. See Kerem Yıldırım, "Clientelism and Dominant Incumbent Parties: Party Competition in an Urban Turkish Neighbourhood," *Democratization* 27, no. 1 (2020): 81–99, https://doi.org/10.1080/13510347.2019.1658744.
5. See Ahmet Öncü and Erol Balkan, "Nouveaux Riches of the City of Minarets and Skyscrapers: Neoliberalism and the Reproduction of the Islamic Middle Class in İstanbul," *Research and Policy on Turkey* 1, no. 1 (2016): 29–45, https://doi.org/10.1080/23760818.2015.1099780.
6. See Çetin Çelik and Tuğçe Özdemir, "When Downward Mobility Haunts: Reproduction Crisis and Educational Strategies of Turkish

Middle Class Under the AK Party Rule," *British Journal of Sociology of Education* 43, no. 2 (2021): 260–77, https://doi.org/10.1080/01425692.2021.2018652.

7. See John Ehrenreich and Barbara Ehrenreich, "The Professional-Managerial Class," in *Between Labor and Capital*, ed. Pat Walker (South End Press, 1979).

8. See Cihan Tuğal, "'Resistance Everywhere': The Gezi Revolt in Global Perspective," *New Perspectives on Turkey* 49 (2013): 157–72, https://doi.org/10.1017/S0896634600002077; Erdem Yörük and Murat Yüksel, "Class and Politics in Turkey's Gezi Protests," *New Left Review* 89, no. September–October (2014): 103–23.

9. Note that the Turkish middle class's counterparts around the globe, from Iran to Brazil, were also putting their marks on the global revolt wave of the 2010s. See Cihan Tuğal, "Elusive Revolt: The Contradictory Rise of Middle-Class Politics," *Thesis Eleven* 130, no. 1 (2015): 87–88, https://doi.org/10.1177/0725513615602183.

10. See Çağlar Keyder, "The New Middle Class (Yeni Orta Sınıf)," *Science Academy*, 2013, http://bilimakademisi.org/wp-content/uploads/2013/09/Yeni-Orta-Sinif.pdf.

11. See Stephanie Lee Mudge, "What Is Neo-Liberalism?," *Socio-Economic Review* 6, no. 4 (2008): 704–5, https://doi.org/10.1093/ser/mwn016. I also want to highlight here that the U.S. hegemony in the latest neoliberal wave of globalization since the 1980s—as the worldwide adherence to the Washington Consensus suggests—encourages us to spotlight U.S. transnational corporations in particular: we need further research to examine how U.S. work culture—the paradigmatic work culture of advanced capitalism that prioritizes a strong allegiance to work at the expense of nonwork spheres of life—spread to and interacted with the rest of world. U.S. transnational corporations, with their increasingly international activities and the ascendance of their branches as primary employers of high-skilled labor in various host-country outposts, are likely suspects.

12. See Christine Barwick and Patrick Le Galès, "Work in London, Love in Paris: Middle Class Mobility over the Channel Tunnel," *Journal of Ethnic and Migration Studies* 47, no. 17 (2021): 4023–39, https://doi.org/10.1080/1369183X.2020.1763787.

13. Neil Fligstein, *Euroclash: The EU, European Identity, and the Future of Europe* (Oxford University Press, 2008), 78–88, https://doi.org/10.1093/acpro f:oso/9780199580859.001.0001.

14. See Fligstein, *Euroclash*, 27.

15. See Alberta Andreotti, Patrick Le Galès, and Francisco Javier Moreno-Fuentes, *Globalised Minds, Roots in the City: Upper Middle Classes in European Cities* (Wiley, 2014), https://doi.org/10.1002/9781118330791.

16. See Sam Scott, "The Social Morphology of Skilled Migration: The Case of the British Middle Class in Paris," *Journal of Ethnic and Migration Studies* 32, no. 7 (2006): 1105–29, https://doi.org/10.1080/13691830600821802.

17. See Barwick and Le Galès, "Work in London, Love in Paris"; Fligstein, *Euroclash*, 18.

18. See Andreotti, Le Galès, and Moreno-Fuentes, *Globalised Minds, Roots in the City*.

19. See Adrian Favell, *Eurostars and Eurocities: Free Movement and Mobility in an Integrating Europe* (Blackwell, 2008), xi, https://doi.org/10.1002 /9780470712818.

20. See Jonathan V. Beaverstock, "Transnational Elites in the City: British Highly-Skilled Inter-Company Transferees in New York City's Financial District," *Journal of Ethnic and Migration Studies* 31, no. 2 (2005): 245–68, https://doi.org/10.1080/1369183042000339918.

21. See Anouk de Koning, *Global Dreams: Space, Class, and Gender in Middle-Class Cairo* (American University in Cairo Press, 2009); Shana Cohen, *Searching for a Different Future: The Rise of a Global Middle Class in Morocco* (Duke University Press, 2004).

22. See de Koning, *Global Dreams*; Cohen, *Searching for a Different Future*; Smitha Radhakrishnan, *Appropriately Indian: Gender and Culture in a New Transnational Class* (Duke University Press, 2011), respectively, for the Egyptian, Moroccan, and Indian transnational middle-class formations.

23. See Marion Fourcade-Gourinchas and Sarah L. Babb, "The Rebirth of the Liberal Creed: Paths to Neoliberalism in Four Countries," *American Journal of Sociology* 108, no. 3 (2002): 561–62, https://doi.org /10.1086/367922.

24. See Kevan Harris, "Unraveling the Middle Classes in Postrevolutionary Iran," *Political Power and Social Theory* 37 (2020): 130, https://doi.org /10.1108/S0198-871920200000037006.

25. For an account of how Iran's auto industry developed despite, see Darius Bozorg Mehri, "The Role of Engineering Consultancies as Network-Centred Actors to Develop Indigenous, Technical Capacity: The Case of Iran's Automotive Industry," *Socio-Economic Review* 13, no. 4 (2015): 747–69, https://doi.org/10.1093/SER/MWU041.

26. See Harris, "Unraveling the Middle Classes in Postrevolutionary Iran," 120.

27. See Akbar E. Torbat, "The Brain Drain from Iran to the United States," *Middle East Journal* 56, no. 2 (2002): 272–95.

28. See Nina Bandelj, "The Global Economy as Instituted Process: The Case of Central and Eastern Europe," *American Sociological Review* 74, no. 1 (2009): 134, https://doi.org/10.1177/000312240907400107.

29. See Lawrence P. King and Iván Szelényi, "Post-Communist Economic Systems," in *The Handbook of Economic Sociology*, 2nd ed., ed. Richard Swedberg and Neil J. Smelser (Princeton University Press, 2010), 213.

30. See Elizabeth Cullen Dunn, *Privatizing Poland: Baby Food, Big Business, and the Remaking of Labor* (Cornell University Press, 2015), https://doi.org/10.7591/9781501702204.

31. See Gil Eyal, Ivan Szelenyi, and Eleanor Townsley, *Making Capitalism Without Capitalists* (Verso, 1998), 13.

32. See King and Szelényi, "Post-Communist Economic Systems," 218.

33. Here and in the remainder of the conclusion, I emphasize not the equality of opportunity principle of the American dream but rather its widespread and glorified prescription of the pursuit of happiness via a materialistic, individualistic, competitive, and achievement-oriented understanding and conduct of life.

34. See Michael L. Siciliano, *Creative Control: The Ambivalence of Work in the Culture Industries* (Columbia University Press, 2021).

35. For a modern take on crafts labor, see Richard Sennett, *The Craftsman* (Yale University Press, 2008), 9. Sennett defines "craftsmanship" rather broadly and highlights its key characteristic as a "basic human impulse, the desire to do a job well for its own sake." For how crafts labor enables transformation of old manual labor into chic and meaningful careers, see also Richard E. Ocejo, *Masters of Craft: Old Jobs in the New Urban Economy* (Princeton University Press, 2017).

36. The language of postmaterialism or self-expression may allude to the use of modernization theory. See Ronald Inglehart, *Cultural Evolution: People's Motivations Are Changing, and Reshaping the World* (Cambridge University Press, 2018). But here, I focus solely on postmaterialism at the level of individuals instead of nations. I also strongly disagree with the modernization theory's understanding of postmaterialism (e.g., gender equality or same-sex marriage should be thought of not as a matter of self-expression but rather as a matter of social justice).

37. For an elaboration on the concept of human flourishing beyond well-being or happiness, see Philip Gorski, "Human Flourishing and Human Morphogenesis: A Critical Realist Interpretation and Critique," in *Morphogenesis and Human Flourishing*, ed. Margaret S. Archer (Springer, 2017), 29–43, https://doi.org/10.1007/978-3-319-49469-2.

38. Abraham H. Maslow, *Motivation and Personality* (Harper & Row, 1954). Note that my aim in using Maslow's hierarchy of needs is not for its precision, and I am not interested in applying it directly to my case. Rather, I use it to emphasize the importance of the postmaterial values, such as a search for meaning and authenticity, and a pursuit of self-actualization. I mainly drew from Maslow's theory instead of others because of its widespread recognition.

39. Freelancing white-collar workers, for example, lack a stable social environment, which lowers their quality of working life. See Gianpiero Petriglieri, Susan J. Ashford, and Amy Wrzesniewski, "Agony and Ecstasy in the Gig Economy: Cultivating Holding Environments for Precarious and Personalized Work Identities," *Administrative Science Quarterly* 64, no. 1 (2018): 1–47, https://doi.org/10.1177/0001839218759646.

40. It could be fruitful to think of Maslow's hierarchy of needs visually as idiosyncratic pyramids with varying shapes and heights. Thinking of them as made of Jenga blocks, for instance, allows us to consider a life lacking health, esteem, and friendship as having these blocks removed, which leads to unstable structures. A pyramid lacking self-actualization is short and incomplete and portrays an unfulfilling life.

41. See Robert C. Tucker, "Introduction," in *The Marx-Engels Reader*, 2nd ed., edited by Robert C. Tucker (Norton, 1978), xxii.

42. See Tucker, "Introduction," xxiii.

43. For an interesting case of how the relative deprivation of engineers in some Muslim majority countries, coupled with the engineering mindset prioritizing order and hierarchy, fueled violent jihadist movements, see Diego Gambetta and Steffen Hertog, *Engineers of Jihad: The Curious Connection Between Violent Extremism and Education* (Princeton University Press, 2016).

44. See Robert K. Merton, "Social Structure and Anomie," *American Sociological Review* 3, no. 5 (1938): 672, https://doi.org/10.2307/2084686.

45. See Ted Robert Gurr, *Why Men Rebel* (Princeton University Press, 1970), 23, https://doi.org/10.4324/9781315631073.

46. Gurr, *Why Men Rebel*, 24.

47. Paul Willis, *Learning to Labor: How Working Class Kids Get Working Class Jobs* (Cambridge University Press, 2017).

48. Amy J. Binder, Daniel B. Davis, and Nick Bloom, "Career Funneling: How Elite Students Learn to Define and Desire 'Prestigious' Jobs," *Sociology of Education* 89, no. 1 (2016): 20–39, https://doi.org/10.1177/0038040715610883.

49. See Michèle Lamont, "From 'Having' to 'Being': Self-Worth and the Current Crisis of American Society," *British Journal of Sociology* 70, no. 3 (2019): 660–707, https://doi.org/10.1111/1468-4446.12667.

50. Michael Burawoy, *Manufacturing Consent: Changes in the Labor Process Under Monopoly Capitalism* (University of Chicago Press, 1979).

51. See Amy Wrzesniewski and Jane E. Dutton, "Crafting a Job: Revisioning Employees as Active Crafters of Their Work," *Academy of Management Review* 26, no. 2 (2001): 179, https://doi.org/10.2307/259118.

52. Emile Durkheim, *The Division of Labor in Society* (Free Press, 1997 [1893]).

53. See Max Weber, *The Protestant Ethic and the "Spirit" of Capitalism* (Penguin, 2002 [1905]), 16.

54. See Juliet Schor, *The Overworked American: The Unexpected Decline of Leisure* (Basic Books, 1991); Juliet Schor, *The Overspent American: Upscaling, Downshifting, and the New Consumer* (Basic Books, 1998).

55. See Bertrand Russell, "In Praise of Idleness," *Harper's Magazine*, October 1932; John Maynard Keynes, "Economic Possibilities for Our Grandchildren," in *Essays in Persuasion* (Palgrave Macmillan UK, 2010 [1930]), 321–32, https://doi.org/10.1007/978-1-349-59072-8_25.

56. See Karl Marx, "Economic and Philosophic Manuscripts of 1844," in *The Marx-Engels Reader*, 2nd ed., edited by Robert C. Tucker (Norton, 1978), 80.

57. See Jason Hickel et al., "Degrowth Can Work—Here's How Science Can Help," *Nature* 612, no. 7940 (2022): 400–403, https://doi.org/10.1038/d41586-022-04412-x.

58. Paul Lafargue, *The Right to Be Lazy* (Solidarity Publications, 1969 [1883]).

59. See Patricia Findlay, Arne L. Kalleberg, and Chris Warhurst, "The Challenge of Job Quality," *Human Relations* 66, no. 4 (2013): 441–51, https://doi.org/10.1177/0018726713481070; Paul Osterman, "Introduction to the Special Issue on Job Quality: What Does It Mean and How Might We Think about It?," *ILR Review* 66, no. 4 (2013): 739–52, https://doi.org/10.1177/001979391306600401.

60. See Steven Peter Vallas and Anne Kovalainen, "Introduction: Taking Stock of the Digital Revolution," in *Research in the Sociology of Work*, vol. 33 (Emerald, 2019), 1–12, https://doi.org/10.1108/S0277-283320190000033001.

61. See Shelley J. Correll et al., "Redesigning, Redefining Work," *Work and Occupations* 41, no. 1 (2014): 3–17, https://doi.org/10.1177/0730888413515250; Leslie A. Perlow and Erin L. Kelly, "Toward a Model of Work Redesign for Better Work and Better Life," *Work and Occupations* 41, no. 1 (2014): 111–34, https://doi.org/10.1177/0730888413516473.

62. See Jared B. Fitzgerald, Juliet B. Schor, and Andrew K. Jorgenson, "Working Hours and Carbon Dioxide Emissions in the United States, 2007–2013," *Social Forces* 96, no. 4 (2018): 1851–74, https://doi.org/10.1093/sf/soy014; Kyle W. Knight, Eugene A. Rosa, and Juliet B. Schor, "Could Working Less Reduce Pressures on the Environment? A Cross-National Panel Analysis of OECD Countries, 1970–2007," *Global Environmental Change* 23, no. 4 (2013): 691–700, https://doi.org/10.1016/j.gloenvcha.2013.02.017.

63. See Binder, Davis, and Bloom, "Career Funneling."

64. See Daniel Davis and Amy J. Binder, "Selling Students: The Rise of Corporate Partnership Programs in University Career Centers," *Research in the Sociology of Organizations* 46 (2016): 395–422, https://doi.org/10.1108/S0733-558X20160000046013.

65. Lamont, "From 'Having' to 'Being,'" 661.

66. Herbert Marcuse, *One Dimensional Man: Studies in the Ideology of Advanced Industrial Society* (Beacon, 1964).

METHODOLOGICAL APPENDIX

1. Barney G. Glaser and Anselm L. Strauss, *The Discovery of Grounded Theory: Strategies for Qualitative Research* (Aldine, 1967).

2. Nicole M. Deterding and Mary C. Waters, "Flexible Coding of In-Depth Interviews," *Sociological Methods & Research* 50, no. 2 (2018), https://doi.org/10.1177/0049124118799377.

3. See Laura Empson, "Elite Interviewing in Professional Organizations," *Journal of Professions and Organization* 5, no. 1 (2018): 58–69, https://doi.org/10.1093/jpo/jox010; Brooke Harrington, "Studying Elite Professionals in Transnational Settings," in *Professional Networks in Transnational Governance*, ed. Leonard Seabrooke and Lasse Folke Henriksen (Cambridge University Press, 2017), 39–49, https://doi.org/10.1017/9781316855508.003; Rosanna Hertz and Jonathan Imber, eds., *Studying Elites Using Qualitative Methods* (Sage, 1995), https://doi.org/10.4135/9781483327341.

4. See Amy Wrzesniewski et al., "Jobs, Careers, and Callings: People's Relations to Their Work," *Journal of Research in Personality* 31, no. 1 (1997): 24, https://doi.org/10.1006/jrpe.1997.2162.

5. Most of my human resources (HR) respondents were female; however, this overlaps with the overall gender disparity in HR departments. Thus, I believe my main findings would not have changed significantly if I were able to have more interviews with male HR professionals. The structural reasons for this gender disparity stem from occupational status hierarchies that are partly driven by a gendered hard versus soft sciences distinction and the resulting hierarchy in college majors in Turkey: HR departments often prefer social science majors, particularly psychology, which are in the lower echelons of prestige compared to engineering or economics.

BIBLIOGRAPHY

Abbott, Andrew Delano. "On the Concept of Turning Point." In *Time Matters: On Theory and Method*. University of Chicago Press, 2001.

Acar, Elif Öznur. "Türkiye'den OECD Ülkelerine Nitelikli İşgücü Göçü: Bir Panel Veri Analizi." *Uluslararası Ekonomi ve Yenilik Dergisi* 3, no. 1 (2017): 1–16. https://doi.org/10.20979/ueyd.266025.

Ade, Maren, dir. *Toni Erdmann*. Germany-Austria: Komplizen Film, 2016.

Aksakal, Erdem. *Mezeleri Güzel: Bir Beyaz Yakalının İtirafları*. Ot Kitap, 2016.

Aksoy, Asu. *Küreselleşme ve İstanbul'da İstihdam*. Friedrich-Ebert Stiftung, 1996.

Al-Dabbagh, May. "Serial Migrant Mothers and Permanent Temporariness in Dubai." *Migration Studies*, 2022. https://doi.org/10.1093/MIGRATION/MNAC020.

Alderson, Arthur S., and Jason Beckfield. "Power and Position in the World City System." *American Journal of Sociology* 109, no. 4 (2004): 811–51. https://doi.org/10.1086/378930.

Altan-Olcay, Özlem, and Evren Balta. *The American Passport in Turkey: National Citizenship in the Age of Transnationalism*. University of Pennsylvania Press, 2020. https://doi.org/10.9783/9780812297065.

Andreotti, Alberta, Patrick Le Galès, and Francisco Javier Moreno-Fuentes. *Globalised Minds, Roots in the City: Upper Middle Classes in European Cities*. Wiley, 2014. https://doi.org/10.1002/9781118330791.

Aneesh, Aneesh. "Global Labor: Algocratic Modes of Organization." *Sociological Theory* 27, no. 4 (2009): 347–70.

——. "Skill Saturation: Rationalization and Post-Industrial Work." *Theory and Society* 30, no. 3 (2001): 363–96.

——. *Virtual Migration: The Programming of Globalization.* Duke University Press, 2006.

Anteby, Michel, and Nicholas Occhiuto. "Stand-In Labor and the Rising Economy of Self." *Social Forces* 98, no. 3 (2019): 1287–1310. https://doi.org/10.1093/sf/soz028.

Appelbaum, Eileen, Thomas Bailey, Peter Berg, and Arne L. Kalleberg. *Manufacturing Advantage: Why High-Performance Work Systems Pay Off.* Cornell University Press, 2000.

Arat, Yeşim, and Şevket Pamuk. "Uneven Economic Development and Domestic Politics." In *Turkey Between Democracy and Authoritarianism*, 130–61. Cambridge University Press, 2019. https://doi.org/10.1017/9781139022385.006.

Archibald, Peter W. "Using Marx's Theory of Alienation Empirically." *Theory and Society* 6, no. 1 (1978): 119–32. https://doi.org/10.1007/BF01566160.

Arthur, Michael B., and Denise M. Rousseau, eds. *The Boundaryless Career: A New Employment Principle for a New Organizational Era.* Oxford University Press, 1996.

Ayata, Sencer. "The New Middle Class and the Joys of Suburbia." In *Fragments of Culture: The Everyday of Modern Turkey*, edited by Deniz Kandiyoti and Ayşe Saktanber, 25–42. I. B. Tauris, 2002.

Babb, Sarah. *Managing Mexico: Economists from Nationalism to Neoliberalism.* Princeton University Press, 2001. https://doi.org/10.2307/j.ctv36zrv2.

Babb, Sarah, and Alexander Kentikelenis. "Markets Everywhere: The Washington Consensus and the Sociology of Global Institutional Change." *Annual Review of Sociology* 47, no. 1 (2021): 521–41. https://doi.org/10.1146/annurev-soc-090220-025543.

Bair, Jennifer. "Global Commodity Chains: Genealogy and Review." In *Frontiers of Commodity Chain Research*, edited by Jennifer Bair, 1–34. Stanford University Press, 2009. https://doi.org/10.1515/9780804779760-003.

Balkan, Neşecan, Erol Balkan, and Ahmet Öncü, eds. *The Neoliberal Landscape and the Rise of Islamist Capital in Turkey.* Berghahn, 2015.

Ballakrishnen, Swethaa S. *Accidental Feminism: Gender Parity and Selective Mobility Among India's Professional Elite.* Princeton University Press, 2021.

Bandelj, Nina. *From Communists to Foreign Capitalists.* Princeton University Press, 2008. https://doi.org/10.1515/9781400841257.

——. "The Global Economy as Instituted Process: The Case of Central and Eastern Europe." *American Sociological Review* 74, no. 1 (2009): 128–49. https://doi.org/10.1177/000312240907400107.

Banks Association of Türkiye, The. "24.12.2022 Tarihi İtibarıyla Gruplar Bazında, Banka ve Bankaların Şube Sayıları." December 12, 2024. https://www.tbb.org.tr/modules/banka-bilgileri/banka_sube_bilgileri.asp.

——. "Banking Sector in Turkey 1960–2020." June 2021. https://www.tbb.org.tr/en/Content/Upload/Dokuman/1188/Banking_Sector_In_Turkey_1960-2020.pdf.

Barley, Stephen R. "Careers, Identities, and Institutions: The Legacy of the Chicago School of Sociology." In *Handbook of Career Theory*, edited by Michael B. Arthur, Douglas T. Hall, and Barbara S. Lawrence, 41–65. Cambridge University Press, 1989. https://doi.org/10.1017/CBO9780511625459.005.

Barley, Stephen R., and Gideon Kunda. *Gurus, Hired Guns, and Warm Bodies: Itinerant Experts in a Knowledge Economy*. Princeton University Press, 2004.

Bartley, Tim. "Transnational Corporations and Global Governance." *Annual Review of Sociology* 44, no. 1 (2018): 145–65. https://doi.org/10.1146/annurev-soc-060116-053540.

Barwick, Christine, and Patrick Le Galès. "Work in London, Love in Paris: Middle Class Mobility over the Channel Tunnel." *Journal of Ethnic and Migration Studies* 47, no. 17 (2021): 4023–39. https://doi.org/10.1080/1369183X.2020.1763787.

Bauman, Zygmunt. *Liquid Modernity*. Polity, 2000.

Beaverstock, Jonathan V. "Transnational Elites in the City: British Highly-Skilled Inter-Company Transferees in New York City's Financial District." *Journal of Ethnic and Migration Studies* 31, no. 2 (2005): 245–68. https://doi.org/10.1080/1369183042000339918.

Beck, Ulrich. *Risk Society: Towards a New Modernity*. Sage, 1992.

Belkin, Lisa. "The Opt-Out Revolution." *New York Times Magazine*, October 26, 2003. https://www.nytimes.com/2003/10/26/magazine/the-opt-out-revolution.html.

Bertaux, Daniel, and Paul Richard Thompson. "Introduction." In *Pathways to Social Class: A Qualitative Approach to Social Mobility*, edited by Daniel Bertaux and Paul Richard Thompson, 1–31. Clarendon, 1997.

Biese, Ingrid. *Opting Out and In: On Women's Careers and New Lifestyles*. Routledge, 2017. https://doi.org/10.4324/9781315637006.

Bilici, Mücahit. "Black Turks, White Turks: On the Three Requirements of Turkish Citizenship." *Insight Turkey* 11, no. 3 (2009): 23–35.

Binder, Amy J., and Andrea R. Abel. "Symbolically Maintained Inequality: How Harvard and Stanford Students Construct Boundaries Among Elite

Universities." *Sociology of Education* 92, no. 1 (2019): 41–58. https://doi .org/10.1177/0038040718821073.

Binder, Amy J., Daniel B. Davis, and Nick Bloom. "Career Funneling: How Elite Students Learn to Define and Desire 'Prestigious' Jobs." *Sociology of Education* 89, no. 1 (2016): 20–39. https://doi.org/10.1177/0038040715610883.

Birtek, Faruk. "The Rise and Fall of Etatism in Turkey, 1932–1950: The Uncertain Road in the Restructuring of a Semiperipheral Economy." *Review (Fernand Braudel Center)* 8, no. 3 (1985): 407–38.

Blair-Loy, Mary. *Competing Devotions: Career and Family Among Women Executives*. Harvard University Press, 2003.

Blair-Loy, Mary, and Jerry A. Jacobs. "Globalization, Work Hours, and the Care Deficit Among Stockbrokers." *Gender & Society* 17, no. 2 (2003): 230–49. https://doi.org/10.1177/0891243202250777.

Blauner, Robert. *Alienation and Freedom: The Factory Worker and His Industry*. University of Chicago Press, 1964.

Boltanski, Luc, and Eve Chiapello. *The New Spirit of Capitalism*. Verso, 2005.

Bourdieu, Pierre. *Distinction: A Social Critique of the Judgement of Taste*. Harvard University Press, 1984.

——. "Forms of Capital." In *Handbook of Theory and Research for the Sociology of Education*, edited by J. G. Richardson, 241–58. Greenwood, 1986.

Bowles, Samuel, and Herbert Gintis. *Schooling in Capitalist America: Educational Reform and the Contradictions of Economic Life*. Basic Books, 1976.

Bozkurt, Ödül, and Alexander T. Mohr. "Forms of Cross-Border Mobility and Social Capital in Multinational Enterprises." *Human Resource Management Journal* 21, no. 2 (2011): 138–55. https://doi.org/10.1111/J.1748-8583.2010 .00147.X.

Braverman, Harry. *Labor and Monopoly Capital: The Degradation of Work in the Twentieth Century*. Monthly Review Press, 1974.

Brown, Andrew, Andy Charlwood, and David A. Spencer. "Not All That It Might Seem: Why Job Satisfaction Is Worth Studying Despite It Being a Poor Summary Measure of Job Quality." *Work, Employment and Society* 26, no. 6 (2012): 1007–18. https://doi.org/10.1177/0950017012461837.

Buchholz, Larissa. "What Is a Global Field? Theorizing Fields Beyond the Nation-State." *Sociological Review Monographs* 60, no. 2016 (2016): 31–60. https://doi.org/10.1111/2059-7932.12001.

Budig, M. J., and P. England. "The Wage Penalty for Motherhood." *American Sociological Review* 66, no. 2 (2001): 204–25. https://doi.org/10.2307 /2657415.

Burawoy, Michael. *Manufacturing Consent: Changes in the Labor Process Under Monopoly Capitalism.* University of Chicago Press, 1979.

——. *The Politics of Production: Factory Regimes Under Capitalism and Socialism.* Verso, 1985.

Carroll, William K. *The Making of a Transnational Capitalist Class: Corporate Power in the Twenty-First Century.* Zed, 2010.

Caterine, Christopher L. *Leaving Academia.* Princeton University Press, 2020. https://doi.org/10.1515/9780691209869.

Çelik, Çetin, and Tuğçe Özdemir. "When Downward Mobility Haunts: Reproduction Crisis and Educational Strategies of Turkish Middle Class Under the AK Party Rule." *British Journal of Sociology of Education* 43, no. 2 (2021): 260–77. https://doi.org/10.1080/01425692.2021.2018652.

Centeno, Miguel A., and Joseph N. Cohen. "The Arc of Neoliberalism." *Annual Review of Sociology* 38, no. 1 (2012): 317–40. https://doi.org/10.1146/annurev-soc-081309-150235.

Chase-Dunn, Christopher, and Marilyn Grell-Brisk. "World-System Theory." In *International Relations.* Oxford University Press, 2019. https://doi.org/10.1093/obo/9780199743292-0272.

Chiaburu, Dan S., Tomas Thundiyil, and Jiexin Wang. "Alienation and Its Correlates: A Meta-Analysis." *European Management Journal* 32, no. 1 (2014): 24–36. https://doi.org/10.1016/j.emj.2013.06.003.

Cohen, Shana. *Searching for a Different Future: The Rise of a Global Middle Class in Morocco.* Duke University Press, 2004.

Colpan, Asli M., and Geoffrey Jones. "Business Groups, Entrepreneurship and the Growth of the Koç Group in Turkey." *Business History* 58, no. 1 (2016): 69–88. https://doi.org/10.1080/00076791.2015.1044521.

Conradson, David, and Alan Latham. "Transnational Urbanism: Attending to Everyday Practices and Mobilities." *Journal of Ethnic and Migration Studies* 31, no. 2 (2005): 227–33. https://doi.org/10.1080/1369183042000339891.

Correll, Shelley J., Stephen Benard, and In Paik. "Getting a Job: Is There a Motherhood Penalty?" *American Journal of Sociology* 112, no. 5 (2007): 1297–1338. https://doi.org/10.1086/511799.

Correll, Shelley J., Erin L. Kelly, Lindsey Trimble O'Connor, and Joan C. Williams. "Redesigning, Redefining Work." *Work and Occupations* 41, no. 1 (2014): 3–17. https://doi.org/10.1177/0730888413515250.

Costas, Jana, and Peter Fleming. "Beyond Dis-Identification: A Discursive Approach to Self-Alienation in Contemporary Organizations." *Human Relations* 62, no. 3 (2009): 353–78. https://doi.org/10.1177/0018726708101041.

Cuzzocrea, Valentina, and Dawn Lyon. "Sociological Conceptualisations of 'Career': A Review and Reorientation." *Sociology Compass* 5, no. 12 (2011): 1029–43. https://doi.org/10.1111/j.1751-9020.2011.00429.x.

Davis, Daniel, and Amy J. Binder. "Selling Students: The Rise of Corporate Partnership Programs in University Career Centers." *Research in the Sociology of Organizations* 46 (2016): 395–422. https://doi.org/10.1108/S0733-558X20160000046013.

Davis, Diane E. *Discipline and Development: Middle Classes and Prosperity in East Asia and Latin America.* Cambridge University Press, 2004. https://doi.org/10.1017/CBO9780511499555.

——. "The Sociospatial Reconfiguration of Middle Classes and Their Impact on Politics and Development in the Global South: Preliminary Ideas for Future Research." *Political Power and Social Theory* 21 (2010): 241–67. https://doi.org/10.1108/S0198-8719(2010)0000021014.

de Koning, Anouk. *Global Dreams: Space, Class, and Gender in Middle-Class Cairo.* American University in Cairo Press, 2009.

Demir, Ömer, Mustafa Acar, and Metin Toprak. "Anatolian Tigers or Islamic Capital: Prospects and Challenges." *Middle Eastern Studies* 40, no. 6 (2004): 166–88. https://doi.org/10.1080/0026320042000282937.

Derne, Steve. "Globalization and the Making of a Transnational Middle Class: Implications for Class Analysis." In *Critical Globalization Studies*, edited by Richard P. Appelbaum and William I. Robinson, 177–86. Routledge, 2005.

——. "Making the Transnational Middle Class in India." In *Globalization on the Ground: Media and the Transformation of Culture, Class, and Gender in India*, 90–126. Sage, 2008. https://doi.org/10.4135/9788132100386.n3.

Deterding, Nicole M., and Mary C. Waters. "Flexible Coding of In-Depth Interviews." *Sociological Methods & Research* 50, no. 2 (2018). https://doi.org/10.1177/0049124118799377.

Devine, Fiona, and Mike Savage. "The Cultural Turn, Sociology and Class Analysis." In *Rethinking Class: Culture, Identities and Lifestyle*, 1–23. Bloomsbury, 2005.

Devlet Planlama Teşkilatı. "Dördüncü Beş Yıllık Kalkınma Planı 1979–1983." 1979.

——. "Doğrudan Yabancı Sermaye Yatırımları Özel İhtisas Komisyonu Raporu." *Sekizinci Beş Yıllık Kalkınma Planı.* 2000.

Duhigg, Charles. "Wealthy, Successful and Miserable." *New York Times Magazine*, February 21, 2019. https://www.nytimes.com/interactive/2019/02/21/magazine/elite-professionals-jobs-happiness.html.

Dunn, Elizabeth Cullen. *Privatizing Poland: Baby Food, Big Business, and the Remaking of Labor*. Cornell University Press, 2015. https://doi.org/10.7591/9781501702204.

Durkheim, Emile. *The Division of Labor in Society*. Free Press, 1997.

Ebaugh, Helen Rose Fuchs. *Becoming an Ex: The Process of Role Exit*. University of Chicago Press, 1988.

Ehrenreich, Barbara. *Fear of Falling: The Inner Life of the Middle Class*. Pantheon, 1990.

Ehrenreich, John, and Barbara Ehrenreich. "The Professional-Managerial Class." In *Between Labor and Capital*, edited by Pat Walker, 5–45. South End Press, 1979.

Empson, Laura. "Elite Interviewing in Professional Organizations." *Journal of Professions and Organization* 5, no. 1 (2018): 58–69. https://doi.org/10.1093/jpo/jox010.

——. *Leading Professionals: Power, Politics, and Prima Donnas*. Oxford University Press, 2017.

Emrence, Cem. "After Neo-Liberal Globalization: The Great Transformation of Turkey." *Comparative Sociology* 7, no. 1 (2008): 51. https://doi.org/10.1163/156913308X260466.

Erikson, Robert, and John H. Goldthorpe. *The Constant Flux: A Study of Class Mobility in Industrial Societies*. Oxford University Press, 1992.

Erkmen, T. Deniz. "Houses on Wheels: National Attachment, Belonging, and Cosmopolitanism in Narratives of Transnational Professionals." *Studies in Ethnicity and Nationalism* 15, no. 1 (2015): 26–47. https://doi.org/10.1111/sena.12122.

——. "Stepping into the Global: Turkish Professionals, Employment in Transnational Corporations, and Aspiration to Transnational Forms of Cultural Capital." *Current Sociology* 66, no. 3 (2016): 412–30. https://doi.org/10.1177/0011392116653236.

Espeland, Wendy Nelson, and Michael Sauder. *Engines of Anxiety: Academic Rankings, Reputation, and Accountability*. Russell Sage Foundation, 2016.

Eyal, Gil, Ivan Szelenyi, and Eleanor Townsley. *Making Capitalism Without Capitalists*. Verso, 1998.

Farrugia, David. "Class and the Post-Fordist Work Ethic: Subjects of Passion and Subjects of Achievement in the Work Society." *Sociological Review*, no. 2011 (2019): 1–16. https://doi.org/10.1177/0038026118825234.

——. "The Formation of Young Workers: The Cultivation of the Self as a Subject of Value to the Contemporary Labour Force." *Current Sociology* 67, no. 1 (2019): 47–63. https://doi.org/10.1177/0011392118793681.

Favell, Adrian. *Eurostars and Eurocities: Free Movement and Mobility in an Integrating Europe*. Blackwell, 2008. https://doi.org/10.1002/9780470712818.

Felstead, Alan, Duncan Gallie, and Francis Green. *Unequal Britain at Work*. Oxford University Press, 2015.

Findlay, Patricia, Arne L. Kalleberg, and Chris Warhurst. "The Challenge of Job Quality." *Human Relations* 66, no. 4 (2013): 441–51. https://doi.org/10.1177/0018726713481070.

Fitzgerald, Jared B., Juliet B. Schor, and Andrew K. Jorgenson. "Working Hours and Carbon Dioxide Emissions in the United States, 2007–2013." *Social Forces* 96, no. 4 (2018): 1851–74. https://doi.org/10.1093/sf/soy014.

Fligstein, Neil. *Euroclash: The EU, European Identity, and the Future of Europe*. Oxford University Press, 2008. https://doi.org/10.1093/acprof:oso/9780199580859.001.0001.

Fourcade-Gourinchas, Marion, and Sarah L. Babb. "The Rebirth of the Liberal Creed: Paths to Neoliberalism in Four Countries." *American Journal of Sociology* 108, no. 3 (2002): 533–79. https://doi.org/10.1086/367922.

Frege, Carola, and John Godard. "Varieties of Capitalism and Job Quality: The Attainment of Civic Principles at Work in the United States and Germany." *American Sociological Review* 79, no. 5 (2014): 942–65. https://doi.org/10.1177/0003122414548194.

Fromm, Erich. *Escape from Freedom*. Farrar & Rinehart, 1941.

Gallie, Duncan, ed. *Economic Crisis, Quality of Work, and Social Integration: The European Experience*. Oxford University Press, 2013. https://doi.org/10.1093/acprof:oso/9780199664719.001.0001.

——, ed. *Employment Regimes and the Quality of Work*. Oxford University Press, 2007. https://doi.org/10.1093/acprof:oso/9780199230105.001.0001.

——. "Production Regimes and the Quality of Employment in Europe." *Annual Review of Sociology* 33, no. 1 (2007): 85–104. https://doi.org/10.1146/annurev.soc.33.040406.131724.

Gambetta, Diego, and Steffen Hertog. *Engineers of Jihad: The Curious Connection Between Violent Extremism and Education*. Princeton University Press, 2016.

General Directorate of Foreign Investment. "Foreign Direct Investments in Turkey 2006." 2007.

Giddens, Anthony. "Class Structuration and Class Consciousness." In *Classes, Power, and Conflict: Classical and Contemporary Debates*, edited by Anthony Giddens and David Held, 157–74. Macmillan Education UK, 1982.

Glaser, Barney G., and Anselm L. Strauss. *The Discovery of Grounded Theory: Strategies for Qualitative Research.* Aldine, 1967.

Go, Julian, and Monika Krause. "Fielding Transnationalism: An Introduction." *Sociological Review Monographs* 30 (2016): 6–30. https://doi.org/10.1111/2059-7932.12000.

Gök, Fatma. "The Privatization of Education in Turkey." In *The Ravages of Neo-Liberalism: Economy, Society, and Gender in Turkey*, edited by Neşecan Balkan and Sungur Savran, 93–104. Nova Science, 2002.

Goldthorpe, John H. "On the Service Class, Its Formation and Future." In *Social Class and Division of Labor*, edited by Anthony Giddens and Gavin Mackenzie, 162–85. Cambridge University Press, 1982.

Goldthorpe, John H., David Lockwood, Frank Bechhofer, and Jennifer Platt. *The Affluent Worker: Industrial Attitudes and Behaviour.* Cambridge University Press, 1968.

——. *The Affluent Worker in the Class Structure.* Cambridge University Press, 1969.

Göle, Nilüfer. *Mühendisler ve İdeoloji Öncü Devrimcilerden Yenilikçi Seçkinlere.* Metis Yayınları, 1986.

Gorski, Philip. "Human Flourishing and Human Morphogenesis: A Critical Realist Interpretation and Critique." In *Morphogenesis and Human Flourishing*, edited by Margaret S. Archer, 29–43. Springer, 2017. https://doi.org/10.1007/978-3-319-49469-2.

Green, Francis. "Assessing Job Quality in the Affluent Economy." In *Demanding Work: The Paradox of Job Quality in the Affluent Economy*, 1–23. Princeton University Press, 2007.

Grigoriadis, Ioannis N. "Türk or Türkiyeli? The Reform of Turkey's Minority Legislation and the Rediscovery of Ottomanism." *Middle Eastern Studies* 43, no. 3 (2007): 423–38. https://doi.org/10.1080/00263200701246116.

Grusky, David. "Foundations of a Neo-Durkheimian Class Analysis." In *Approaches to Class Analysis*, edited by Erik Olin Wright, 51–81. Cambridge University Press, 2005. https://doi.org/10.1017/CBO9780511488900.004.

Guhin, Jeffrey, and Joseph Klett. "School Beyond Stratification: Internal Goods, Alienation, and an Expanded Sociology of Education." *Theory and Society* 51, no. 3 (2022): 371–98. https://doi.org/10.1007/S11186 -022-09472-6.

Gurr, Ted Robert. *Why Men Rebel.* Princeton University Press, 1970. https:// doi.org/10.4324/9781315631073.

Haggard, Stephan, and Robert R. Kaufman. *Development, Democracy, and Welfare States.* Princeton University Press, 2009. https://doi.org/10.1515 /9780691214153.

Hall, Douglas T., Jeffrey Yip, and Kathryn Doiron. "Protean Careers at Work: Self-Direction and Values Orientation in Psychological Success." *Annual Review of Organizational Psychology and Organizational Behavior* 5, no. 1 (2018): 129–56. https://doi.org/10.1146/annurev-orgpsych-032117 -104631.

Halpin, Brian W., and Vicki Smith. "Employment Management Work: A Case Study and Theoretical Framework." *Work and Occupations* 44, no. 4 (2017): 339–75. https://doi.org/10.1177/0730888417720714.

Harrington, Brooke. "Studying Elite Professionals in Transnational Settings." In *Professional Networks in Transnational Governance*, edited by Leonard Seabrooke and Lasse Folke Henriksen, 39–49. Cambridge University Press, 2017. https://doi.org/10.1017/9781316855508.003.

Harris, Kevan. "Unraveling the Middle Classes in Postrevolutionary Iran." *Political Power and Social Theory* 37 (2020): 103–34. https://doi.org/10.1108 /S0198-871920200000037006.

Hazır, Irmak Karademir. "Boundaries of Middle-Class Identities in Turkey." *Sociological Review* 62, no. 4 (November 1, 2014): 675–97. https://doi.org /10.1111/1467-954X.12114.

Heiman, Rachel, Carla Freeman, and Mark Liechty, eds. *The Global Middle Classes: Theorizing Through Ethnography.* School for Advanced Research, 2012. https://doi.org/10.1177/0094306114531284u.

Hersch, Joni. "Opting Out Among Women with Elite Education." *Review of Economics of the Household* 11, no. 4 (2013): 469–506. https://doi.org /10.1007/s11150-013-9199-4.

Hertz, Rosanna, and Jonathan Imber, eds. *Studying Elites Using Qualitative Methods.* Sage, 1995. https://doi.org/10.4135/9781483327341.

Hickel, Jason, Giorgos Kallis, Tim Jackson, Daniel W. O'Neill, Juliet B. Schor, Julia K. Steinberger, Peter A. Victor, and Diana Ürge-Vorsatz. "Degrowth Can Work—Here's How Science Can Help." *Nature* 612, no. 7940 (2022): 400–403. https://doi.org/10.1038/d41586-022-04412-x.

Ho, Karen. *Liquidated.* Duke University Press, 2009. https://doi.org/10.1215/9780822391371.

Hochschild, Arlie Russell. *The Managed Heart: Commercialization of Human Feeling.* University of California Press, 1979.

Hom, Peter W., Thomas W. Lee, Jason D. Shaw, and John P. Hausknecht. "One Hundred Years of Employee Turnover Theory and Research." *Journal of Applied Psychology* 102, no. 3 (2017): 530–45. https://doi.org/10.1037/apl0000103.

Horkheimer, Max, and Theodor W. Adorno. "The Culture Industry: Enlightenment as Mass Deception." In *Dialectic of Enlightenment: Philosophical Fragments*, 94–136. Stanford University Press, 2002 (1944).

Howell, David R., and Arne L. Kalleberg. "Declining Job Quality in the United States: Explanations and Evidence." *RSF: The Russell Sage Foundation Journal of the Social Sciences* 5, no. 4 (2019): 1. https://doi.org/10.7758/rsf.2019.5.4.01.

Hung, Ho-fung. "Recent Trends in Global Economic Inequality." *Annual Review of Sociology* 47, no. 1 (2021): 349–67. https://doi.org/10.1146/annurev-soc-090320-105810.

Ibarra, Herminia. *Working Identity: Unconventional Strategies for Reinventing Your Career.* Harvard Business School Press, 2003.

Igarashi, Hiroki, and Hiro Saito. "Cosmopolitanism as Cultural Capital: Exploring the Intersection of Globalization, Education and Stratification." *Cultural Sociology* 8, no. 3 (2014): 222–39. https://doi.org/10.1177/1749975514523935.

İlhan, Deniz. "Turkish Transnational Business Professionals in Istanbul: Globalization, Cosmopolitanism and the Emerging Elite." Master's thesis, Bogazici University, 2010.

Inglehart, Ronald. *Cultural Evolution: People's Motivations Are Changing, and Reshaping the World.* Cambridge University Press, 2018.

Jones, Geoffrey. "Learning to Live with Governments: Unilever in India and Turkey, 1950–80." In *Entrepreneurship and Multinationals: Global Business and the Making of the Modern World*, 165–89. Edward Elgar, 2013.

Kahneman, Daniel, and Angus Deaton. "High Income Improves Evaluation of Life but Not Emotional Well-Being." *Proceedings of the National Academy of Sciences* 107, no. 38 (2010): 16489–93. https://doi.org/10.1073/pnas.1011492107.

Kalekin-Fishman, Devorah, and Lauren Langman. "Alienation: The Critique That Refuses to Disappear." *Current Sociology* 63, no. 6 (2015): 916–33. https://doi.org/10.1177/0011392115591612.

———. "Introductory Background." *Current Sociology* 56, no. 4 (2008): 507–16. https://doi.org/10.1177/0011392108090938.

Kalleberg, Arne L. *Good Jobs, Bad Jobs: The Rise of Polarized and Precarious Employment Systems in the United States, 1970s–2000s.* Russell Sage Foundation, 2011.

———. *The Mismatched Worker.* Norton, 2007.

———. "Precarious Work, Insecure Workers: Employment Relations in Transition." *American Sociological Review* 74, no. 1 (2009): 1–22. https://doi.org/10.1177/000312240907400101.

———. "Work Values and Job Rewards: A Theory of Job Satisfaction." *American Sociological Review* 42, no. 1 (1977): 124. https://doi.org/10.2307/2117735.

Kalleberg, Arne L., and Ted Mouw. "Occupations, Organizations, and Intragenerational Career Mobility." *Annual Review of Sociology* 44, no. 1 (2018): 283–303. https://doi.org/10.1146/annurev-soc-073117-041249.

Kandiyoti, Deniz, and Ayşe Saktanber, eds. *Fragments of Culture: The Everyday of Modern Turkey.* I. B. Tauris, 2002.

Karataşlı, Şahan Savaş. "The Origins of Turkey's 'Heterodox' Transition to Neoliberalism: The Özal Decade and Beyond." *Journal of World-Systems Research* 21, no. 2 (2015): 387–416. https://doi.org/10.5195/jwsr.2015.8.

Karpat, Kemal H., ed. *Social Change and Politics in Turkey: A Structural-Historical Analysis.* Brill, 1973.

Kaya, Yunus. "Proletarianization with Polarization: Industrialization, Globalization, and Social Class in Turkey, 1980–2005." *Research in Social Stratification and Mobility* 26, no. 2 (2008): 161–81. https://doi.org/10.1016/j.rssm.2007.11.003.

Kelly, Erin L., and Phyllis Moen. *Overload: How Good Jobs Went Bad and What We Can Do About It.* Princeton University Press, 2020.

Kelly, Erin L., Phyllis Moen, J. Michael Oakes, Wen Fan, Cassandra Okechukwu, Kelly D. Davis, Leslie B. Hammer, et al. "Changing Work and Work-Family Conflict." *American Sociological Review* 79, no. 3 (2014): 485–516. https://doi.org/10.1177/0003122414531435.

Keyder, Çağlar. "Globalization and Social Exclusion in Istanbul." *International Journal of Urban and Regional Research* 29, no. 1 (2005). https://doi.org/10.1111/j.1468-2427.2005.00574.x.

Keyder, Çağlar, ed. *Istanbul: Between the Global and the Local.* Rowman & Littlefield, 1999.

——. "The New Middle Class (Yeni Orta Sınıf)." *Science Academy*, 2013. http:// bilimakademisi.org/wp-content/uploads/2013/09/Yeni-Orta-Sinif.pdf.

——. *State and Class in Turkey: A Study in Capitalist Development*. Verso, 1987.

Keynes, John Maynard. "Economic Possibilities for Our Grandchildren." In *Essays in Persuasion*, 321–32. Palgrave Macmillan UK, 2010. https://doi .org/10.1007/978-1-349-59072-8_25.

Khurana, Rakesh. *From Higher Aims to Hired Hands: The Social Transformation of American Business Schools and the Unfulfilled Promise of Management as a Profession*. Princeton University Press, 2007.

King, Lawrence P., and Iván Szelényi. "Post-Communist Economic Systems." In *The Handbook of Economic Sociology*, 2nd ed., edited by Richard Swedberg and Neil J. Smelser, 205–30. Princeton University Press, 2010.

——. *Theories of the New Class: Intellectuals and Power*. University of Minnesota Press, 2004.

Knight, Kyle W., Eugene A. Rosa, and Juliet B. Schor. "Could Working Less Reduce Pressures on the Environment? A Cross-National Panel Analysis of OECD Countries, 1970–2007." *Global Environmental Change* 23, no. 4 (2013): 691–700. https://doi.org/10.1016/j.gloenvcha.2013.02.017.

Koo, Hagen. "The Global Middle Class: How Is It Made, What Does It Represent?" *Globalizations* 13, no. 4 (2016): 440–53. https://doi.org/10.1080 /14747731.2016.1143617.

Köse, Ahmet Haşim, and Ahmet Öncü. "A Class Analysis of the Professional and Political Ideologies of Engineers in Turkey." In *The Ravages of Neo-Liberalism: Economy, Society, and Gender in Turkey*, edited by Nesecan Balkan and Sungur Savran, 145–64. Nova Science, 2002.

Kozanoğlu, Hayri. *Yuppieler, Prensler ve Bizim Kuşak*. İletişim, 1993.

Kunda, Gideon. *Engineering Culture: Control and Commitment in a High-Tech Corporation*. Rev. ed. Temple University Press, 2006.

Lafargue, Paul. *The Right to Be Lazy*. Solidarity Publications, 1969.

Lamont, Michèle. "From 'Having' to 'Being': Self-Worth and the Current Crisis of American Society." *British Journal of Sociology* 70, no. 3 (2019): 660–707. https://doi.org/10.1111/1468-4446.12667.

——. *Money, Morals, and Manners: The Culture of the French and American Upper-Middle Class*. University of Chicago Press, 1992.

Lareau, Annette. *Unequal Childhoods: Class, Race, and Family Life*, 2nd ed. University of California Press, 2011.

Lilly, Irani. *Chasing Innovation: Making Entrepreneurial Citizens in Modern India.* Princeton University Press, 2019.

López, A. Ricardo, and Barbara Weinstein, eds. *The Making of the Middle Class: Toward a Transnational History.* Duke University Press, 2012. https://doi .org/10.1080/03071022.2013.807637.

Mainiero, Lisa A., and Sherry E. Sullivan. *The Opt-Out Revolt: Why People Are Leaving Companies to Create Kaleidoscope Careers.* Davies-Black, 2006.

Marcuse, Herbert. *One Dimensional Man: Studies in the Ideology of Advanced Industrial Society.* Beacon, 1964.

Marx, Karl. "Economic and Philosophic Manuscripts of 1844." In *The Marx-Engels Reader*, 2nd ed., edited by Robert C. Tucker, 66–125. Norton, 1978.

Marx, Karl, and Friedrich Engels. "Manifesto of the Communist Party." In *The Marx-Engels Reader*, 2nd ed., edited by Robert C. Tucker, 469–500. Norton, 1978.

Maslow, Abraham H. *Motivation and Personality.* Harper & Row, 1954.

Mears, Ashley. "Working for Free in the VIP: Relational Work and the Production of Consent." *American Sociological Review* 80, no. 6 (2015): 1099–1122. https://doi.org/10.1177/0003122415609730.

Mehri, Darius Bozorg. "The Role of Engineering Consultancies as Network-Centred Actors to Develop Indigenous, Technical Capacity: The Case of Iran's Automotive Industry." *Socio-Economic Review* 13, no. 4 (2015): 747–69. https://doi.org/10.1093/SER/MWU041.

Meier, Lars, and Hellmuth Lange, eds. *The New Middle Classes: Globalizing Lifestyles, Consumerism and Environmental Concern.* Springer, 2009.

Menger, Pierre-Michel. "Artistic Labor Markets and Careers." *Annual Review of Sociology* 25 (1999): 541–74.

Merton, Robert K. "Social Structure and Anomie." *American Sociological Review* 3, no. 5 (1938): 672. https://doi.org/10.2307/2084686.

Michel, Alexandra. "Participation and Self-Entrapment: A 12-Year Ethnography of Wall Street Participation Practices' Diffusion and Evolving Consequences." *Sociological Quarterly* 55, no. 3 (2014): 514–36. https://doi.org /10.1111/tsq.12064.

——. "Transcending Socialization." *Administrative Science Quarterly* 56, no. 3 (2011): 325–68. https://doi.org/10.1177/0001839212437519.

Milliyet. "İş Dünyası Katar'la İş Birliğini Güçlendirecek." *Milliyet*, September 26, 2020. Accessed September 13, 2021. https://www.milliyet.com.tr /ekonomi/is-dunyasi-katarla-is-birligini-guclendirecek-6315720.

Mills, Wright C. *White Collar: The American Middle Classes.* Oxford University Press, 1956.

Moen, Phyllis, Jack Lam, Samantha Ammons, and Erin L. Kelly. "Time Work by Overworked Professionals." *Work and Occupations* 40, no. 2 (2013): 79–114. https://doi.org/10.1177/0730888413481482.

Mogan, Sarp. *Beyaz Yalaka: Kariyer İçin Hayat Feda Etme Sanatı.* Okuyan Us Yayınları, 2017.

Mudge, Stephanie Lee. "What Is Neo-Liberalism?" *Socio-Economic Review* 6, no. 4 (2008): 703–31. https://doi.org/10.1093/ser/mwn016.

Murray, Joshua. "Interlock Globally, Act Domestically: Corporate Political Unity in the 21st Century." *American Journal of Sociology* 122, no. 6 (2017): 1617–63. https://doi.org/10.1086/691603.

Nader, Laura. "Up the Anthropologist—Perspectives Gained from Studying Up." In *Reinventing Anthropology*, edited by Dell Hymes, 284–311. Pantheon, 1972.

Neubert, Dieter, and Florian Stoll. "The Narrative of 'the African Middle Class' and Its Conceptual Limitations." In *Middle Classes in Africa: Changing Lives and Conceptual Challenges*, edited by Lena Kroeker, David O'Kane, and Tabea Scharrer, 57–79. Palgrave Macmillan, 2018. https://doi.org/10.1007/978-3-319-62148-7_3.

Newman, Katherine S. *Falling from Grace: Downward Mobility in the Age of Affluence.* University of California Press, 1999.

Neyzi, Nezih. "The Middle Classes in Turkey." In *Social Change and Politics in Turkey: A Structural-Historical Analysis*, edited by Kemal Karpat, 123–50. Brill, 1973.

Ocejo, Richard E. *Masters of Craft: Old Jobs in the New Urban Economy.* Princeton University Press, 2017.

OECD. "Employment in Foreign Affiliates." In *OECD Factbook 2010: Economic, Environmental and Social Statistics*, 82–83. OECD Publishing, 2010. https://doi.org/10.1787/factbook-2010-29-en.

——. "How Do OECD Countries Compare in Their Attractiveness for Talented Migrants?" *Migration Policy Debates*, 2019. https://www.oecd.org/migration/mig/migration-policy-debates-19.pdf.

——. "OECD FDI Regulatory Restrictiveness Index (Edition 2020)." OECD International Direct Investment Statistics (database), 2021. Accessed April 2, 2022. https://www.oecd-ilibrary.org/finance-and-investment/data/oecd-international-direct-investment-statistics/oecd-fdi-regulatory-restrictiveness-index-edition-2020_06c5b964-en.

Olsen, Karen M., Therese E. Sverdrup, and Arne L. Kalleberg. "Turnover and Transferable Skills in a Professional Service Firm." *Journal of Professions and Organization* 6, no. 1 (2019): 2–16. https://doi.org/10.1093/JPO/JOY022.

Öncü, Ahmet, and Erol Balkan. "Nouveaux Riches of the City of Minarets and Skyscrapers: Neoliberalism and the Reproduction of the Islamic Middle Class in İstanbul." *Research and Policy on Turkey* 1, no. 1 (2016): 29–45. https://doi.org/10.1080/23760818.2015.1099780.

Öncü, Ayşe, and Deniz Gökçe. "Macro-Politics of De-Regulation and Micro-Politics of Banks." In *Strong State and Economic Interest Groups*, edited by Metin Heper, 99–117. De Gruyter, 1991. https://doi.org/10.1515/9783110859966.99.

Öniş, Ziya. "The Dynamics of Export-Oriented Growth in a Second Generation NIC: Perspectives on the Turkish Case, 1980–1990." *New Perspectives on Turkey* 9 (1993): 75–100. https://doi.org/10.1017/s0896634600002223.

——. "International Context, Income Distribution and State Power in Late Industrialization: Turkey and South Korea in Comparative Perspective." *New Perspectives on Turkey* 13 (1995): 25–49. https://doi.org/10.1017/s089663460000234x.

——. "Liberalization, Transnational Corporations and Foreign Direct Investment in Turkey: The Experience of the 1980s." In *Recent Industrialization Experience of Turkey in a Global Context*, edited by Fikret Şenses, 91–109. Greenwood, 1994.

Osterman, Paul, ed. *Broken Ladders: Managerial Careers in the New Economy*. Oxford University Press, 1996.

——. "Introduction to the Special Issue on Job Quality: What Does It Mean and How Might We Think About It?" *ILR Review* 66, no. 4 (2013): 739–52. https://doi.org/10.1177/001979391306600401.

——. "In Search of the High Road: Meaning and Evidence." *ILR Review* 71, no. 1 (2018): 3–34. https://doi.org/10.1177/0019793917738757.

Osterman, Paul, and Beth Shulman. "Introduction." In *Good Jobs America*, 1–22. Russell Sage Foundation, 2011.

Pamuk, Şevket. *Uneven Centuries: Economic Development of Turkey Since 1820*. Princeton University Press, 2018. https://doi.org/10.23943/princeton/9780691166377.001.0001.

——. "Uneven Centuries: Turkey's Experience with Economic Development Since 1820." *Economic History Review* 72, no. 4 (2019): 1129–51. https://doi.org/10.1111/ehr.12938.

Parker, Kim, and Juliana Menasce Horowitz. "Majority of Workers Who Quit a Job in 2021 Cite Low Pay, No Opportunities for Advancement, Feeling Disrespected." *Pew Research Center*, March 9, 2022. https://www.pewresearch.org /short-reads/2022/03/09/majority-of-workers-who-quit-a-job-in-2021-cite -low-pay-no-opportunities-for-advancement-feeling-disrespected/.

Parreñas, Rhacel Salazar. *Servants of Globalisation: Migration, Women and Domestic Work*. Stanford University Press, 2015.

Peiperl, Maury, and Yehuda Baruch. "Back to Square Zero: The Post-Corporate Career." *Organizational Dynamics* 25, no. 4 (1997): 7–22. https://doi .org/10.1016/S0090-2616(97)90033-4.

Percheski, Christine. "Opting Out? Cohort Differences in Professional Women's Employment Rates from 1960 to 2005." *American Sociological Review* 73, no. 3 (2008): 497–517. https://doi.org/10.1177/000312240807300307.

Perlow, Leslie A., and Erin L. Kelly. "Toward a Model of Work Redesign for Better Work and Better Life." *Work and Occupations* 41, no. 1 (2014): 111–34. https://doi.org/10.1177/0730888413516473.

Petriglieri, Gianpiero, Susan J. Ashford, and Amy Wrzesniewski. "Agony and Ecstasy in the Gig Economy: Cultivating Holding Environments for Precarious and Personalized Work Identities." *Administrative Science Quarterly* 64, no. 1 (2018): 1–47. https://doi.org/10.1177/0001839218759646.

Petriglieri, Gianpiero, Jennifer Louise Petriglieri, and Jack Denfeld Wood. "Fast Tracks and Inner Journeys: Crafting Portable Selves for Contemporary Careers." *Administrative Science Quarterly* 63, no. 3 (2018): 479–525. https://doi.org/10.1177/0001839217720930.

Polanyi, Karl. *The Great Transformation: The Political and Economic Origins of Our Time*. Beacon, 2001.

Portes, Alejandro. *Economic Sociology: A Systematic Inquiry*. Princeton University Press, 2010.

Potter, Jesse. "The Ghost of the Stable Path: Stories of Work-Life Change at the 'End of Career.'" *Work, Employment and Society* 34, no. 4 (2019): 1–16. https://doi.org/10.1177/0950017019870751.

Poulantzas, Nicos. *Classes in Contemporary Capitalism*. New Left Books, 1975. https://doi.org/10.2307/2063170.

Presidency of the Republic of Turkey Investment Office. "Business Services Sector in Turkey." 2018.

——. "Invest in Türkiye." *Invest in Türkiye*. February 2020.

——. "Why Invest in Turkey?" 2021.

Prieur, Annick, and Mike Savage. "Emerging Forms of Cultural Capital." *European Societies* 15, no. 2 (2013): 246–67. https://doi.org/10.1080/14616696 .2012.748930.

Radhakrishnan, Smitha. *Appropriately Indian: Gender and Culture in a New Transnational Class*. Duke University Press, 2011.

Rivera, Lauren A. "Go with Your Gut: Emotion and Evaluation in Job Interviews." *American Journal of Sociology* 120, no. 5 (2015): 1339–89. https://doi.org/10.1086/681214.

——. "Hiring as Cultural Matching: The Case of Elite Professional Service Firms." *American Sociological Review* 77, no. 6 (2012): 999–1022. https://doi.org/10.1177/0003122412463213.

——. *Pedigree: How Elite Students Get Elite Jobs*. Princeton University Press, 2015.

Robinson, William I. "Global Capitalism Theory and the Emergence of Transnational Elites." *Critical Sociology* 38, no. 3 (2012): 349–63. https://doi.org/10.1177/0896920511411592.

——. "Social Theory and Globalisation: The Rise of a Transnational State." *Theory and Society* 30, no. 2 (2001): 157–200.

——. *A Theory of Global Capitalism: Production, Class, and State in a Transnational World*. Johns Hopkins University Press, 2004.

Rosa, Hartmut. *Resonance: A Sociology of Our Relationship to the World*. Polity, 2019.

——. *Social Acceleration: A New Theory of Modernity*. Columbia University Press, 2013.

——. *The Uncontrollability of the World*. Polity, 2020.

Rosenfeld, Rachel A. "Job Mobility and Career Processes." *Annual Review of Sociology* 18, no. 1 (1992): 39–61. https://doi.org/10.1146/annurev.so.18 .080192.000351.

Roth, Silke. *The Paradoxes of Aid Work: Passionate Professionals*. Routledge, 2015.

Russell, Bertrand. "In Praise of Idleness." *Harper's Magazine*, October 1932.

Rutz, Henry J., and Erol M. Balkan. "Globalization, Middle-Class Formation, and 'Quality' Education: Hyper-Competition in Istanbul, Turkey." *International Journal of Diversity in Organisations, Communities and Nations* 3, no. 1 (2003): 1–6. https://doi.org/10.18848/1447-9532/CGP/v03i01.

——. *Reproducing Class: Education, Neoliberalism, and the Rise of the New Middle Class in Istanbul*. Berghahn, 2009.

Sallaz, Jeffrey J. "Labor and Capital in the Twenty-First Century: Rereading Braverman Today." *Employee Responsibilities and Rights Journal* 26, no. 4 (2014): 299–311. https://doi.org/10.1007/s10672-014-9251-4.

——. *Labor, Economy, and Society*. Polity, 2013.

Sassen, Saskia. *The Global City: New York, London, Tokyo*. Princeton University Press, 1991.

——. *Globalization and Its Discontents*. New Press, 1998.

——. *The Mobility of Labor and Capital: A Study in International Investment and Labor Flow*. Cambridge University Press, 1988. https://doi.org/10.1017/CBO9780511598296.

——. *A Sociology of Globalization*. Norton, 2006.

Schieman, Scott, Paul Glavin, and Melissa A. Milkie. "When Work Interferes with Life: Work-Nonwork Interference and the Influence of Work-Related Demands and Resources." *American Sociological Review* 74, no. 6 (2009): 966–88. https://doi.org/10.1177/000312240907400606.

Schor, Juliet. *The Overspent American: Upscaling, Downshifting, and the New Consumer*. Basic Books, 1998.

——. *The Overworked American: The Unexpected Decline of Leisure*. Basic Books, 1991.

Schwartz, Christine R. "Trends and Variation in Assortative Mating: Causes and Consequences." *Annual Review of Sociology* 39, no. 1 (2013): 451–70. https://doi.org/10.1146/annurev-soc-071312-145544.

Scott, Sam. "The Social Morphology of Skilled Migration: The Case of the British Middle Class in Paris." *Journal of Ethnic and Migration Studies* 32, no. 7 (2006): 1105–29. https://doi.org/10.1080/13691830600821802.

Seeman, Melvin. "Alienation Studies." *Annual Review of Sociology* 1, no. 1 (1975): 91–123. https://doi.org/10.1146/annurev.so.01.080175.000515.

——. "On the Meaning of Alienation." *American Sociological Review* 24, no. 6 (1959): 783–91. https://doi.org/10.1126/science.135.3503.554.

Sekban, Kaan. *Tebrikler Kovuldunuz!* Okuyan Us Yayınları, 2017.

Şener, Meltem Yilmaz. "Turkish Managers as a Part of the Transnational Capitalist Class." *Journal of World-Systems Research* 13, no. 2 (2008): 119–41.

Şener, Sefer. "Osmanlı'dan Günümüze Türkiye'de Yabancı Sermaye." *Bilgi Sosyal Bilimler Dergisi* 16, no. 1 (2008): 38. https://dergipark.org.tr/tr/pub/bilgisosyal/issue/29126/311561.

Sennett, Richard. *The Craftsman*. Yale University Press, 2008.

Şenses, Fikret. "Structural Adjustment Policies and Employment in Turkey." *New Perspectives on Turkey* 15 (July 21, 1996): 65–93. https://doi.org/10.1017/S0896634600002491.

Sharone, Ofer. "Why Do Unemployed Americans Blame Themselves While Israelis Blame the System?" *Social Forces* 91, no. 4 (2013): 1429–50. https://doi.org/10.1093/sf/sot050.

Siciliano, Michael L. *Creative Control: The Ambivalence of Work in the Culture Industries.* Columbia University Press, 2021.

Silva, Jennifer M. "Constructing Adulthood in an Age of Uncertainty." *American Sociological Review* 77, no. 4 (2012): 505–22.

Simmel, Georg. "The Triad." In The Sociology of Georg Simmel, edited by Kurt H. Wolff, 145–77. Free Press, 1950.

Sklair, Leslie. *The Transnational Capitalist Class.* Blackwell, 2001.

Skotnicki, Tad, and Kelly Nielsen. "Toward a Theory of Alienation: Futurelessness in Financial Capitalism." *Theory and Society* 50, no. 6 (2021): 837–65. https://doi.org/10.1007/s11186-021-09440-6.

Small, Mario Luis, and Jessica McCrory Calarco. *Qualitative Literacy.* University of California Press, 2022. https://doi.org/10.1525/9780520390676.

Spilerman, Seymour. "Careers, Labor Market Structure, and Socioeconomic Achievement." *American Journal of Sociology* 83, no. 3 (1977): 551–93. https://doi.org/10.1086/226595.

Stone, Pamela. *Opting Out? Why Women Really Quit Careers and Head Home.* University of California Press, 2007.

Stone, Pamela, and Meg Lovejoy. *Opting Back In.* University of California Press, 2019. https://doi.org/10.2307/j.ctvpb3w8p.

Streib, Jessi. *The Power of the Past: Understanding Cross-Class Marriages.* Oxford University Press, 2015. https://doi.org/10.1093/acprof:oso/9780199364428.001.0001.

Sullivan, Sherry E., and Michael B. Arthur. "The Evolution of the Boundaryless Career Concept: Examining Physical and Psychological Mobility." *Journal of Vocational Behavior* 69, no. 1 (2006): 19–29. https://doi.org/10.1016/j.jvb.2005.09.001.

Sullivan, Sherry E., and Yehuda Baruch. "Advances in Career Theory and Research: A Critical Review and Agenda for Future Exploration." *Journal of Management* 35, no. 6 (2009): 1542–71. https://doi.org/10.1177/0149206309350082.

Therborn, Göran. "Class in the 21st Century." *New Left Review*, no. 78 (November–December 2012): 5–29.

Thompson, E. P. *The Making of the English Working Class*. Pantheon, 1963.

Timmermans, Stefan, and Iddo Tavory. "Theory Construction in Qualitative Research: From Grounded Theory to Abductive Analysis." *Sociological Theory* 30, no. 3 (2012): 167–86. https://doi.org/10.1177/0735275112457914.

Tomaskovic-Devey, Donald, and Dustin Avent-Holt. *Relational Inequalities*. Oxford University Press, 2019. https://doi.org/10.1093/oso/9780190624422.001.0001.

Tomaskovic-Devey, Donald, Anthony Rainey, Dustin Avent-Holt, Nina Bandelj, István Boza, David Cort, Olivier Godechot, et al. "Rising Between-Workplace Inequalities in High-Income Countries." *Proceedings of the National Academy of Sciences of the United States of America* 117, no. 17 (2020): 9277–83. https://doi.org/10.1073/PNAS.1918249117/SUPPL_FILE/PNAS.1918249117.SAPP.PDF.

Torbat, Akbar E. "The Brain Drain from Iran to the United States." *Middle East Journal* 56, no. 2 (2002): 272–95.

Tucker, Robert C. "Introduction." In *The Marx-Engels Reader*, 2nd ed., edited by Robert C. Tucker. Norton, 1978.

Tuğal, Cihan. "Elusive Revolt: The Contradictory Rise of Middle-Class Politics." *Thesis Eleven* 130, no. 1 (2015): 74–95. https://doi.org/10.1177/0725513615602183.

——. "'Resistance Everywhere': The Gezi Revolt in Global Perspective." *New Perspectives on Turkey* 49 (2013): 157–72. https://doi.org/10.1017/S0896634600002077.

Türem, Z. Umut. "Engineering Competition and Competitive Subjectivities: 'Self' and Political Economy in Neoliberal Turkey." In *The Making of Neoliberal Turkey*, edited by Cenk Özbay, Maral Erol, Ayşecan Terzioğlu, and Z. Umut Türem, 33–52. Routledge, 2016. https://doi.org/10.4324/9781315562766-10.

Turkish Statistical Institute. "Labor Force Microdata Statistics 2017," 2017.

Twining, James E. "Alienation as a Social Process." *Sociological Quarterly* 21, no. 3 (1980): 417–28. https://doi.org/10.1111/j.1533-8525.1980.tb00622.x.

United Nations Conference on Trade and Development. "World Investment Report 1994: Transnational Corporations, Employment and the Workplace." United Nations, 1994.

——. "World Investment Report 1999: Foreign Direct Investment and the Challenge of Development." United Nations Conference on Trade and Development (UNCTAD) World Investment Report (WIR). United Nations, 1999. https://doi.org/10.18356/8e79f24c-en.

Vallas, Steven Peter. "New Technology, Job Content, and Worker Alienation: A Test of Two Rival Perspectives." *Work and Occupations* 15, no. 2 (May 17, 1988): 148–78. https://doi.org/10.1177/0730888488015002002.

——. "White-Collar Proletarians? The Structure of Clerical Work and Levels of Class Consciousness." *Sociological Quarterly* 28, no. 4 (1987): 523–40. https://doi.org/10.1111/j.1533-8525.1987.tb00310.x.

——. "Work and Employment." In *The Wiley-Blackwell Companion to Sociology*, edited by George Ritzer and William Yagatich, 418–43. Wiley, 2012. https://doi.org/10.1002/9781444347388.ch23.

Vallas, Steven Peter, and Angèle Christin. "Work and Identity in an Era of Precarious Employment: How Workers Respond to 'Personal Branding' Discourse." *Work and Occupations* 45, no. 1 (2018): 3–37. https://doi .org/10.1177/0730888417735662.

Vallas, Steven Peter, and Emily R. Cummins. "Personal Branding and Identity Norms in the Popular Business Press: Enterprise Culture in an Age of Precarity." *Organization Studies* 36, no. 3 (2015): 293–319. https://doi .org/10.1177/0170840614563741.

Vallas, Steven Peter, and Andrea L. Hill. "Reconfiguring Worker Subjectivity: Career Advice Literature and the 'Branding' of the Worker's Self." *Sociological Forum* 33, no. 2 (2018): 287–309. https://doi.org/10.1111/socf.12418.

Vallas, Steven Peter, and Anne Kovalainen. "Introduction: Taking Stock of the Digital Revolution." In *Research in the Sociology of Work*, vol. 33, 1–12. Emerald, 2019. https://doi.org/10.1108/S0277-283320190000033001.

Vallas, Steven Peter, and Juliet B. Schor. "What Do Platforms Do? Understanding the Gig Economy." *Annual Review of Sociology* 46, no. 1 (2020): 273–94. https://doi.org/10.1146/annurev-soc-121919-054857.

Villegas, Celso M. "The Middle Class as a Culture Structure: Rethinking Middle-Class Formation and Democracy Through the Civil Sphere." *American Journal of Cultural Sociology* 7, no. 2 (2019): 135–73. https://doi.org /10.1057/s41290-018-0061-2.

Wacquant, Loïc J. D. "Making Class: The Middle Class(es) in Social Theory and Social Structure." In *Bringing Class Back In: Contemporary and Historical*

Perspectives, edited by Scott G. McNall, Rhonda F. Levine, and Rick Fantasia, 39–64. Westview, 1991.

Walker, Louise. *Waking from the Dream: Mexico's Middle Classes After 1968*. Stanford University Press, 2013.

Wallerstein, Immanuel. "Class-Formation in the Capitalist World-Economy." *Politics & Society* 5, no. 3 (1975): 367–75. https://doi.org/10.1177/003232927500500304.

Weber, Max. *The Protestant Ethic and the "Spirit" of Capitalism*. Penguin, 2002.

Weeden, Kim A., and David B. Grusky. "The Case for a New Class Map." *American Journal of Sociology* 111, no. 1 (2005): 141–212. https://doi.org/10.1086/428815.

Weenink, D. "Cosmopolitanism as a Form of Capital: Parents Preparing Their Children for a Globalizing World." *Sociology* 42, no. 6 (2008): 1089–1106. https://doi.org/10.1177/0038038508096935.

Weisshaar, Katherine. "From Opt Out to Blocked Out: The Challenges for Labor Market Re-Entry After Family-Related Employment Lapses." *American Sociological Review* 83, no. 1 (2018): 34–60. https://doi.org/10.1177/0003122417752355.

Wharton, Amy S. "The Sociology of Emotional Labor." *Annual Review of Sociology* 35, no. 1 (2009): 147–65. https://doi.org/10.1146/annurev-soc-070308-115944.

Wharton, Amy S., and Mary Blair-Loy. "Long Work Hours and Family Life." *Journal of Family Issues* 27, no. 3 (2006): 415–36. https://doi.org/10.1177/0192513X05282985.

——. "The 'Overtime Culture' in a Global Corporation: A Cross-National Study of Finance Professionals' Interest in Working Part-Time." *Work and Occupations* 29, no. 1 (2002): 32–63. https://doi.org/10.1177/0730888402029001003.

Wheaton, Blair, and Ian H. Gotlib. "Trajectories and Turning Points over the Life Course: Concepts and Themes." In *Stress and Adversity over the Life Course: Trajectories and Turning Points*, edited by Blair Wheaton and Ian H. Gotlib, 1–26. Cambridge University Press, 1997. https://doi.org/10.1017/CBO9780511527623.001.

Wilensky, Harold L. "Orderly Careers and Social Participation: The Impact of Work History on Social Integration in the Middle Mass." *American Sociological Review* 26, no. 4 (1961): 521. https://doi.org/10.2307/2090251.

Wilhoit, Elizabeth D. "Opting Out (Without Kids): Understanding Non-Mothers' Workplace Exit in Popular Autobiographies." *Gender, Work & Organization* 21, no. 3 (2014): 260–72. https://doi.org/10.1111/gwao.12034.

Willis, Paul. *Learning to Labor: How Working Class Kids Get Working Class Jobs.* Cambridge University Press, 2017.

World Bank. "Foreign Direct Investment, Net Inflows (% of GDP)—Turkey, Middle Income." World Development Indicators (database), 2022. Accessed April 3, 2022. https://data.worldbank.org/indicator/BX.KLT.DINV.WD.GD.ZS?locations=TR-XP.

Wright, Erik Olin. "The Biography of a Concept: Contradictory Class Locations." In *Classes*, 19–63. Verso, 1985.

——. "Class Analysis." In *Class Counts*, 1–40. Cambridge University Press, 2000. https://doi.org/10.1017/cbo9780511488917.

——. *Class Structure and Income Determination.* Academic Press, 1979.

——. "The Comparative Project on Class Structure and Class Consciousness: An Overview." *Acta Sociologica* 32, no. 1 (1989): 3–22.

Wrzesniewski, Amy, and Jane E. Dutton. "Crafting a Job: Revisioning Employees as Active Crafters of Their Work." *Academy of Management Review* 26, no. 2 (2001): 179. https://doi.org/10.2307/259118.

Wrzesniewski, Amy, Clark McCauley, Paul Rozin, and Barry Schwartz. "Jobs, Careers, and Callings: People's Relations to Their Work." *Journal of Research in Personality* 31, no. 1 (1997): 21–33. https://doi.org/10.1006/jrpe.1997.2162.

Yanaşmayan, Zeynep. "Does Education 'Trump' Nationality? Boundary-Drawing Practices Among Highly Educated Migrants from Turkey." *Ethnic and Racial Studies* 39, no. 11 (2016): 2041–59. https://doi.org/10.1080/01419870.2015.1131315.

Yavaş, Mustafa. "White-Collar Opt-Out: How 'Good Jobs' Fail Elite Workers." *American Sociological Review* 89, no. 4 (2024): 761–88. https://doi.org/10.1177/00031224241263497.

Yıldırım, Kerem. "Clientelism and Dominant Incumbent Parties: Party Competition in an Urban Turkish Neighbourhood." *Democratization* 27, no. 1 (2020): 81–99. https://doi.org/10.1080/13510347.2019.1658744.

Yörük, Erdem, and Murat Yüksel. "Class and Politics in Turkey's Gezi Protests." *New Left Review* 89, no. September–October (2014): 103–23.

Zaloom, Caitlin. *Indebted: How Families Make College Work at Any Cost.* Princeton University Press, 2019.

Zerey, Yüce. *Fabrika Ayarlarına Dön.* Doğan Yayıncılık, 2016.

——. *The Profesyonel.* Doğan Yayıncılık, 2014.

INDEX

abductive reasoning, 12, 110, 217
Abel, Andrea, 90
accents, 85, 92–93
Adalet ve Kalkınma Partisi (AKP/
Justice and Development Party),
93, 196–98
Adorno, Theodor W., 141
AKP. *See* Adalet ve Kalkınma Partisi
algocratic governance, 260n48
alienated judgment, 116
alienation, 8–9, 110, 195;
entrepreneurship and,
186–87; escaping, 170–79;
extended theory of, 203–16;
job satisfaction and, 118–20;
justification failures, 131–37;
labor process and, 112–20;
beyond manual labor, 114–18;
middle-class, 15, 158–59;
occupational regret and,
126–31, 218; opt-out decisions
and, 148, 157–59; overwork and,
117, 206, 213–15; processual
understanding of, 122, 125;
of professional-managerial

labor, 115; as relative
deprivation, 209–11; research
on, 112–13; self, 135, 207; as
self-domination, 16, 24, 207,
211; in service-sector jobs,
115; technology and, 113;
underemployment and, 126–31,
211–12; work-life balance and,
125
Althusser, Louis, 33
anomie, 110, 209
Aristotle, 29
Armenians, 93
Arthur, Michael B., 153
artisans, 127. *See also* crafts labor
Asian financial crisis, 35
assortative mating, 142. *See also*
class homophily
austerity measures, 23, 35, 43
authorship, 114, 116, 204
autonomy, 16, 168; class schemas
and, 31–32; of the body, 140;
over labor, 109, 111, 113–14,
116, 168–69, 183, 190, 260n48;
worker autonomy 118, 127, 159

Horkheimer, Max, 141
housing costs, 235n4
HR professionals, 231–32, 276n5
human body, as defense against
    overwork, 139–40
human capital, 16, 207
human flourishing, 122, 204–6, 215,
    273n37
humanism, 207
Hungary, 201

Ibarra, Herminia, 155
ideal white-collar employees, 74–81
identity: career changes and, 156;
    class, 237n15, 260n40; European,
    199; golden handcuffs and,
    170, 173–74; occupational, 160;
    opting out as change in, 173–74
identity workspaces, 153
ideological mismatch, 135–36
ideology of the ladder, 52, 158. *See
    also* careerism
IELTS. *See* International English
    Language Testing System
ILO. *See* International Labour
    Organization
IMF. *See* International Monetary
    Fund
immigration: Eurostars and,
    199–200; to global cities, 99; to
    Global North, 49, 56–58, 106,
    197, 212; of labor, 40, 56–58;
    upward mobility and, 10
impactfulness, 132–33
import substitution industrialization
    (ISI), 35, 42–43, 248n117

India, 27, 36–37, 201
individualism, 20; competitive, 52
industrialization, 45–46, 113;
    globalization overlap with, 59;
    import substitution, 35, 42–43,
    248n117; state-led, 35
inequality, 16; hiring
    discrimination and, 255n32;
    organizational approach to,
    17; reproduction of, 64–65, 76;
    status anxiety and, 210
information hoarding, 94
INGO. *See* international
    nongovernmental organization
"In Praise of Idleness"
    (Russell), 215
Instagram, 56
instrumentalization of labor, 120,
    214–15
intellectual challenge, 127, 129
intellectual labor, 15, 24, 158, 208.
    See also knowledge work
intergenerational mobility, 153
International English Language
    Testing System (IELTS), 80
international experience, 77–79,
    91–92
International Labour Organization
    (ILO), 111
International Monetary Fund
    (IMF), 35, 43; loan conditions, 35
international nongovernmental
    organization (INGO), 40, 180
international travel, 56
internships, 101
Interrail passes, 56, 78–79

interviews, 12, 221; corporate opt-
outs, 225, 230; elite workers,
222, 224–25; HR professionals,
231–32; psychotherapists,
230; socioeconomic and
demographic details from,
226–29; supplemental, 232;
undergraduates, 230–31
intra-North mobility, 200
intrinsic satisfaction, 16; career
prioritization over, 214; lack
of, 126–31; opt-out decisions
and lack of, 148; post opt-out,
187–88
introspection, 180–81
Iran, 34, 201
ISI. *See* import substitution
industrialization
Islamization, 197
isomorphism, 40, 202
Istanbul Technical University, 71

job candidates: emotional
resonance with, 21; evaluation
of, 81–87
job crafting, 211
job interviews, 21, 73, 104, 194; class
background and, 93–94; cultural
matching and fit assessment
and, 84–86; extracurricular
activities and, 84; international
experience and, 78
job orientation, 124–26, 188, 224,
233. *See also* work orientations
job quality, 109, 111–12, 116, 216
job rewards, 118–20

job satisfaction, 111–12, 124, 225,
260n42; alienation and, 118–20;
lack of intrinsic, 126–31
job security, 109, 216
job-specific training, 76
Justice and Development Party. *See*
Adalet ve Kalkınma Partisi
justification failures, 131–37

Kahneman, Daniel, 117
kaleidoscope careers, 153–54
Kalleberg, Arne, 109, 118
kariyer kasmak, 91
Keynes, John Maynard, 215
knowledge work, 18, 128, 211. *See
also* professional-managerial
labor
Koç University, 71
Köse, Ahmet Haşim, 52
Kozanoğlu, Hayri, 52
Kunda, Gideon, 116
Kurds, 93

labor migration, 56–58
labor process, 21, 31, 40, 82, 87, 92,
106, 112–20, 208, 212, 260n48
Lange, Hellmuth, 36
late modernity, 153
Latin American debt crisis, 35
Law on Encouragement and
Protection of Foreign
Investment (2002) (Iran), 201
lean manufacturing, 76
Learning to Labor (Willis), 63, 209
leisure time, 140–41, 204. *See also*
free time

universities, 69–71; career centers,
219; CV screening and, 72;
student exchange programs
and, 79–80
university entrance exams, 70, 73,
131
university-to-work transitions, 62
UN World Investment Report, 50
upward mobility, 13, 23, 153,
254n27; expectations of, 103–4;
immigration and, 10
urban flight, 182
urbanization, 42, 46; globalization
overlap with, 59

value chains, 34
value mismatches, 133–34
visas, 57; H-1B visa, 57–58, 212; L-1
visa, 57

Wacquant, Loïc, 31
Wall Street, 1, 5, 133, 140, 174
Washington Consensus, 19, 35, 43,
194, 270n11
"Wealthy, Successful and
Miserable" (*New York Times
Magazine*), 110
Weber, Max, 213–14, 217
Weberian approaches, to middle-
class analyses, 32
Weinstein, Barbara, 36
welfare: austerity policies and, 35;
neoliberalism and, 194, 208;
privatization and, 58; safety
nets and, 176; social, 52; states,
160, 208, 219

well-being, 18, 65, 110, 117–18,
139–40, 162, 173, 189, 205, 214,
217, 219, 273n37
well rounded-ness, 74, 89–91
WhatsApp groups, 94
white-collar blues, 6, 19, 21, 193;
studying, 12–15
white-collar consent, withdrawal
of, 160–79
white-collar jobs, 61, 110
white-collar labor, 128–29, 153, 208,
210, 246n87, 258n23
white-collar opt-out, 147–48,
195–96; aftermath of, 185–89;
economic security and,
177–78; gender and work-family
conflict and, 150–52; intrinsic
satisfaction and, 187–88; job
crafting as alternative to, 211;
neoliberalism and boundaryless
careers and, 152–54; popular
culture narratives of, 190;
process of, 160–62; pull factors
in, 167–70; push factors in, 162–
67; as turning points, 154–56;
turnover and, 150; withdrawal
of consent and, 160–79; work
orientation shifts and, 188
white-collar workers, 6, 9, 30–32,
118, 122, 127, 208, 210, 258n23;
emotional labor and, 115;
habitus of ideal, 75–76; ideal,
74–81; in Turkey, 45–46
White Turks, 93
Willis, Paul, 63, 209
Wood, Jack Denfeld, 153

GPSR Authorized Representative: Easy Access System Europe, Mustamäe tee
50, 10621 Tallinn, Estonia, gpsr.requests@easproject.com

www.ingramcontent.com/pod-product-compliance
Lightning Source LLC
Chambersburg PA
CBHW022137020426
42334CB00015B/930